A UNIQUELY CORNISH CONCEPT

The Story of the 'Old Cornwall' Movement
1 9 2 0 - 2 0 2 0

by Merv Davey, Andrew Langdon, Peter W Thomas
and others, edited by Peter W Thomas

Ⓟ Federation of 'Old Cornwall' Societies

A UNIQUELY CORNISH CONCEPT

The Story of the 'Old Cornwall' Movement

1920 - 2020

978-0-902660-52-6

Cover Photo: Coutesy of Phil Ellery, this image shows St Columb OCS members being shown Wheal Coates

Contents

Preface

During the year 2020, the Federation of Old Cornwall Societies would have been celebrating the centenary of the foundation of the Old Cornwall movement which started in St Ives in 1920. Instead the centenary year became the coronavirus year. In March the country was in lockdown and many events had to be postponed or cancelled because of Covid-19.

It gradually became apparent that social distancing would have to continue for many months to come. The Federation's Summer and Winter Festivals were cancelled and local societies had to put their meetings and events on hold. Fortunately the project to produce a centenary book celebrating the development of the Old Cornwall movement and its many achievements was already underway. This book is the result of many hours of travel, communications and painstaking research to show as much as possible about the activities of Old Cornwall societies over the past one hundred years. The Publications Committee and its researchers have worked diligently to provide the information for each chapter. It is fascinating to see how the movement was created and how quickly it developed, its aim being to record the everyday life of people, their holidays, work and home life, folk traditions and seasonal celebrations, language and dialect and to help preserve Cornwall's archaeological and historic sites. This work continues today so that the individuality of Cornwall can be preserved for the future, not in an antiquarian way or in an effort to keep things the same forever, but to remain as a living tradition that adjusts to the changes in society but retains Cornish ethnicity. For example, we now welcome people who have become Cornish by adoption and who want to learn more about Cornwall's heritage and culture.

It is interesting to read that the concerns of the past are similar to those expressed at Federation meetings now. The interpretation of the name "Old Cornwall" has been discussed at length over the years. Robert Morton Nance provides the reason for the name choice in his introduction to the first *Old Cornwall* journal.

> *It is for such a "New Cornwall" that we work, but it is "Old Cornwall" that provides us with all this essence of Cornishness that we mean to hand on to it, so "Old Cornwall Societies" we have been ever since, and OLD CORNWALL is the obvious name for our journal.*

The current use of **Kernow Goth** (the Cornish for Old Cornwall, the adjective being placed after the noun in Cornish) would seem to help to remedy this dichotomy of opinion.

Evidence provided by this centenary book shows how much the Old Cornwall movement has been a pathfinder over the years. Many organisations have been initiated by its efforts, the Gorsedh in particular. The Federation website gives examples of organisations to which we are affiliated and associated as well as links to many others.

In the last 100 years the work of the Old Cornwall movement has always been to collect, preserve and share Cornish heritage and culture. Congratulations to everyone involved past and present in this work. I feel sure this will continue with interest and enthusiasm throughout the next 100 years.

Karin Easton
President - Federation of Old Cornwall Societies

July 2020

Introduction

Garry Tregidga

The launch of the first Old Cornwall Society at St Ives on 21 January 1920 was a pivotal moment in the historical development of the Cornish movement.

By the second half of the previous century there had been clear signs of a growing interest in the identity of Cornwall as a Celtic nation. In 1865, for example, the Revd WS Lach-Szyrma had given a lecture to the Liskeard Literary Institution on the subject of 'Cornish Nationality' and in the following decade he played a prominent if sometimes forgotten role in organising the 1877 centenary commemorations of Dolly Pentreath with a public event that brought together lectures, short presentations in the Cornish language, Cornish Carols, and the singing of *Trelawny*.[1]

The Cornish language research of Henry Jenner at this time was to lead to *A Handbook of the Cornish Language* in 1904 and in the same year Cornwall was formally accepted as a Celtic nation by the Pan-Celtic Congress.[2] But progress depended on the often isolated activities of individuals rather than the long-term benefits of promoting Celtic Cornwall through an association or institution.

The late nineteenth century had witnessed the formation of a number of cultural and political organisations in the other Celtic nations including Cymru Fydd for Wales in 1886 and Conradh na Gaeilge (more commonly known as the Gaelic League) and An Comunn Gàidhealach in the early 1890s in Ireland and Scotland respectively. In comparison the revival of the Penzance Natural History and Antiquarian Society in 1880 merely provided a local focus for pioneers like Lach-Szyrma, MA Courtney and GB Millett to discuss subjects like archaeology, folklore and the Cornish language since from a geographical perspective the group was to be restricted to West Cornwall and lost direction in subsequent decades.[3] The creation in 1901 of Cowethas Kelto-Kernuak (Celtic-Cornish Society) meant that a specific group for the so-called Cornish Revivalists finally existed. However, despite playing an active role in the publication of *A Handbook of the Cornish Language* and the campaign for Celtic nationality the group failed to establish a permanent presence and had ceased to exist by the time of the First World War.[4] In these circumstances the subsequent development of the Old Cornwall movement in the inter-war period was to create a new model to promote Cornish culture that has essentially stood the test of time for the past one hundred years. That approach was to link the appeal of individual societies at the community level with a Cornwall-wide federation providing co-ordination

The banner parade to the Plain-an-Gwarry at St Just & Pendeen's Summer Festival for the Federation, 2019. Courtesy of Tony Mansell.

and an overall sense of direction.[5] In this much needed study of the history of Old Cornwall a prominent team of contributors associated with the movement explore its chronological story since 1920, practical work in preserving ancient sites, and the public engagement with Cornish folk traditions.

Peter Thomas introduces the study with an overview of the history of Old Cornwall from its early days to the present. He shows how a series of societies were created in the far west in the early 1920s at Camborne, Hayle, Redruth and Truro following the initial lead of St Ives. The formation of a Federation of the societies took place in 1924 leading over time to the expansion of the movement into other parts of Cornwall with the launch of the *Old Cornwall* journal in 1925 providing another early sign of progress. As Thomas notes, it was Robert Morton Nance who was the dominant figure in the early decades of expansion. Even Jenner who provided the iconic leadership of the Cornish Revival as Federation president declared in 1932 'that the real awakening was very largely due to Mr. R. Morton Nance. He started the first Old Cornwall Society … and there were now 20

of them with a membership of 1,500'.[6] Nance's vision of an active group that could popularise the Cornish language, develop stronger links with the other Celtic nations and promote an interest in a wide variety of other aspects of the Duchy's culture from dialect and music to history provided an appealing agenda at the community level. Yet Thomas notes that problems were still evident in subsequent decades. By the late 1930s there was concern that some societies were becoming inactive, while initial activities like promoting dialect studies and links with the other Celtic nations were perhaps being neglected.

An ongoing debate down to the present relates to how far the name itself makes it difficult to present a dynamic image and attract a younger membership. The launch of Tyr ha Tavas (Land and Language) in 1932 was seen as a practical way of attracting the support of younger activists to the Federation.[7] It was followed by the launch in the 1940s of Young Cornwall under the leadership of university students like Richard Jenkin and Mary Foss, which initiated local branches at places like Penzance, Redruth, Helston and Truro usually in association with Old Cornwall.[8] Priscilla Oates writes in the book about her personal memories of a subsequent attempt in the early 1960s to develop a Young Cornwall group at Helston Grammar School and the way in which it provided an introduction to the Old Cornwall movement.

The preservation of Cornwall's tangible heritage has long been a concern of the Cornish movement. Even Cowethas Kelto-Kernuak with its focus on the language actually listed its first core aim in 1901 as the need 'To preserve from damage and destruction and to study the stone-circles, cromlechs, menhirs, hut circles, beehive dwellings, camps, hill forts, castles, logan and crick stones, crosses, oratories, holy wells, cemeteries, barrows, and inscribed stones'.[9] Andrew Langdon describes the practical ways in which from its early days Old Cornwall was able to develop a plan for individual societies to start taking responsibility for sites at the local level. Repair and preservation were linked to promotion of that heritage through talks and reports with good use made of the network of societies at the grassroots. Consideration is given to key personalities like Albert de Castro Glubb, CK Croft Andrew and Nicholas Bray who were pioneers of fieldwork conservation in the middle decades of the twentieth century alongside collaboration with local government and specialist groups like the Cornwall Archaeological Society. Langdon's study develops into a detailed account of the work of the Federation and individual societies over the past one hundred years.

Cornish folklore has also been a recurring theme during these years. Merv Davey writes of the pioneering approach of Old Cornwall in the 1920s for the way in which it challenged the assumption that folk traditions only had relevance for antiquarian or academic study. Along with articles in *Old Cornwall* were performances of songs, stories and dialect. Midsummer bonfires and Crying the Neck ceremonies added a communal dimension to the Revival that continues to the present day. Moreover, the movement's emphasis on pageantry through banners and tartan created a powerful context for presenting Cornish folklore. From the early days of the movement there was an appeal to the power of spectacle with a report on the Winter Festival at Penzance in 1929 noting that

'The decorations of the hall were in keeping with the event. Banners of the various branches were hung round the balcony, interspersed with mottos in old Cornish. On one side of the platform, "One and All" was written in old Cornish, and "Cornwall for ever" on the other'.[10] Davey's reference to the importance of banners is developed further by David Stark who highlights the importance of the visual imagery of the movement both in a short piece for this book and in his earlier study.[11]

But this centenary record is not just about the achievements of the past. Langdon concludes with an appeal to local societies to be ever more vigilant at a time when our tangible heritage continues to be threatened, while Davey still sees the movement playing an important role in maintaining Cornish culture as a 'living tradition'. Thomas similarly brings the story of Old Cornwall up to the present with reference to the movement's greater engagement in recent years with the medium of the Internet that is evident, for example, through an active Facebook presence both for the Federation and individual societies. The creation of new Kernow Goth Interest Groups can be seen as an innovative way to focus research on particular topics and part of a renewed focus on the vital if sometimes neglected role of the Recorder. Indeed, it is that emphasis on researching the culture and history of Cornwall that can still be regarded as a vital component of the work of Old Cornwall. There is a proud tradition of democratic scholarship west of the Tamar that the movement is well placed to develop in partnership with bodies like Cornwall Heritage Trust, Institute of Cornish Studies and Kresen Kernow. Education is not just about abstract academic theories but a desire to ensure that knowledge can be shared and passed on to future generations. It was that commitment that led the new St Ives society in 1920 to declare that 'it is high time to try to rouse the interest of the young people in the old dialect, customs, beliefs, and spirit of Cornwall'.[12] Such an approach must be ongoing since a knowledge of Cornish heritage now needs to be passed on to present and future generations.

Cornish dancing on Perranporth Beach at Lowender Peran. Courtesy of Perran Tremewan.

The first 100 years of 'Old Cornwall'

Peter W Thomas

Redruth OCS members at Trenethick Barton, Helston, 1922. Courtesy of the late Paddy Bradley.

This account is an attempt to give a general overview of the story of the Old Cornwall Movement since its foundation, particularly in its early years, as much with respect to its aims, character and ideals as to specific events and achievements.

These are so many and varied that a much longer account would be needed to do them justice. Indeed, a book would be needed for each Old Cornwall Society, at least for those which have not already produced one, and no attempt is made to incorporate such accounts here, though many of the references indicate where additional details may be found. The amount of available information on Old Cornwall and individual Societies is enormous, and more accessible than ever thanks to such research

tools as online searches of newspapers, quite apart from the wealth of data to be found in the *Old Cornwall* journal. Later chapters of this book will provide more detailed outlines of practical work undertaken by Old Cornwall Societies and the movement's significance within Cornwall's rich folk tradition. The Cornish language in an Old Cornwall context is discussed in the chapter following this one.

The Constitution of the Federation of Old Cornwall Societies[1] incorporates a formal statement of the movement's aims, of which the following are central: to 'collect, record and publish information concerning Cornwall's culture and heritage, to include Cornish history, topography, place names, folklore, traditions, dialect, music, industries and similar subjects'; to 'protect, record and publicise the natural beauty and culture of Cornwall'; to

'encourage the study and use of the Cornish language'; and to 'preserve Cornish antiquities and relics'. For all lovers of Cornwall they must be laudable aims, and the story of the movement behind them worth telling.

1920-1959: *The era of Robert Morton Nance*

1920: Origins

The story of the first Old Cornwall century could begin with a person and a place: May James,[2] St Ives. A group of local enthusiasts used to meet in the town to discuss topics of Cornish interest, and at one of these meetings, in Anne Pool's house, it was Mrs James who was sufficiently inspired by the discussion on Cornish dialect words to suggest

that it would be an excellent idea if their talks could be shared with a wider circle. This idea was taken up and, at 3 pm on January 21st 1920 in the Council Chamber, St Ives, the inaugural meeting of the first Old Cornwall Society took place, the Mayor of St Ives presiding. Another member of the group, Robert Morton Nance, contacted the press about the concept of the movement.[3] In his letter, printed in the *St Ives Times* of January 30th and elsewhere, he expressed a wish to bridge the gap between the articles published by learned societies, inaccessible or off-putting to many people, and the traditional knowledge possessed by those who are often shy about passing it on to young people 'who have the best right to it.' The name 'Old Cornwall' had already been settled on, but even at this very early stage Nance was concerned to transmit knowledge to the young. If the St Ives society is successfully

A HANDBOOK OF THE CORNISH LANGUAGE

CHIEFLY IN ITS LATEST STAGES WITH SOME ACCOUNT OF ITS HISTORY AND LITERATURE

BY

HENRY JENNER

MEMBER OF THE GORSEDD OF THE BARDS OF BRITTANY
FELLOW OF THE SOCIETY OF ANTIQUARIES

"Never credit me but I will spowt some Cornish at him.
Peden bras, vidne whee bis cregas."
The Northern Lass, by RICH. BROME, 1632.

LONDON
DAVID NUTT, AT THE SIGN OF THE PHŒNIX
57–59 LONG ACRE
MCMIV

"Handbook of the Cornish Language" (1904). Courtesy of Toby Nicholson.

launched, he says, 'meetings of all kinds, grave, gay, with summer excursions, etc., would provide something for 'one and all'.' This is a hopeful message indeed for a time when the 'Spanish flu' pandemic had not yet run its course and the Great War had ended barely a year before. As Nance saw it, '[w]ith peace it became possible for the idea of Cornish nationality to rise again, and starting inconspicuously the Old Cornwall movement and the Cornish Revival as a whole began.'[4]

Though he was ably supported by dedicated fellow-workers, Nance was indisputably the principal founder of the Old Cornwall Movement and a towering figure within the Cornish Revival as a whole for over half a century. He and his wife had moved to Nancledra in 1906, and in the following few years he wrote a series of Cornish dialect plays, originally for acting by the local schoolchildren. When some of them were eventually published in book form as The Cledry plays[5] about 50 years later, he wrote in the preface: 'It was a performance of "Duffy" [the first play in the collection] at St. Ives that led to the formation there in 1920 of the first Old Cornwall Society – and so in time to the Federation of Old Cornwall Societies and to the Cornish Gorsedd.'[6] To him, the Cornish dialect was 'the key to Old Cornwall.'[7]

AK Hamilton Jenkin, Cornish historian and member of the first Society, tells the origin story in the 50th anniversary commemoration issue of the Old Cornwall journal.[8] As he put it, the movement 'came into being through a happy accident rather than design.' He recalls the reading of one of Nance's Cledry Plays and subsequent reminiscences by the St Ives group, which led to the decision to hold similar meetings at monthly intervals: 'Our original meeting place was eminently suited to the character of the Society, being a net loft over a fish cellar ... which stood at the top of Pudding Bag Lane.' Over time they accumulated 'a small collection of relics illustrative of the life, customs and industries of the town' which were later housed in St Ives Museum. (The Museum, now containing a rich collection of local artefacts, was closely bound up with St Ives Old Cornwall Society, played an important role in

its history and continues as a vital partner, having surmounted many difficulties on its way. It was opened at its original premises in 1951, Nance having played a prominent part in its creation, and includes a 'Nance Room' in his honour as well as a portrait of him by Leonard John Fuller which was commissioned as a tribute to his memory.)[9] The first meetings of the Society were informal, comprising the reading of a short paper followed by discussion. Even at this stage the Recorder played a vital part, taking down in writing the various contributions. Several early achievements of St Ives OCS are mentioned by Jenkin, including the revival of Christmas guise dancing there, the rescue and recording of local 'curls' (carols) to be sung at their Winter Festival and the revival of the Midsummer Eve Bonfire celebration.[10]

The Old Cornwall Movement did not of course emerge fully formed from nowhere. The publication of Henry Jenner's[11] Handbook of the Cornish language in 1904 is often used as a convenient starting point for the Cornish Revival, but Jenner himself and others had been interesting themselves with the Cornish language and Cornish issues since the 19th century, building on the work of scholars of the previous two centuries. As well as the publication of the Handbook, the first few years of the 20th century saw, for example, the foundation of the important but short-lived Cowethas Kelto-Kernuak (Celtic-Cornish Society) (1901), Jenner's installation as a bard of the Breton Gorsedd (1903) and Cornwall's admission to the Pan-Celtic Congress (1904). The Cowethas is particularly noteworthy since its stated aims were similar in many ways to those of Old Cornwall. On his retirement from the British Museum in 1909 Jenner returned to Cornwall, where he and Nance quickly formed a friendship based on mutual interests and enthusiasms. Jenner and his wife Kitty Lee, as well as Nance's wife Maud, were members of the group which met in St Ives.

The time was ripe for the formation of the Old Cornwall Movement – 'a uniquely Cornish concept' in the memorable words of Brian Coombes[12] – which was in turn to lead to the foundation of other Cornwall-centred organisations.

A production of Robert Morton Nance's dialect play **Duffy and the Devil** *(l to r: Miss R Frazier, AK Hamilton Jenkin, Nance, May James). Courtesy of Carola Nance Scupham.*

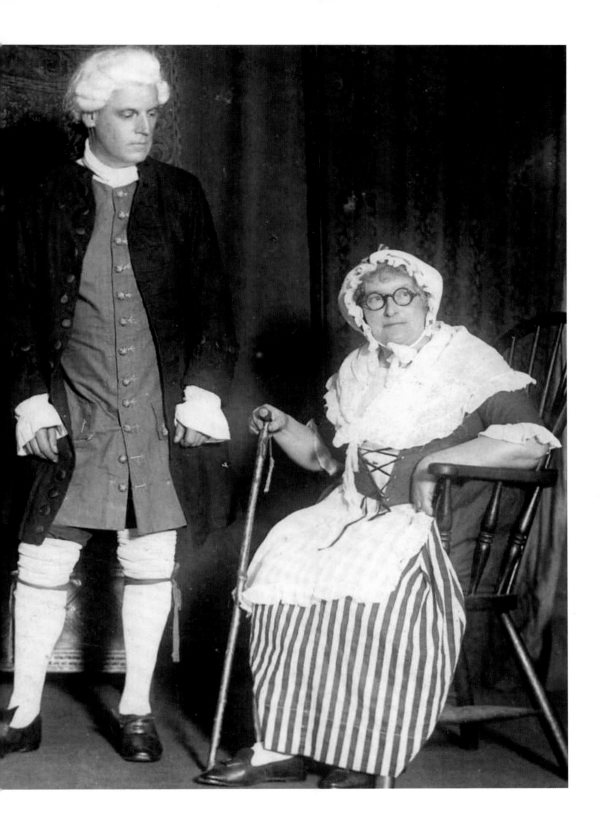

At that first St Ives meeting in January 1920, attended by the Jenners, the Nances, Mrs James, Mrs Pool and others, 'Mr Jenner followed by Mr Nance explained at length the aims and object [sic] of the Society & after discussion – It was decided to form a Society & that it be called The 'St Ives Old Cornwall Society'. It was also decided to call a Public Meeting at an early date ...'[13] This meeting was duly held on February 11th, when Jenner and Nance sought to awake public interest and enthusiasm. If longevity is any guide their endeavour was successful, since in January 2020 the Society triumphantly celebrated its centenary.[14]

Nance filled the important office of Recorder in the St Ives Society, while Jenner, as the patriarch of the Cornish Revival, was inevitably elected as its first President, just as he was to become the first President of the Federation of Old Cornwall Societies four years later and first Grand Bard of the Cornish Gorsedh in 1928. (In addition, in 1923 he had founded the OCS in Hayle, where he lived, becoming its first President, and he was also first President of Redruth OCS.)[15] Shortly after the formation of the St Ives Society, Jenner expressed his support for its approach: "Why not have Old Cornwall Societies all over the county?' he asked. Run on different lines, they would not clash with the old existing societies and 'might indeed be worked on lines similar to those of those excellent things, the Women's Institutes, with perhaps eventually a similar collective organisation'."[16]

For well over two years, until the founding of the Truro Old Cornwall Society at the beginning of June 1922, the St Ives OCS and the Old Cornwall Movement were formally one and the same. The first 'official' meeting, in March 1920, was announced in the local press. Rules were discussed and adopted, and working methods considered at length. The importance of Recording was already being stressed: 'It was hoped that all members would cultivate the note book habit.' The minutes of the following meeting, in April, include the decision by all present 'that no one be elected a member of the Executive Committee unless they be Cornish.'

By the time of the Annual Meeting in March 1922 the membership had reached 70, though only 24 attended the meeting. At the equivalent meeting a year later Nance took up a position which was to become familiar and perennially necessary as he 'spoke of the work of the Society during the year & incited the Members to further effort especially in the matter of dialect words & Place names, & was very desirious [sic] of every member feeling his or her personal responsibility in contributing to the general information.' It was at this meeting that a committee was formed to work towards the Museum which the Society hoped to found.

In the range of its work the St Ives Old Cornwall Society showed the way right from the start, as its early minute books show. A selection of its activities might include: archaeological and restoration work, and lobbying to save sites and buildings; purchase of traditional farm implements which would otherwise have been lost; transcription of church records; outreach to village communities with the Old Cornwall message; outreach to the wider Celtic world; co-operation with other OCSs and with outside organisations for the common good; numerous local pilgrimages, festivals and Cornish-language classes; advice on appropriate and grammatical Cornish names for new developments; regular dialect meetings and classes, and performance of dialect plays; musical performances; involvement in local events and engagement with the town; erecting commemorative plaques; revival of folk customs; donations to appropriate causes; members' evenings, at which those present were encouraged to be providers of instruction and entertainment rather than mere recipients; establishing a Society library; and money-raising activities.

The original Society was regarded as a model for others to follow – at the October 1931 AGM of the Federation of Old Cornwall Societies, for instance, it was recommended that the rules of the St Ives Society should be adopted by all other Societies.

1924: The Federation of Old Cornwall Societies

Jenner's 'collective organisation' was to come about sooner than he had anticipated. Moves towards inter-Society links can be discerned as early as September 1922, at which stage only the St Ives, Truro and Redruth Societies had been formed, though preparations for setting up other Societies were clearly being made. The time had come to meet the need for a unifying agency to keep the different Societies in contact and facilitate the exchange of information. At a committee meeting of the St Ives Society that month it was decided to 'hold an Open Session on ... Oct 7th at our Club Room & invite the various societies to come & join us visiting places of interest about St Ives ... & then all joining in a meeting to be held after tea.' At the St Ives Annual Meeting in March 1924, by which time Hayle and Camborne OCSs had also been founded, the proposal that a 'Central Federation of Old Cornwall Societies' should be formed was discussed. One month later the proposal was ratified, as recorded in a low-key statement signed by Jenner at the beginning of the first Federation minute book:

> At a meeting of Old Cornwall Societies held at Camborne 22 April 1924, it was decided to form a Central Federation of the Societies, for the purpose of seeing that all were working on similar lines, and to prevent overlapping.[17]

This modest declaration marked the beginning of an organisation which has acted as a reference point for the individual OCSs ever since, co-ordinating activities, offering advice, publicity and financial help, supporting other Cornish bodies with similar aims and using its collective strength to lobby on Cornwall's behalf. Delegates from the St Ives, Redruth, Hayle and Camborne Societies attended this preliminary meeting (26 people in all), and the Officers elected were Henry Jenner (President), Revd J Sims Carah (Vice-President), Robert Morton Nance (Recorder) and AK Hamilton Jenkin (Secretary). Each Society would have the right to send representatives to Federation meetings. The Officers would meet and draw up 'rules of Council'.

The first meeting of the new Federation was held at Redruth on July 22nd 1924 and was attended by one or more delegates from the five Societies which had so far been formed and from Helston, where a Society would not be officially founded till later that year. The meeting agreed to draw up rules and suggestions for the guidance of the Societies, which stipulated that Society officials 'should be Cornish, except under exceptional circumstances' and that the annual affiliation fee should be not less than 1d per member. The official version of the Rules, sent to Society Secretaries in September 1924, also required that those Secretaries should keep in touch with the Secretary of the Central Committee and that each Society 'shall have as its main object the collection of details of the past life of Cornwall.' The Recommendations listed in the same document are: that great care be taken to ensure that notices to the press about Old Cornwall Societies are duly authorised in order to prevent the publication of inaccurate reports; that since pilgrimages (preferably with a knowledgeable guide) are undertaken with the object of learning more about Old Cornwall, all members should take an active interest in them;[18] that every member should endeavour to know and make a point of using the correct pronunciation of Cornish personal and place names.

The requirement that Society officers should be Cornish whenever possible could hardly be met today and seems indeed to sit uneasily with the Constitution's policy that '[t]he Federation will be non-political, non-sectarian, non-discriminatory and operate a policy of equal opportunity.' In any case, though most Cornish people know who they are, to define precisely what 'being Cornish' means is not so easy. Whatever definition is used, the Cornish have become a minority within Cornwall, but thankfully a person's ethnicity does not determine their enthusiasm or preparedness to work for Old Cornwall. The feeling reflected by the 1924 Rules, however, was genuine and strong. It can also be seen in WA Pascoe's words to the Liskeard Society shortly after its formation,

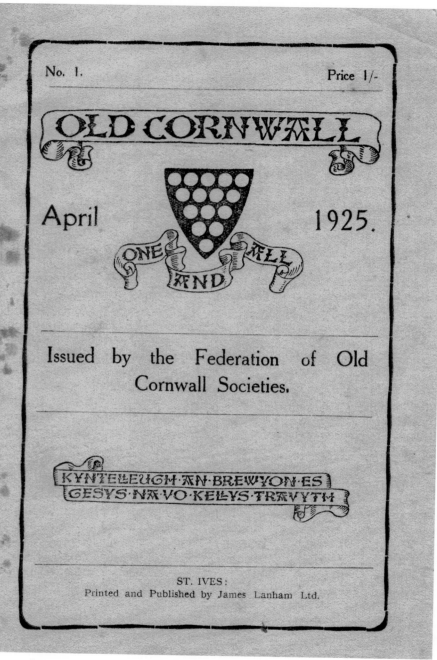

No. 1.   Price 1/-

OLD CORNWALL

April   1925.

ONE AND ALL

Issued by the Federation of Old Cornwall Societies.

KYNTELLEUGH AN BREWYON ES GESYS NA VO KELLYS TRAVYTH

ST. IVES:
Printed and Published by James Lanham Ltd.

Old Cornwall, no 1, April 1925. Courtesy of Terry Knight.

at its monthly meeting in December 1928. The immediate success of the Society 'among all classes of local Cornish men and women,' he said, 'went to show that such a society filled … a place in their lives and a demand in their hearts which had hitherto remained empty and unsatisfied' and gave them 'the opportunities and the privilege to assert their somewhat dormant national consciousness and voice their racial aspirations.'[19] Though the sentiment would be expressed somewhat differently today, the heartfelt desire to save something precious in imminent danger of being lost for ever is palpable and has never disappeared.

At the second Federation meeting, at Hayle in November 1924, it was resolved that an Old Cornwall Journal should if feasible be printed and that Nance and Hamilton Jenkin should be responsible for the first issue. Jenkin was asked to sound out the Societies to obtain some idea of the number of sales they might expect. The committee also authorised the printing and distribution of a circular to estate agents and solicitors, inviting them to deposit obsolete documents of Cornish interest in the library of the Royal Institution of Cornwall – this modest item appears to have been the first 'publication' of the Federation.

1925: The Old Cornwall Journal

Old Cornwall, the journal of the Federation of Old Cornwall Societies,[20] is a rich source of information about the history, activities and character of the movement it represents. It has always retained something of its original essence, though it has certainly changed over the years. If it had not, perhaps it would not have proved uniquely durable – despite some rocky moments – compared to other Cornish periodicals. Two of the many recurring motifs in the history of the movement are the need for a larger circulation for the journal and appeals for contributions to it. Unique in some ways, it has nonetheless been compared to other publications, Devon & Cornwall Notes & Queries being one, but the closest to it in spirit are surely the two 'Notes and Queries' series published in the Cornish Telegraph and

the Western Morning News, edited by Peter Penn (E Whitfield Crofts) and Joseph Hambley Rowe respectively. Selections of the former appeared in printed form as Cornish Notes & Queries (1906). The Telegraph series started in 1903, and after it had run its course the WMN series took up the idea, starting before Old Cornwall first appeared in 1925 and continuing for some years afterwards. Nance was a contributor to it and references to Old Cornwall are found within it. Rowe himself, surgeon and Cornish activist, was a stalwart of Old Cornwall and other Cornish organisations who would later become Deputy Grand Bard of the Cornish Gorsedh.[21]

The first number of Old Cornwall appeared in April 1925, with a cover price of 1/- (5 p). It was published in St Ives by James Lanham, included advertisements before and after the main text, and bore on its cover and title-page the Cornish arms and motto ('One and All') as well as the motto of the Old Cornwall Movement, in the Cornish spelling of the time: 'Kyntelleugh an brewyon es gesys na vo kellys travyth' ('Gather up the fragments that remain, that nothing be lost'),[22] a biblical injunction which encapsulates well a fundamental purpose of the movement. (The text has nevertheless been used as a criticism of a 'soft' approach to achieving Cornish aspirations: '"a gathering of the fragments" – antiquarianism tinged with nostalgia and romanticism.')[23] The precise layout of the first Old Cornwall cover was never used again. The editorship of Nance and Hamilton Jenkin was intended to be a temporary arrangement pending the appointment of a permanent editorial staff, according to the note preceding the main contents. This refers to the journal as an 'experimental' issue and acknowledges that it presents 'an undue representation of St. Ives,' but suggests that individual Societies should take their turn in compiling subsequent issues. (In the event, though Truro, Redruth and Camborne were responsible for the second to fourth issues respectively, this idea did not last beyond four issues.) It was proposed that two issues should appear in the first year, with the hope that four would be published the following year and that ideally the journal would be issued monthly in

The Old Cornwall Societies were instrumental in maintaining traditional customs like Crying the Neck.
Courtesy of the late Paddy Bradley.

due course 'for lovers of Cornwall throughout the world.' If attained, this should be most useful 'in binding together the scattered little Cornish Nation.' In retrospect, this seems hugely optimistic, but on the other hand the fact that the journal has appeared annually since 1925 (usually twice a year) is a remarkable achievement. The note also refers to the 'vast amount of Cornish matter that ought to be printed,' the only difficulty being in making a selection. 'Urgency, the unique character of the information given, and the appeal made by them to Cornish patriotic feeling, have been the chief grounds for including the articles here printed.' This first issue sold so well that, uniquely, a 'second edition' of it (really a corrected reprint) was published, with a one-off cover price of 2/-, after the second issue had already appeared (October 1925). In June 1990, a 'Special Edition' of the journal was issued, to mark the 70th anniversary of the formation of the St Ives Society, comprising principally a facsimile reprint of the original issue.

It is fitting that the first article in the first journal is a statement of principle by Robert Morton Nance, entitled 'What we stand for', which can be seen as a founding document of the movement. Interestingly, his first point refers to the fact that various suggestions of name for the original group at St Ives had been rejected in favour of Old Cornwall Society, which 'was thought exactly to meet the case, for we had come together to strengthen one another in our devotion to all those ancient things that make the spirit of Cornwall – its traditions, its old words and ways, and what remains to it of its Celtic language and nationality.'

Several times over the years the suggestion has been made that the name of the movement should be changed, specifically to avoid the supposed negative connotations of the word 'old' in the minds of potential younger members who should not be put off from joining a Society because of it. In fact, it could be said that Nance addresses this very question as the next point in his manifesto. Referring to the OC motto, he states:

[T]hese fragments we set ourselves to gather, not in the spirit of collectors of quaint and useless curios, but as gleaners of the folk-culture of Cornwall, upon which all really Cornish art and literature of the future must be based, and hoping that future generations will arise, Cornish still, to make good use of them. It is for such a "New Cornwall" that we work, but it is "Old Cornwall" that provides us with all this essence of Cornishness that we mean to hand on to it, so "Old Cornwall Societies" we have been ever since, and OLD CORNWALL is the obvious name for our journal.

He goes on to contrast the aims of the Old Cornwall Movement with those of the long-established learned societies which concern themselves with Cornish antiquities. Both he and Jenner held office in organisations such as the Royal Cornwall Polytechnic Society and the Royal Institution of Cornwall and contributed to their journals, and he acknowledges that they 'have done much to uphold the honour of Cornwall' but

[t]o them … Cornwall's past is a subject for antiquarian discussions; to us it holds a living spirit, and in our unlearned way we aim at spreading a knowledge of this past amongst Cornish people of every sort as a thing that is necessary to them if they would remain Cornish. From these learned societies, to which we may serve as recruiting bodies perhaps, but which we do not rival, we differ also in that we are as much interested in the holiday, workaday and home life of older generations – the festivals, the hearthside tales, the printed dialect literature, and the old songs and words – as in any other side of the past of Cornwall, and are as ready to honour the teller of a good Cornish story in the good old way, as we are [to] recognise the value of more difficult but less love-inspired research on Cornish Antiquities.[24]

He reflects ruefully on the changes that had transformed Cornwall in the 60 to 70 years prior to that point, writing that

> *… all this traditional knowledge is the very savour and Cornishness of Cornwall, without which the name is but an empty one; and it is this that we seek to gather up, bit by bit, and to hand on again to those of Cornish origin who are in danger of growing up without any of it … for all this traditional Cornishness is apt to be cast away in ignorance, that self-blinding ignorance that despises all knowledge lying near at hand for the sake of standardized book-learning from a distance.*

He then discusses the merits of the Cornish language and dialect, lamenting the fact that the former was allowed to fall into general disuse and looking to the latter as a means of regaining and retaining Cornish distinctiveness. He states that the dialect 'happily is still far from being a dead language' (which was unfortunately no longer true by the end of the 20th century though dialect stories remained popular as entertainment). He also mentions old customs, which should be documented and if possible revived. (The Old Cornwall Movement has in fact been instrumental over the years in breathing new life into old customs, two of the most prominent being Crying the Neck and Midsummer Bonfires, first staged by the Federation in 1928 and 1929 respectively.) Old methods of working are full of interest, he says, and should be recorded – 'here is work that awaits Old Cornwall workers in every parish.'

Incorrect ways of pronouncing place-names, and even their disappearance, are also causes of concern for Nance, and again it is notable how the same issues are still with us today: 'We often have,' he says, 'an uncertain feeling as to whether it is not "common," or still worse, "affected," to be true and natural in speaking what is left of our own Ancient British language in such names, and we must encourage each other to be firmer …'

Nance ends his declaration with his portrait of the typical Old Cornwall member, 'a person who is first of all on the watch for anything that is not generally known of the words and ways of the Cornish people of old times.' Such people 'are the salt of the movement, without which no merely antiquarian, linguistic, or historical members, however brilliant, could long keep it from perishing.' He concludes:

> *This movement has but one enemy – that ugly thing Snobbery. It concerns itself in no way with questions of religion and politics, and has no anti-foreign side to its pro-Cornish propaganda. It asks the comradeship and help of true lovers of Cornwall, "one and all" …*

AK Hamilton Jenkin later wrote,[25] 'With such a programme of tasks as is outlined [in 'What we stand for'] it is small wonder that our ambitions often outran our achievements. It should be remembered, however, to what extent we were then in the position of pioneers.' To emphasise this he went on to list several organisations which came into being in later years to take on specific areas of activity which Old Cornwall had already included in its remit, including the Cornwall Record Office itself (now part of Kresen Kernow, Redruth). Cornwall has changed enormously in many ways – not least in its demographic make-up – since Nance wrote his Old Cornwall statement of principle but his words ring with conviction, and practical results were achieved: 'Within limits,' wrote Hamilton Jenkin, 'the Old Cornwall Societies saved much that might have been lost for ever.' As well as appearing in the 1990 'Special Edition' of the first number of *Old Cornwall*, 'What we stand for' was reprinted again in 2010[26] in connection with the 90th anniversary of St Ives OCS that year.

This founding number of the journal includes articles on mining, Cornish language and dialect, folk songs and drama, as well as reports from the Federation and from Societies, roughly in order of their formation: St Ives, Truro (1922), Redruth (1922), Hayle (1923), Camborne (1923), Helston (1924) and Madron (1924). The range of activities already undertaken by these early Societies, the personnel forming their committees, the speakers at their meetings and the size of their membership are impressive. (Nance was tireless in his close involvement with new Societies as they were set up, speaking at inaugural meetings or delivering lectures to their members.)

A report on 'Sympathisers and Supporters' underlines the point that the movement has always been keen to foster links and working relationships with other organisations having compatible aims, such as the Royal Institution of Cornwall, the Royal Cornwall Polytechnic Society and the London Cornish Association, and willing to welcome them as affiliated members. There was no wish to compete with them. The printing of a letter from a Cornish 'exile' in Australia exemplified the backing of members of the Cornish diaspora, and the encouragement of Cornish newspapers, 'whose reports have unfailingly approved of all that we do or dream of,' was welcomed.

The Federation report in this first journal outlines the relationship which should exist between the central body and the individual Societies, which remained independent but were happy to work together to further the Old Cornwall ideal. The publication of the journal was itself made possible through setting up the Federation. Interestingly, the report also states that another long-cherished objective which the Federation may also be able to realise is the establishment in Cornwall of 'something akin to the Welsh National Eisteddfod' because 'something in which an appeal would be made to the best side of local patriotism in the mass should exist here as it has existed in Wales.' This aim of Nance's was partially fulfilled with the inauguration of the Cornish Gorsedh, under Old Cornwall auspices, in 1928.[27] The Welsh Gorsedd is a component of the Eisteddfod, but the first Cornish Eisteddfod (Esedhvos Kernow) was not held until 1983, 24 years after Nance's death, and in Cornwall the Gorsedh continued to be widely recognised as the foremost Cornish cultural institution.

The report's final point is that the movement should be outgoing and inclusive with respect to other Cornish and Celtic organisations:

The Federation forms a means of keeping its component societies in touch not only with one another, but also with all other Cornish societies throughout the world, and, through the Celtic Congress, with all other Celtic societies, most of which are like ourselves striving to preserve the national traditions of a Celtic people.

Philip Payton's assertion that *Old Cornwall* provided 'an important window into the motives and activities of the Revivalists in this period'[28] could be justified by reference to this first number alone.

As well as songs and dialect, topics covered in the second issue (October 1925) included smuggling, wrestling, charms and witchcraft. Advertisements were charged at a guinea (£1.05) per page. Issue 2 also contained an article headed 'Old Cornwall Societies', describing how they work, calling for more to be formed and setting out their philosophy in visionary terms:

These Societies are being formed as a means of saving before it is quite too late the threatened Cornishness of Cornwall. To each lover of Cornwall this Cornish individuality may seem specially to rest in some one feature – Local History and Architecture, the Cornish Language and Place-names, the Local Dialect, Folk-lore or even Local Gossip … [A]n Old Cornwall Society is not an Antiquarian Association, not a Celtic Society nor even a Cornish Social Club. It may seem all these by turns, but it is always something more. It gathers up these things of the past … as the Living Tradition of the Cornish People; the material in which the Spirit of Cornwall is to be handed on to future generations … Ours is thus the beginning at least of a National Movement …

More practically, the procedures for setting up a new Society are explained, mentioning the small affiliation fee paid to the Federation 'in return for a large amount of potential help.' (Notwithstanding the smallness of the fee, arrears in its payment are another recurring motif in Federation minute books.) A minimum of one meeting a month was desirable, with papers being read and set subjects discussed. Pilgrimages to historic sites often took the place of summer meetings. To a large extent the pattern described here is still maintained today. The article concludes: 'To attempt thus to preserve the individuality of Cornwall is not a reactionary effort to "stop the clock" … Let us be ourselves and live.'[29]

At the Federation meeting in December 1925 it was decided that the next 'All Cornwall Social of the Societies' should take place at Redruth. Each Society was requested to play its part in the general entertainment, and each member asked to wear a ribbon of their Society's colour. Such annual social gatherings of the Societies were clearly features from the start and remain an important part of the Old Cornwall year, notably with the Summer and Winter Festivals (both originating in the 1920s), though across-the-board participation in entertainment and the wearing of ribbons are no longer requirements. Another important matter was also in the Federation's mind at this early stage:

> With a view to getting a better exchange of the many excellent papers now read at local societies (and afterwards passing into oblivion,) it was asked that secretaries should supply the names of those willing to read their papers elsewhere, to the Federation Secretary. It was hoped also by this means to get papers of an Old Cornwall nature more frequently taken out to villages and towns, where as yet Societies do not exist.

Letters of congratulation on the work of Old Cornwall and the journal from members of the Cornish diaspora in different parts of the world were read, as well as the 'good wishes of our Celtic cousins and sympathisers in Brittany.' The Breton link was an ongoing feature of Old Cornwall outreach, particularly in connection with Cornish-Breton wrestling tournaments, and

was to become particularly important during the World War of 1939-45.

The Federation report in the third *Old Cornwall* (April 1926) begins by referring to the Festival at Redruth and repeats the hope that, 'as the only meeting attended by Cornish people simply because they are Cornish and enjoy being as Cornish as possible,' it will be a step towards a Cornish version of the Eisteddfod in Wales. It also mentions the leading part taken by the Federation in preparing for the Celtic Congress, due to take place in Cornwall for the first time the following summer. At the foundation of the Federation Nance had pressed for its admission to the Congress as the only Cornish Society 'that aims at fostering a popular sense of Cornish nationality and Celtic sympathies' and had successfully negotiated a reduced (i.e. affordable) fee.[30] (In the event the Congress could not be held because of the general strike.)

Ten Societies, from Penzance to Padstow, are listed in the report. Also described are the first proper Federation publications (apart from *Old Cornwall* itself): a ballad sheet with the words sung at the Padstow 'Obby 'Oss festival and a leaflet with Jenner's translation into Cornish of the UK and Welsh national anthems. (A version of the latter ('Bro Goth Agan Tasow') is still sung as part of the Cornish Gorsedh ceremony every

The Old Cornwall badge. Courtesy of Toby Nicholson.

September.) It was hoped that other publications would be possible, but support from the membership would be necessary to achieve this. (The bibliography in this book is testament to the long history of publication which the Federation came to achieve.) The Cornish press is again commended for its support of the movement, as are newspapers in Wales and Brittany.

The April 1927 issue of *Old Cornwall* was the first to contain pictures. Tellingly, in contrast to the situation in 1925, it also included an appeal for more copy and Recorders' notes to be submitted for publication. New Societies reported at this time included one at the University College of the South West (the forerunner of the University of Exeter), an institution which also issued an appeal for funds among the advertising material in the journal. Membership was open to all Cornish residents of Exeter as well as to staff and students of the college, but the Society's existence was fleeting. This issue also reported the publication of the first edition of the pamphlet *Old Cornwall Societies: what they are and what they are doing* (priced 2d), which gave a useful outline of the background of the movement and the work of the Societies.[31]

The Federation and the Old Cornwall Movement as a whole clearly gained a strong foothold in Cornwall quite rapidly, the journal reporting the invitation to Old Cornwall from the Secretary of the Cornwall Education Committee to play a part in Cornish education. It was suggested that some children could be admitted to meetings and lectures as appropriate and could take part in summer pilgrimages, and Old Cornwall talks could be given in schools (work which had already begun). The Societies were invited to play a role in Education Week in May and June 1927, and the Federation was invited to submit a panel of lecturers to the Local Education Authority. Overall, Societies continued to report progress in membership and activities, with St Ives holding one dialect evening and two Cornish language classes every month. The spread of Old Cornwall Societies was seen as one of the most noteworthy features in the recent history of Cornwall. 'An interest in Local History, Customs and Folk-lore, always latent in Cornish people is thus finding expression to-day on a scale quite unprecedented in the past.' In a voluntary organisation, however, in which subscriptions were nominal and reserves non-existent, funds were urgently needed for publications and the preservation of objects.

The *Old Cornwall* journal reflected the moves towards the creation of the Cornish Gorsedh. The Federation report in the sixth issue described the Summer Pilgrimage in 1927, which included a visit to Boscawen-Un, where Henry Jenner, in his Breton bardic robes, 'spoke of its associations with the Gorsedd of the Ancient Britons.' 'I should like to throw it out as a hint,' he said, 'that we really ought some day to have a Cornish Gorsedd.'[32] Several Federation representatives had attended the Inter-Celtic Festival at Riec, Brittany, in August 1927, where WD Watson had made a speech in Cornish. This report also mentions the Federation meeting in October 1927, at which the emblem of the chough was adopted as the Old Cornwall badge, with the motto in Nance's 'archaic' script and Cornish spelling of the time: 'Nynsyu marow maghtern Arthur' ('King Arthur is not dead'). (The chough emblem and motto, in slightly amended orthography, has appeared on the back of the journal since 1998.) Though it was 'still living too hand-to-mouth an existence' and needed more copy, *Old Cornwall* had now reached a stage where a published index could be contemplated, though this did not become a reality till 1948.

The record of the meeting in October 1927 also indicates the first instance of the Federation's taking on the role of lobbyist. There was a resolution that Cornwall County Council (as it then was) be requested to revive the sub-committee charged with the preservation of ancient monuments in Cornwall and to take all steps to preserve ancient landmarks and trackways, in fact 'to do everything in their power to preserve the Amenities of Cornwall.' The Federation also pledged to do all they could to encourage the revival of Cornish wrestling, and they did indeed provide consistent support for the Cornish Wrestling Association over the years and promoted tournaments between Cornish and Breton wrestlers.

The Federation meeting in February 1928 was the first of several to be held at Penponds, where James Sims Carah was vicar. After the attendees had visited Richard Trevithick's cottage there, Carah presented a paper about the building, and from then on till well into the 1940s a great deal of Federation work was devoted to the cottage's preservation. The Federation would provide some of the trustees who would join with other organisations to launch a joint appeal to repair the building and set it up as a memorial to Trevithick and a folk museum – an early example of Old Cornwall's willingness to cooperate to achieve desired results.[33]

1928: The first Cornish Gorsedh

The main interest in the April 1928 issue of *Old Cornwall* is again its anticipation of the Cornish Gorsedh. It includes the text of Henry Jenner's address at the previous year's Summer Pilgrimage, and the aspiration expressed in it was fulfilled in September 1928 when the first Gorsedh Kernow ceremony was held at Boscawen-Un, under Old Cornwall auspices. Twelve bards were initiated, including Charles Henderson, AK Hamilton Jenkin and Sir Arthur Quiller-Couch. In preparation for this, eight bards from Cornwall, including Nance, had already been initiated at the Welsh Gorsedd at Treorchy in August, following a request from the Federation. Nance, the Federation Recorder, had assisted in drawing up this petition, in Cornish and English.[34] Henry Jenner was clear that it was the 'unqualified success' of the Old Cornwall Movement which had made the Gorsedh possible 'and there is no doubt that to the Old Cornwall Societies belongs the credit of making it an accomplished fact. We really ought to be pleased with ourselves.'[35] At the time, as the journal makes clear, it was not assumed that the Cornish Gorsedh ceremony would be repeated the following year, but in the event it found the strength to hang on and has been held every year since 1928 in one form or another. Though the Gorsedh is widely regarded as the foremost cultural organisation in Cornwall, it was Old Cornwall that led to its creation, and the connection between the two is maintained and expressed visually every

September at the Gorsedh ceremony, where the banners[36] of OC Societies are employed to good effect in the parade and the display at the Gorsedh site. Material relating to the Gorsedh, including prize essays, have found a regular place in *Old Cornwall*, and in 2010 the links between the two movements were said to be 'ever-closer.'[37] There has always been a marked crossover in the personnel and officers of the two, as well as common aims and interests, and several Grand Bards have served as Federation President or in other OC capacities: Henry Jenner, Robert Morton Nance, EG Retallack Hooper, George Pawley White, Denis Trevanion, Richard Jenkin, Hugh Miners, Brian Coombes, Merv Davey. In the journal issued the month after the first Gorsedh the Federation report drives the point home: '[I]t is safe to say that but for the Old Cornwall movement, there would have been no Gorsedd, and it was thus very much an affair of our own though something wider as well.' Henry Jenner welcomed the Gorsedh while

Commemorative pamphlet for the first Cornish Gorsedh, 1928. Courtesy of Toby Nicholson.

maintaining that its establishment did not remove a duty from the Old Cornwall movement: 'When Cornishmen cease to recognize the existence of their Celtic heritage then only will their Cornish and therefore Celtic nationality cease. It is for the Old Cornwall Societies to see to it that such a calamity never happens.'[38]

The first appearance of book reviews, which would become a regular feature of the journal, also occurred in the issue of April 1928, as did the expressed ambition to achieve Cornwall-wide coverage by the Old Cornwall Movement to make good the 'many missing links in our chain.'

It was in 1928 too that Nance was asked to carry on as sole editor of *Old Cornwall* after Hamilton Jenkin had to step down as joint editor. (Except for a brief period in the early 1930s Nance continued as editor till his death in 1959.) The delegates to the 1928 AGM regarded the journal as 'the most valuable propaganda of the Federation and the strongest link between the Old Cornwall Societies and interested Cornish people at home and abroad.' The future of the publication, however, was clearly not regarded as assured: 'Whilst it was recognised that the journal was in a critical stage of development it was felt … that any premature thought of its abandonment was to be highly deplored;' the 'margin between profit and loss … was a very small one and it only required a slightly increased circulation and a few more advertisements to place it in a satisfactory financial position.' The Societies' representatives agreed to make a special effort to ensure its future.

Two important Cornish books were published in 1929. Nance's *Cornish for all* is discussed in the section on the Cornish language. The other was Ralph Dunstan's *Cornish Song Book (Lyver Canow Kernewek)*,[39] to which Jenner, Nance and Old Cornwall in general made a considerable contribution. Dunstan wrote a piece about the book in *Old Cornwall* in April that year.[40] In the October journal an article by J Hambley Rowe on William Bottrell (the author of *Traditions and hearthside stories of West Cornwall* who died in St Ives in 1881) includes the arresting statement

that Bottrell 'may be said to be the posthumous founder of the Old Cornwall movement: for though he had been dead over sixty years before it started, it was his influence that was paramount on the little group that formed themselves into the pioneer Old Cornwall Society.' And so another name is added to the founding mothers and fathers.

Throughout its life the *Old Cornwall* journal has been regularly used to outline some of the work of individual Societies as well as that of the Federation, and in the Winter 1930 issue 'Old Cornwall in action' reports work in the fields of restoration, renovation, preservation, maintenance, transcription of records and the erection of memorial tablets. There is also a list of OC Secretaries and colours for the 16 Societies

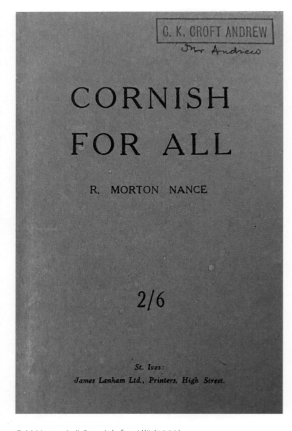

C. K. CROFT ANDREW

CORNISH FOR ALL

R. MORTON NANCE

2/6

St. Ives:
James Lanham Ltd., Printers, High Street.

R M Nance's " Cornish for All" (1929).
Courtesy of Toby Nicholson.

then in existence. (Though not mentioned, there had been attempts to establish Societies in other places but they had not survived, as would happen again.) *Old Cornwall* itself had however reached a crisis point: this issue is described as 'probably the final number of this journal' and it ends with Nance's 'Editorial Ultimatum':

> *Whether this is a farewell or not depends on Old Cornwall members. We have reached our twelfth issue, but in the past five years, which have doubled our membership, our circulation has stood still … [A]ll we can, and do, ask is that Old Cornwall should be loyally supported by those it serves. At present it seems that Cornwall is tired of it.*

This stark declaration goes on to offer ways to prevent the journal from foundering, offering specific suggestions to Secretaries, Journal Secretaries, Recorders and writers; and all readers 'who are wearied by serious articles,' he declares, 'must themselves see that somehow the lighter dialect tales, verse, songs, etc., that are equally welcome are sent to it. If they do not, they may expect to see more notes on Cornish Antiquities, or, still worse, unreadable *Kernewek* [Cornish].' The exasperated tone here may resonate with subsequent editors of the journal, indeed with journal editors in general. The last appeal of the 'Ultimatum' may equally strike a chord with many of the more active Old Cornwall workers:

> *All Members must know that an Old Cornwall Society is no mere social club for summer outings or winter happy-evenings, but exists for a definite end; has before it a next to impossible task – that of keeping Cornwall Cornish – and therefore demands of them more than the occasional wearing of a badge or the payment of a nominal subscription.*[41]

If the baton were not taken up, Nance concluded, *Old Cornwall* would cease. He had felt equally pessimistic about the durability of the Gorsedh, and for similar reasons,[42] yet both have survived various crises and kept going. Such perennial

difficulties as the 'Ultimatum' addresses did not however disappear from the movement.

Despite Nance's misgivings, the next issue of the journal (vol. 2, no. 1) appeared on schedule and, while recognising the pertinency of the problems outlined by him, struck a less pessimistic tone. AA Clinnick had taken over as editor (briefly, as it turned out), but the great debt owed to Nance by the Societies, for the first 12 issues of the journal and for much else, was acknowledged at this stage. The 13th journal included brief extracts from an interesting article by two younger members, M Trewhella Uren and EG Retallack Hooper (the latter of whom would succeed Nance as Grand Bard 28 years later). It is clear that the two men had worked on ideas for shaking up the movement, including the introduction of readings and conversations in Cornish into Society meetings. Among their other suggestions was a National Festival for Cornwall, which has arguably come to pass with the increasingly popular celebration of St Piran's Day each year as well as Esedhvos Kernow (the Cornish Eisteddfod) and other events.

The Celtic Congress eventually came to Cornwall for the first time in 1932, when the Federation played a large part in the proceedings. Its President, Henry Jenner, had also been elected President of the Congress. In the Winter 1932 issue of the journal there was a report on 'Old Cornwall and the Celtic Congress', written by Nance as National Secretary for Cornwall. The event had been a great success, and his report includes the speech by Jenner on the 'Awakening of Celtic Cornwall', which contrasted the few workers for the cause in the early days with 'the vastly improved conditions to-day, when thanks to the Old Cornwall Movement no intelligent Cornish person can remain utterly ignorant of his or her Celtic nationality, and thousands take a real pride in it.' Many OC members had attended the Congress sessions or excursions, and others the Gorsedh ceremony at the Merry Maidens. 'For the special benefit of Old Cornwall members,' too, 'it was arranged that the one Congress paper which most vitally and directly concerned the future of the Old Cornwall Movement should be read to

Robert Morton Nance (in his customary plus-fours, centre) in Brittany in the summer of 1938. He was the head of the first official Cornish delegation to take part in a Breton Gorsedd, where he delivered a speech in Cornish in the name of the bards. Courtesy of St Ives OCS.

them at the assembly at Penzance which followed on the Gorsedd.' Nance links this paper by Maud Quayle with the new Cornish youth movement Tyr ha Tavas ('Land and Language') which

> should prove a very valuable adjunct to the movement of which the Gorsedd is one expression and the Federation of Old Cornwall Societies another … The knowledge of this nucleus of a Youth Movement should … be spread by all our societies, and meanwhile these should all do their utmost to attract young people to themselves, especially by offering them SOMETHING TO DO. "Old Cornwall" is often strangely misinterpreted as meaning "the Cornwall that can only interest old people." If it were more widely known that one "Old Cornwall" object (set out in the Rules of the first society) has always been that of building up a New Cornwall that in spite of all changes shall remain Cornish, it might help to dispel that misunderstanding.

MT Uren was forthright in his criticism of both Old Cornwall and the youth movement in a letter to the press,[43] where he expressed the view that before addressing cultural issues their first responsibility towards the local young unemployed should be to do all they could to help them find work. Commenting on this sentiment in a letter of his own to Retallack Hooper, Wilfred Sarre stated: 'He is right enough, but I fancy many O.C. members are comfortably off themselves, and have little or no sympathy for their less fortunate fellows.' Sarre had personal experience of unemployment, though given the stated aims of Old Cornwall it could be seen as unfair to castigate the whole movement in these terms. The remarks demonstrate nonetheless that even in the early days Old Cornwall was subject to sometimes trenchant criticism. Sarre, moreover, was not without inside knowledge. He acted as Recorder at St Agnes and was a dedicated Old Cornwall worker, as was Hooper, and several articles by both were published in the journal.[44]

In *Old Cornwall* Summer 1933 there are three articles in connection with the formation of Tyr ha Tavas (one of them, by Hooper, in Cornish), where again there is stress on the organisation's not being in competition with Old Cornwall or any other like-minded body. In the event, though Tyr ha Tavas was an important activist organisation, arranged the first few modern church services in Cornish (starting in 1933)[45] and was a forerunner of later developments in the Cornish movement, it did not survive long after the end of the World War in 1945.

In 1933 the Federation was hoping to raise funds for dialect recording and anthropological research, and a proposal that gramophone records of Cornish dialect should be made was accepted. This was not followed through, though the Federation was to issue records of Cornish-language readings by Nance in 1954. The Old Cornwall Movement could be said to have sprung from enthusiasm for Cornish dialect but the membership as a whole has never embraced the subject wholeheartedly, as successive meagre AGM reports from Federation Dialect Recorders testify, though several individual members have actively championed dialect within the movement. At the AGM in September 1933 the Journal Secretary reported that the position of *Old Cornwall* was again far from satisfactory. There was a very small profit margin, fewer copies of the current issue had been ordered, and eight Societies had not yet appointed a Journal Secretary. Inadequate sales of the journal have proved a recurring problem. At some points in its occasionally turbulent history it has not paid its way at all.

The Federation report in the Winter 1933 issue of *Old Cornwall* includes a list of papers read and work accomplished by each of 22 Societies. Many of them are clearly very industrious, including Liskeard, who also have their own troupe of 'Old Cornwall Players'[46] and who were to continue as an impressively active Society. Included in the list are two new Societies: London – formed in connection with the London Cornish Association – and St Agnes. (This was the second St Agnes OCS, which does not appear in the next such list. The current Society is the third.)

1934: Nance as President

Henry Jenner, first President of the Federation and first Grand Bard, died on May 8th 1934: 'The last conscious words uttered by him regarding the movement which was so close to his heart … were, "You will go on," and were answered, for us all, "We will."'[47] Nance succeeded Jenner as Grand Bard and later became the Honorary Secretary of the Jenner Memorial Fund, which was not confined to the Old Cornwall Movement though its aim was to foster 'Old Cornwall Work' and the Federation was one of the trustee organisations. Many Societies committed annual sums towards it.[48] At the Federation AGM in October 1934 Nance was also unanimously elected Federation President in succession to Jenner and at the same time reappointed Federation Recorder and Journal Editor. It was decided in June 1934 that an Executive Council of the Federation should be formed, to which each Society would be entitled to appoint a representative, and it was at an Executive Council meeting in November 1935 that the decision was taken to appoint Special Recorders for particular aspects of Federation activities, to cover the whole of Cornwall. At this stage, the three subject areas decided on were Archaeology, Field & Place Names and Folklore & Dialect. Nance had reported in October that as Federation Recorder he was not receiving as much information as he should and had proposed appointing such Special Recorders. The Field & Place-Names Recorder was Edwin Chirgwin, who was to make the bold claim that he would have collected all the place-names in Cornwall within a short time.[49]

The role of the Federation as a publisher had been growing. The Winter 1934 issue of *Old Cornwall* was the first to feature on its back cover (instead of an advertisement) 'Books of interest to lovers of Cornwall'. Not all of the 16 titles listed were published by the FOCS but they were all 'Issued by the Federation of Old Cornwall Societies' and included some of the first in a long line of FOCS publications, which for a time included Christmas cards. In the journal for Winter 1938 it was announced that Kathleen Jennie (Mrs Ashley) Rowe would be setting up an Old Cornwall bookstall at future Federation Festivals and Pilgrimages, where Cornish publications (from any publisher) would be on sale. The bookstall is still one of the regular stalls that feature at Old Cornwall events, and it crops up on numerous other occasions throughout Cornwall. In the same issue Retallack Hooper put forward the proposition that in the pages of the journal 'a lover of Cornwall finds in the scope of "Old Cornwall work" a veritable university,' in that information provided on aspects of daily life in Cornwall can lead to a deeper interest in, and study of, such subjects as geology, botany and linguistics.

Printed annual reports of the Federation from the 1930s throw some light on the personnel and activities of individual Societies at that time. The 1934-35 report, which was the first to be printed separately, provides data on 18 Societies and on the Bristol and District Cornish Association and the London Cornish. The information provided on the Societies includes details of officers, colours, membership numbers, *Old Cornwall* sales, lecturers and their subjects, pilgrimages, festivals, donations and practical work. The Liskeard Society, under the leadership of its dynamic first President Albert de Castro Glubb, supplies the longest report, with an impressive account of practical projects. Several other Societies are clearly doing well in their different ways, while a few appear to be having a harder time. Penzance has the largest membership (184). Sales of the journal are generally low as a ratio of membership numbers. An additional Society, Newlyn East, appears in the 1936-37 annual report, in which the Newquay Society presents the fullest record, while the Camborne Society states that '[a]ll surplus funds have been expended in maintenance work on Trevithick's Cottage.' Also at Camborne, certain members 'have been doing excellent propaganda work and are arousing considerable interest – especially among the younger generation.'[50]

Newspaper reports are often more forthright and revealing about Old Cornwall meetings than Federation minutes. A report on the 1937 AGM is a case in point: "'As far as folk lore and place names

Old Cornwall Federation meeting circa 1950s. Courtesy of the late TP Roscrow.

are concerned, Old Cornwall Societies are a dead letter, and are not doing anything at all," observed Mr. R. Morton Nance, president …' He thought that since the formation of OCSs even fewer people were interested in Old Cornwall than before. It was therefore resolved that the Special Federation Recorders meet Society Recorders and explain what was wanted – such visits were to form part of the winter programme. Dialect Recorder Jane Kelynack had nothing to report, thinking 'that members were quite content to attend meetings and listen to what other people had to say, but that was about all.' Ashley Rowe pointed out that public transport at night had been cut down so that country people found it impossible to attend meetings in the towns.[51]

In 1938 there was a move by the Federation towards cooperation with the Royal Cornwall Polytechnic Society and the Royal Institution of Cornwall to preserve the most important papers read at their gatherings. There was also agreement that the Societies should cooperate with the Workers' Educational Association in a series of lectures on Cornish history. Plans were in hand for an Old Cornwall group to attend the Breton Gorsedd and the associated Breton-Cornish wrestling that summer, following which they would visit places of interest in Brittany under the guidance of Cornish scholar GH Doble. They had been given permission to travel without passports.

The Federation Secretary Anne Pool took the opportunity at the 1938 AGM to chide members for inaction despite appeals to them for help from outside the movement: 'We are proud to parade around the country wearing our badges and enjoying ourselves, but that is not the object of the Old Cornwall movement. We must pull ourselves together and do something.' Nance himself felt that 'at the present time Cornwall, as it struck a Celt, was a dead land – a tomb haunted with the memory of something which once was alive. All his life he had heard the echoes of that something … and when a small boy he determined to do all he could to bring that back. He was ready now to spend his last breath in bringing that back.'[52]

Nance was no more sanguine at the meeting in February 1939,[53] remarking that one of the few things keeping Old Cornwall alive was the Midsummer Bonfire tradition, and that he seldom if ever received material from the Societies for publication in the journal. (In fact, although the bonfire tradition has often been observed very successfully, the chain of fires has by no means always been complete.) It was agreed that an Old Cornwall representative should have a place within Tyr ha Tavas and vice versa, but the potential for fruitful collaboration was of course nullified by the outbreak of war later that year. It had been hoped that Tyr ha Tavas could have helped in attracting younger members to Old Cornwall:

As a "youth" movement its leaders and members have an almost untouched field in getting those of their own age interested in our "Old Cornwall" programme, which they only word somewhat differently, and in this any help we can give is theirs for the asking. In the one matter of using Cornish their youth has helped them to do what the Old Cornwall Societies seem unable to do, but if anything can be done by the Cornish Movement … towards building up a national spirit this can only be done by working as one body, and it is well that this is being recognized.[54]

The Celtic Congress was scheduled to be held in Cornwall again in September 1939, with strong input and support from the Federation, but events in the wider world meant that the plan, like many others, had to be deferred.

1939-1945: The World War

Nance's pessimism in the months leading up to the outbreak of war may seem to suggest the likelihood of the Old Cornwall Movement foundering in the course of the conflict. The war naturally brought new problems for the movement to tackle – and led to some interesting wartime meetings – but like the Gorsedh it made adjustments to its operations and carried on, despite some members being engaged on war work. Gorsedh activity continued to be reported regularly in *Old Cornwall*.

At the Federation AGM of October 1939, the first since the country went to war, the decision was taken to maintain continuity as far as possible, for which Nance thanked the members present, saying that 'they would not be helping the country in this time by allowing [the] movement … to die.' The suggestion that an attempt should be made to interest wartime incomers in Old Cornwall activities was welcomed. (According to one contributor to the discussion, some people staying in the St Agnes area had been wondering whether they could bear to stay on 'owing to the dullness,' which called forth a protest from Ashley Rowe.) The journal would continue to be published though the Summer and Winter Festivals were in abeyance. At this meeting both Nance as President and Anne Pool as Secretary expressed a wish not to stand for re-election. TH Rogers felt that without Nance at the head the movement would go under, but Nance considered himself responsible for unwise management decisions and 'preferred that someone representing the rank and file should occupy the chair.' Eventually both President and Secretary were prevailed upon to continue, and in the event Nance carried on as President (and Grand Bard) until his death in 1959 and Mrs Pool until her death in 1949.

The *Old Cornwall* issue for Winter 1939 showed little outward sign of the changed conditions (the contents included congratulations to the Liskeard Society for its membership of 200, its contingent of junior members and the popularity of its Saturday rambles), but the Federation meeting in April 1940 was called specifically to review the work of the Societies under wartime restrictions. There had been a suggestion for a series of lectures 'embodying a particular Cornish as well as generally educational interest' to be arranged in cooperation with the adult education movement. Nance welcomed the scheme as very helpful, believing that Old Cornwall work as a whole was educational. The discussion led to yet another proposal for a name change, hence the headline of a newspaper report referring to a '[m]istaken impression about "old fogies and greybeards".' It was suggested that the main problem with OCSs was the 'impression that they existed for "those with grey hairs and bald heads".' (How this applied to the many female members of Old Cornwall was not explained.) The further suggestion was made that the name should be changed to the Cornwall Society, and there was some agreement as to the unsuitability of the traditional name. Clearly there was a lively discussion: 'The new Cornwall could look after itself, with its red-roofed bungalows, etc.,' said Perkins Cowls, adding that he would leave the movement if the name were changed. Ashley Rowe, however, felt that the name belittled Cornwall, 'implying that it had to be kept alive somehow, whereas it was the very heart of western civilisation.' On a more substantive note, Nance again stressed the need to keep organisations like Old Cornwall alive during the war and said that the movement and the Gorsedh had anticipated the government's actions in doing everything possible to foster British-French friendship because they had been cultivating Cornish-Breton connections for many years, notably with the work of GH Doble, thus 'helping to keep civilisation going, and that was the main aim of the war.' He also reminded Societies about using the Royal Institution of Cornwall to deposit material containing information which might otherwise be lost. Society delegates reported that winter meetings had carried on as usual in spite of the blackout, though only their own members were giving papers because of the difficulty in getting speakers from neighbouring Societies. Increased production costs again called the future of *Old Cornwall* into question, but in the event the situation was managed despite the adverse conditions.

At the AGM of 1940[55] there was positive news on various fronts, including heartening reports from the Societies, who were adapting to conditions of blackout and transport restrictions and doing good work. The paucity of information on dialect from the Societies, however, led Nance to the conclusion that Society Recorders were not doing their work properly. The war had also entailed disturbance of ground to build camps and other installations, leading to danger to archaeological remains, and the paper salvage campaign meant that important documents were being destroyed as waste. Members should be vigilant in order to minimise potential loss. The idea of exchanging talks between Societies had been successful and was supported. The question of a name change was carried over to this AGM, where the proposition to drop the word 'Old' was vigorously opposed in a lively discussion. Nance stated that his resignation would be automatic if the change were made, saying, 'We do not want to keep Cornwall from changing, but we want to keep the old tradition going … The idea of the Old Cornwall Society is a Cornwall that is Cornish.' May James was another objector to the proposal for the change, and Anne Pool said that it was the 'most ridiculous thing ever proposed.' One side believed that the name put off people who might have joined the movement, while the other was sure that members would leave if it were changed. There was clear disagreement between Societies about the matter so it was agreed to canvas their views and defer the question again to the following AGM. At that meeting Ashley Rowe's proposal for change had no seconder and was unanimously rejected. Despite this exhaustive airing of the subject it would raise its head again more than once and would again be rejected.

In 1941 the St Ives Society celebrated its coming of age and was as strong as ever, continuing to hold meetings as usual, including the Winter Festival. The St Ives minute books show that in so many ways Nance was not only a mainstay of the Old Cornwall Movement as a whole but of the St Ives

OCS in particular. He even used his artistic talent to design a new banner for the Society – not the only instance of his artist's background being put to good use for the benefit of Old Cornwall. At the meeting in St Ives in April 1941 he gave a talk on the movement's work to date, though a proper celebration of the anniversary could not of course take place at that time. There were some 22 Societies at that point, so an informal meeting in St Ives 21 years earlier had led to a great deal of valuable work throughout Cornwall, which was still continuing. The first Pilgrimage made by the St Ives Society in 1920 had been by four-horse brake to the home of Dolly Pentreath and then to Trewoofe and Lamorna, but '[w]ork near at hand must now take the place of these pleasant and fruitful historic trips which, all anticipate, will be resumed when this land of ours is once again at peace.' During this 21-year period scores of books and articles written (or co-written) by Nance, in

The opening of the St Ives OCS Museum at the Guildhall in 1951. Courtesy of St Ives OCS.

both Cornish and English, had been published, many under the auspices of the Federation of Old Cornwall Societies.[56]

Another casualty of war had been Cornish milestones, and in 1941 the Federation sent a resolution to the Clerk of Cornwall County Council about the unrestrained damage done to them in the process of rendering them useless to the enemy if the country were invaded. The Old Cornwall view was that these 'relics of their ancestors' should be buried and later restored to their original positions. It was reported at the 1942 AGM that the County Surveyor agreed with the Federation position. Also in 1942, it was decided that the Federation affiliation fee due from Societies should be waived for those in abeyance because of the war but not for those still functioning. Nance was however clear that Societies should be kept going wherever possible

even if only a few members could attend.[57]

The reality of the situation for the FOCS is spelled out the following year in Secretary Anne Pool's Federation report in the Summer issue of *Old Cornwall*:

> *Wartime conditions prevent any work being undertaken by the Federation other than the publication of **Old Cornwall**, and it was feared that from increased costs and possibly declining sales, this too might end with the issue of the Winter Number, which completed Volume III.*

She encourages members to try to increase sales, specifically by sending the journal as a gift to Cornish service personnel abroad, and, like Nance, urges Societies to keep at least a skeleton organisation going despite the blackout.

'There are many signs,' she writes, 'that despite curtailed activity, the spirit of "Old Cornwall" is more valued to-day than ever.' (At the Federation AGM in October 1942 she had reported that sales of the journal had not diminished that year.) The principal outward effect of the war on the journal was that only one issue per year was published between 1944 and 1947, the first two of which were markedly shorter and more cheaply produced than usual. Longer articles were in fact discouraged until the return of peacetime. (There was also only one issue published in most years between 1950 and 1960.)

At the 1943 Federation AGM[58] CKC Andrew, as Recorder for documents and archaeology, returned to his concerns for archaeological remains and manuscripts, saying that he was 'searching some of the salvage dumps with startling results.' Nance expressed sadness that salvage work was being taken over by local authorities, which meant that 'the work was being done by people who could not possibly know the value of the things they were destroying' – 'We must make sure the new

Members of the newly-formed Pentewan OCS at the Gorsedh at Castle Dore, September 6th 1954. Courtesy of Robert Evans.

Cornwall does not wipe out the old Cornwall, and that we shall have a solid foundation upon which a new Cornwall can be built.'

In October 1944 there was a Federation appeal for funds for the Friends of Brittany, a group founded by the Cornish Gorsedh the previous year with Old Cornwall support, both for humanitarian reasons and to maintain the old friendship between Celtic cousins. Anne Pool again struck an optimistic note, saying that despite Old Cornwall's enforced inactivity it was garnering more sympathy than it had for a long time, that its post-war activities

would be better than ever and that some Societies were resuming their usual routine – St Ives, for example, had held their Crying the Neck ceremony that year.

1945-1959: a new beginning

The post-war mood in the Old Cornwall Movement remained generally positive. It was reported at the Federation AGM in October 1945 that Penzance was trying to form a Young Cornwall Association. This idea was welcomed by Nance, who hoped it would spread, and the following year he stated that the June meeting had been convened with the idea of making a fresh start in extending the Old Cornwall Movement. Increased attendances at meetings and the formation of new Societies were grounds for optimism, but he also drew attention to the ways in which Old Cornwall had not done enough: in the collection of dialect words 'compared with what the Devon Association had accomplished, Cornwall had done practically nothing.' He also raised the recurring problem of an ageing membership, but Ashley Rowe pointed to the Young Cornwall Associations which had been formed at Redruth and Truro, in which no-one over 20 could hold office, thus gaining, he hoped, valuable recruits for Old Cornwall in the future. Not all Societies were lacking younger members – the recently-formed Launceston Society, for instance, had no members over 60. Resolutions were passed against the threats of ceding part of Cornwall to Plymouth and of merging BBC West with Midland. A protest would be sent from the Federation.

The vigorous restart and optimism for the future were further reflected at the 1946 AGM,[59] with gratifying reports from the Societies. It was reported that three new ones had been formed (Launceston, Probus and Saltash) and the journal was back to full-size (though only one issue was published during the year). The members were keen to restart the Midsummer Bonfire tradition. Nance still had his regrets however: 'We thought when we started the Old Cornwall Movement that we should have at least 20,000 Cornish men and women with us and that there would have been

The opening of St Ives Museum at the Guildhall, 1951. Left to right: Messrs Downing, A K Hamilton Jenkin, Hingston Curnow (Deputy Mayor), R Morton Nance, and C S Murrish. Courtesy of St Ives OCS.

a society in every town in Cornwall, but we are far from reaching those heights yet.' An increase in the affiliation fee from 1d to 2d per member was agreed, to meet the anticipated expenditure in the year to come.

The new spirit continued the following year, with Societies flourishing, membership increasing and activities being resumed, including Federation and Society pilgrimages. Old Cornwall publications, however, apart from the journal, had not yet started to reappear despite the need for them – even the journal was having problems because of paper restrictions and lack of skilled printing workers – and there was clearly a perception that there were still too many non-participating members within Societies. The first price rise for the journal came with the 1947 issue, from 1/- (5 p.) to 1/6 (7½ p.).

A feature headed 'Something Done' in the first issue for 1948 is an impressive seven-page outline of some of the work accomplished to date by nine Old Cornwall Societies, not only as a useful record but to 'encourage further efforts.' It was in this year that the first published index to *Old Cornwall* appeared. Compiled by SW Johns, it covered the first three volumes (36 issues), 1925-1942, and brought out the fact that Nance, unsurprisingly, was by some margin the most prolific contributor to the journal in both Cornish and English. (In due course the first nine volumes (to 1985) were covered by printed indexes.) The October 1948 AGM reported the best financial statement ever, with a credit balance of just over £200.

At the Federation Spring Meeting in 1949[60] there was strong criticism of the reported proposal of the

English Place-Name Society to publish a volume of Cornish place-names.[61] The Federation had long felt the need to produce a comprehensive, popular handbook on the subject, but even Nance with his prodigious work rate had not been able to find the time or devise the methodology to compile one, though he intimated at the meeting that if someone else would do so he would revise it. (In 1941, when FB Cargeeg had pointed to the need for a book on Cornish place-names, Nance had responded that he was 'trying all the time to learn how to do it.')

In 1950 there were moves once again towards more coordination of Recording, as it was felt that the efforts of individual Recorders were largely lost to the Federation because of a lack of central organisation. The proposition to appoint a Central Recorder who could convene meetings was carried, and Dorothy Dudley was appointed. The importance of maintaining links with the wider Celtic world was again stressed at the 1951 Winter Festival. Nance said that 'the Federation of Old Cornwall Societies was the exact equivalent of the national Celtic societies in other Celtic countries. "There is not a breath of anti-English feeling and no politics".' For Ashley Rowe, '[t]he aim of Old Cornwall societies is to keep Cornwall Cornish. To do this Cornwall needs the help of the other Celtic countries. Together they can resist the steam-roller flattening of the B.B.C. and Hollywood.' He returned to the theme at the Spring Conference in March:[62] 'I am looking to the Old Cornwall Societies as being the backbone of the Celtic Movement in Cornwall.' He felt that 'with the ballyhoo going on about the Festival of Britain, there is a risk and even a very grave danger that our Cornish nationality may be swamped entirely in people's minds. We must remember that we are a different race from the Anglo-Saxon. We have a greater tradition. We are the custodians of the art and the literature of the fringe of Europe.' Nance as Chairman felt that the Cornish spirit was also being swamped by the flood of people coming into Cornwall every year. AK Hamilton Jenkin described the very important step forward represented by the County Council decision to establish a muniments room for Cornwall in Truro, as there was an enormous number of documents in danger of being lost through a lack of appreciation of their value. This refers to the foundation of the Cornwall Record Office, later part of Kresen Kernow, Redruth.

Progress with new Societies, mounting interest in Cornish and enthusiasm for the Midsummer Bonfires was maintained the following year. Nance, however, was typically uncompromising in his concluding remarks at the AGM in 1952:[63] 'Cornwall depends upon each of you individually as to whether it is going to survive or be wiped out.' He also warned that the journal would cease publication owing to rising printing costs unless each member made an individual effort to save it.

A particular complication arose with respect to the 1953 Bonfires, in that there were also to be bonfires

Lady of Cornwall Phyllis Bray, with Colin Roberts and Phillip Harvey at the 1957 Gorsedh at Predannack, Mullion. Colin Roberts is now President of Mullion OCS. Courtesy of Colin Roberts.

to mark the coronation of Queen Elizabeth II a few weeks before Midsummer. The suggestion that a telegram of congratulation in Cornish should be sent to the new queen received unanimous support, but Nance was keen that the Old Cornwall Bonfires should go ahead as usual to maintain the ancient custom and as a token of solidarity with the Federation and between Societies: 'Burn a newspaper if you cannot do anything better, but have something.' The fear was expressed that Old Cornwall programmes sometimes had little or no relevance to the movement's aims, but it was felt that these aims should be adhered to even if it meant smaller attendances. The St Ives OCS organised the Gorsedh ceremony on Trencrom in 1953, and the two boys chosen as pages were the Society's youngest members. At nine years old, it seems very likely that they were the youngest members of any OCS ever.[64] The St Ives Society also performed Cornish drama at the Gorsedh – the fourth successive year in which Cornish plays had been staged.

Familiar themes continue to be aired through the 1950s, such as the importance of Recorders: they 'should put down anything unlikely to be printed, sometimes just a phrase, or it might be lost for ever' (1954); the Midsummer Bonfires: 'People who are lighting their own bonfire will see their friends' fires all through the county and feel that they all belong to one another' (1955); Cornish dialect: Nance's *Cledry Plays* 'should act as a blood transfusion' (1956). (Despite the merits of the book and the hopes it aroused, however, it was reported that there had been no orders from Cornish libraries and very few from Old Cornwall Societies, though orders had started to arrive from outside Cornwall within a few days of publication.) The depleted Publications Fund was again one of the issues discussed at the Spring Conference in March 1957. Nance's view was that '100 years hence, when all present had been forgotten, what would remain of the Old Cornwall movement would be what had been published. By getting things in print the movement would have done something for the future of Cornwall and not for themselves.'[65] At the Federation Spring Conference in March 1958 AK Hamilton Jenkin

stressed the importance of reporting discoveries of antiquarian interest to the Cornwall Record Office or the RIC rather than trying to acquire them for one's own Society. The County Archivist should be informed of any valuable antiquities held by individual Societies.

1959-2020: *Towards the future*

Robert Morton Nance died on May 27th 1959.[66] His extended term as Federation President was paralleled exactly by his uniquely long service as Grand Bard (1934-1959). His energy and zeal on behalf of Cornwall were extraordinary and sometimes led him to feel considerable disappointment when his vision was not realised as he had hoped. He quite rightly saw dangers for Old Cornwall on every side, dangers which in some ways became far more pressing after his time. The Old Cornwall Movement continued, though it may not quite be the fulfilment of Nance's dreams. His own achievements, however, were remarkable, as were those of the dedicated Old Cornwall members and groups who helped him or followed in his footsteps. Nance did not escape criticism during his lifetime, and his work and approach have been subject to critical scrutiny since his death, but his accomplishments are manifold and his place within the Old Cornwall Movement, and the Cornish Movement as a whole, is assured.

The story of Old Cornwall in the decades following his death is one of progress, achievement, change, reappraisal and differing views as to the work and place of the movement, from within its membership and from outside. Work continued in the numerous fields with which Old Cornwall had always concerned itself, but with less emphasis than before on some aspects of that work, notably the Cornish language and the maintenance of links with the wider Celtic world. Interest in and support for the language have grown since Nance's day, but (as with the pan-Celtic dimension) not so much within Old Cornwall as in other more narrowly focused organisations, and Nance could not have foreseen, and presumably would not have approved of, certain directions which the language has taken. Some of these independent organisations of course, notably the Cornish Gorsedh, were created at the instigation of Old Cornwall while others have benefited from Federation support, practical and financial. As to Cornish dialect, interest in it, except at academic level, is now largely confined to its use as humorous entertainment, though it is good that it remains popular in that context and is thereby preserved in spoken as well as written form. (Even in 1935, the Federation publication of dialect stories *Echoes from carn, cove & cromlech* by Tom Newall ('Nicky Trevaylor') had not sold well.) In the years following Nance's death as in his lifetime, certain themes recurred, such as the prime importance of Recording (understood in different ways) and the vexed question of a change of name for the movement. This question seems almost irrelevant compared to the changes which Old Cornwall had to make in a rapidly developing technological age which bore little relationship to Cornwall or the wider world in the first half of the 20th century. The present section will consider various appraisals of the movement made in the post-Nance era as well as a few of the huge number of individual activities and projects undertaken by Old Cornwall in those 60 years.

At the Federation AGM in October 1959 AK Hamilton Jenkin was unanimously elected to succeed Nance as President. He served for two years, after which he was elected to the new post of 'Life Past President' (later 'Life Vice-President'), and ever since then the President has served for a fixed term. For about four years after Nance's death the editorship of *Old Cornwall* was taken over by the Publications Editorial Board, until LR Moir assumed sole responsibility. Nance's death clearly marked the end of an era for the movement, and arguably a low point in its history, but Old Cornwall business went on. At the 1959 meeting, concern was expressed that the Tamar road bridge, the construction of which had begun that year, would lead to even more dilution of Cornwall's individuality, and Ivor Thomas felt that bilingual signs for towns and villages throughout Cornwall would go some way to counteract this trend. (The Gorsedh lobbied for the same cause,

and the campaign eventually achieved some success, on the bridge itself and elsewhere. Bilingual signage was later undertaken pro-actively by Cornwall Council.)

Like any long-standing organisation, the St Ives Old Cornwall Society had its unhappier moments and it certainly went through a difficult time after Nance's death, since at around the same time two other former office holders also died and another two resigned. As to the movement as a whole, one view held that '[a]t the start of the 1960s the conservatism of the Old Cornwall Society [sic] was beginning to become even more evident. The introduction to an issue from 1961 indicates some of the pessimism of the ... membership.'[67]

The issue in question was the Autumn 1961 number of *Old Cornwall*, and the rueful message in it is summed up as 'eyes look Eastward still': the young in particular are often not looking to Cornwall, or Old Cornwall, but beyond the Tamar. On the other hand, at the 1961 Federation AGM the Secretary LR Moir referred to 'another year of quiet progress' and PAS Pool expressed the opinion that the growth of the movement meant that it would soon be necessary to consider holding two Winter Festivals and two Summer Pilgrimages each year. The new President JA Shearme stated that the Federation membership of about 2,600 'was more than that of the other three learned societies put together.' Perhaps the movement became less radical without Nance's heroic championing of so many aspects of the Old Cornwall cause, such as wider Celtic links, the Cornish language and Cornish dialect, but these aspects – particularly the latter two – have at least remained part of Old Cornwall's remit.

Professor Charles Thomas, who was to become the first Director of the Institute of Cornish Studies in 1971, was an invaluable critical friend of the Old Cornwall Movement. His address to the Celtic Congress held in Cornwall in 1963, as President and Chairman of the Cornish National Branch of the Congress, was printed in *Old Cornwall* that year under the title 'An Dasserghyans Kernewek' ('The Cornish Revival').[68] He discusses the Revival in its many aspects, covering numerous Cornish organisations and including some thought-provoking comments about 'that unique creation of Jenner and Nance, the Federation of Old Cornwall Societies:'

These, now 32 in all, widely divergent in numbers and character, cover pretty well all of Cornwall ... No one has commented on the remarkable resemblance of the Federation to a circuit of the Methodist Church ...: there is food for thought here, including the distinct possibility that the founders may have copied about the only form of self-governing organisation that has ever been known to have worked successfully in Cornwall. The Federation has lofty aims, and owns and publishes **Old Cornwall***: I should be failing in my duty to scholarship if I said that all those aims were persistently accomplished, but there is no doubt that the Federation has been instrumental in bringing the revival to a vast number of persons who would otherwise have felt it the exclusive domain of the* **literati** *...*

The annual Gorsedd, the Federation of Old Cornwall Societies, and this Congress are now taken seriously by the bulk of Cornish people. I wonder how many of us realise that this ... represents a major achievement: and that, as well as to all those countless un-named workers, whom Nance called "the Old Cornwallites, the salt of the movement," so much of this is due to Nance's own example ...

Cornish dialect ... has been sadly neglected ... The Federation of Old Cornwall Societies possesses a system of recorders of dialect at various levels though in practice this has not made much contribution ...

The uninformed regard the entire Old Cornwall and Gorsedd movement as a waste of time, bogus to the core and simply an excuse for an annual escapist junket of *picturesque appearance. All that one can say is that it is the business of the movement to see that the uninformed become the informed, and I think that slowly this is being accomplished ...*

What is now the role of the Old Cornwall movement? If the revival is an accomplished fact, what is there for them to do except have pasty suppers and coach outings? ...

This is clearly a matter for discussion ...

The danger of the movement's becoming more of a social club than a workforce for the good of Cornwall had often been pointed out by Nance and others, and would be pointed out again, but there have always been within the movement those who are dedicated to doing real work for the preservation of Cornwall's heritage, in one particular field or more generally, though they may be a minority within the movement as a whole. Individual Societies are largely independent, and some of them, too, are more active than others.[69] Nonetheless, reports on the activities of Societies have appeared regularly in *Old Cornwall* throughout its long history, representing a huge body of work, especially considering that the reports represent only part of what Societies have achieved. The need to keep the movement active and relevant is a perennial one and common, in different ways, to many organisations.

Thomas also contrasts the activities of the movement with those of Mebyon Kernow and the viewpoint of the *New Cornwall* journal (which had started in 1952 and continued till 1973): 'Am I right in thinking that the active preservation of our amenities, or the safeguarding of our regional affairs or civil liberties, is considered outside the scope of *Old Cornwall*?' In his view, in 1963 MK was 'perhaps the only part of the Cornish revival that has faced the world.'

At the Spring Conference in 1964 it was reported that Nance's *Glossary of Cornish sea-words*, a memorial volume published the previous year thanks to diligent work by PAS Pool, was selling well. The Federation was granted charitable status in 1965, and in the following year the Winter Festival in Plymouth was the first Old Cornwall event to be held beyond the Tamar, arranged at the instigation of the Plymouth Cornish Association. In the Spring 1967 issue of *Old Cornwall* the journal is reported to be in a healthy state: 'It is a far cry to the early days when the Editor, starved of contributions, faced the prospect of abandoning the production of the journal. Nowadays, more articles are submitted than can be immediately printed – a healthy index of revived practical interest in our work.' There is also, however, a familiar appeal for scripts of Society talks to be sent in with a view to publication and a rueful list of earlier talks of which only the titles survive but which would seem to have been worthy of permanent record.

The first piece in the Autumn 1968 issue of *Old Cornwall* appears under the heading 'Whither bound?' and is another periodical assessment of the purpose and aims of the movement in an attempt to 'capture the enthusiasm and interest of the generations which will follow us.' It quotes the address given by George Pawley White, Grand Bard of the Gorsedh 1964-70, at the Spring Meeting of the Federation in March 1968. (Pawley White was also a Vice-President of the Federation at the time and would later become President.) He in turn quotes from Nance's manifesto 'What we stand for' in the first issue of the journal and continues:

> [W]e must recognise that mere preservation is of little avail, for we cannot live in the present or the future by having a nostalgia for the past. We need to build for the future with the inspiration of the past. This means that we must be adventurous and experimental.

He goes on to enumerate the various fields in which this approach can be exercised (art, music, craft, literature both Cornish and English) and the exponents who are showing the way in Cornwall. The fields of local government, industry and service to the community are also proper ones in which to operate. He concludes:

> We live in the present – we cannot live in Old Cornwall. It is past, but in building the New Cornwall we can use all the heritage of the past and preserve our identity and self-expression in all things. A new motto might be **Bedheugh bynytha Kernewek** ['Be forever Cornish'].[70]

In the 50th year of the Old Cornwall Movement, the editorial in the Spring 1970 journal commemorated in positive terms the establishment of the first Old Cornwall Society:

> It is unlikely that anyone concerned in that venture could have foreseen the extent of the growth of interest in 'Old Cornwall'. Nance and his contemporaries no doubt had their dreams and hopes and these, with the passage of time, have been exceeded beyond their expectations. The revival of a language, moribund for centuries, the collection and preservation of a county's folk-lore, the resurgence of interest in Cornwall's heritage of old churches, manor houses, antiquities and lost history are all achievements of which we should be proud.

The following issue[71] was a special one to commemorate the 50th anniversary, with covers printed in blue ink instead of the usual black. AK Hamilton Jenkin's 'How it started' is the opening article. It concludes:

> Today, with thirty-three societies comprising some 3,500 members, the Old Cornwall movement has an established place in the life of the county. Inevitably it has changed in character as Cornwall itself has changed. Due in a large measure to television and "canned" entertainment, the passing on of oral tradition from one generation to the next has virtually ceased and with this the scope for "gathering up the fragments" of the past. This is not to say that the Old Cornwall Societies have no further purpose to fulfill [sic]. Much good work is still being done ...

This special number of *Old Cornwall* also reprints Nance's 'What we stand for' from the first issue and continues with reports from the 33 Societies. Though similar reports had often appeared in the journal before, these are of particular interest and importance as a concise record of the history and achievements of those individual Societies to date. In addition, Ruth Hirst, then Newquay OCS Recorder, gives an account of her recording methods, making it clear once more how important an office a Recorder occupies (though the first group meeting for Society Recorders did not take place till 1982).[72]

As well as a message from Federation President John Rosewarne, the issue also contains a further address from Grand Bard George Pawley White, conveying greetings from the Gorsedh to the Old Cornwall movement on its golden jubilee. After reminding readers that the first two Grand Bards, Jenner and Nance, were also the founders of Old Cornwall and thanking the Societies for their support for the Gorsedh during its 42 years he goes on:

That the past half-century has seen a transformation in the attitude of Cornish people to their own separate identity is largely due to the spirit which the Old Cornwall Societies have engendered – the interest and pleasure of re-discovering the history, language and customs of the past, the pride of being Cornish and the fellowship which folk enjoy in sharing common interests. We must make use of the material gathered together and of the spirit awakened, so that, in future, these valuable assets shall not again be lost, buried or forgotten. May the next half-century see the spirit of Old Cornwall grow in influence and scope![73]

The press coverage of Old Cornwall at this milestone in its history included an article[74] in which it was claimed that the movement had had more success than the Royal Cornwall Polytechnic Society and The Royal Institution of Cornwall 'in preserving our antiquities, traditions and folk culture from oblivion.' It also contains a positive review of the anniversary issue of *Old Cornwall* and mentions Alfred Lane-Davies's *Holy wells of Cornwall*, the commemorative publication issued by the Federation that year. The Federation Winter Festival in November 1970 was held at St Ives and was also a celebration for the 50th anniversary of the formation of the first Old Cornwall Society there. It was on that occasion that John Rosewarne was invested with the first presidential badge of office of the FOCS.

The following issue of the journal is equally noteworthy, containing as it does another important assessment by Charles Thomas, this time the transcript of his address 'The next fifty years' which was delivered after the 1970 Winter Festival.[75] This runs to 13 closely argued pages and though some of his points have been overtaken by events, the paper should be regarded as essential reading by anyone interested in the history and (changing) character of the Old Cornwall Movement. Thomas starts by expressing the surprise he felt earlier in the year when close friends assured him that his remarks about the Cornish language in his 1963 address had led to the formation of the Cornish Language Board ('one of our more successful recent ventures') in 1967. In any event, his intention at this point is unashamedly to give explicit guidance for positive action on behalf of Old Cornwall, his sole concern being 'that we should maintain, and improve, the contribution that we can make to the sum total of human knowledge and understanding' though 'without proper planning, adequate techniques, a sense of purpose, and appropriate direction, ability and good-will can sometimes be a poor substitute for actual performance.'

He sets out first to examine the stated aims and philosophies of the movement, believing 'that these aims must be modernised, modified, and enlarged if the movement is to play a constructive rôle in the years ahead' and hoping for an acceptance that the Federation faces a dilemma which must be tackled:

We have a splendid Federation, a record of

steady growth, a great potential; but based on aims which were, to my mind, never entirely clarified even when first set out, and never subsequently explored in adequate detail. Do these aims hold good today? I believe that, in large part, they do not; and that the expression of fresh aims, on our fiftieth birthday, is an urgent and imperative duty.

He has no wish to 'set at naught' the 50-year history of the movement, quite the contrary: the 'establishment of a sense of national identity has been well and truly undertaken' and the resuscitation of the Cornish language brought about; numerous important specialist societies, none of which existed in the 1920s, stem from the early years of the Old Cornwall Movement, as do the Cornish language periodicals which appeared after that time. The *non*-specialist nature of Old Cornwall is in fact the problem, but there are still important needs which Old Cornwall should work to meet, as Nance wished right from the start: a national folk-museum and a properly conducted survey of folk-life, a complete place-name survey,[76] and a rigorously conducted Cornish dialect survey, i.e. one that goes far beyond the production of word lists.

This leads to the crux of Thomas's talk: 'the potential of the Federation's Recordership scheme, ever since its general lines were first laid down; its progressive breakdown after the first decade; and the possibilities of starting afresh, on rather different lines.' He has 'little doubt that it is one of the most useful potential contributions in the Federation's hands.' He sees three functions ahead for the movement, which can be summarised as publication, conservation and recording. 'In a sense,' he says, 'they should replace the older aims of Cornish revival and of linguistic salvage – both of which have been accomplished.'

Regarding publication, he commends unreservedly the current *Old Cornwall* editor, LR Moir, who had rescued the journal from the doldrums and to whom Cornish studies owed

a great deal. He further recommends that a definitive bibliography of all Federation and Society publications should be compiled by a professional librarian, and that the mechanics of publication should be conducted on the basis of expert knowledge, this being necessary just to keep up with competitors. (The first point has now been tackled by the bibliography in the present volume, and there is no doubt that the publications arm of Old Cornwall has become increasingly professional over the years since Thomas's address.)[77] Thomas has suggestions for increasing the sales of *Old Cornwall*, finding the low uptake by some Societies 'disgraceful'.

In the matter of conservation he refers to the 50th Anniversary Exhibition in Truro in November 1970, which highlighted the impressive number of projects undertaken by Societies, though there were still more which the Societies had persuaded other agencies to tackle. His one caveat is that

Old Cornwall members, seen here at Ennistymon, Co. Clare, Ireland, enjoying a holiday planned by Joan Rendell who took the photo. Courtesy of John Neale.

archaeological excavation is too specialist a procedure to be engaged in by Old Cornwall, which more than fulfils its duty in this respect through its donations to such organisations as the Cornwall Archaeological Society. In the wider field of conservation, threats to Cornish heritage are ever present, and the network of Societies throughout Cornwall could help those devoted individuals who participate in public enquiries by deploying members with detailed local knowledge.

He goes on to say that Nance's predominant wish was to preserve Cornwall's character and heritage, and to record its 'folk-life' in a permanent form in *Old Cornwall*, as well as to promote the linguistic revival in its pages, but since his time the nature of the journal has changed. Recording was conceived as a scheme whereby Society Recorders would gather a myriad 'scraps' of information of every kind, either first- or second-hand, and pass them on to the Federation Recorder. The

impossibility of the task for one person was conceded by the creation, over time, of the offices of Archaeology, Dialect, Place-Names and Folk-Song Recorders.[78] Furthermore, the scheme was never properly thought out and the processes by which it was supposed to work were never specified. Archaeological, dialect and place-name studies are highly skilled and technical matters, and the recording of them can only proceed meaningfully on that basis. Thomas sees the future of Recording as lying in the fields of '[f]olk-life, immediate and primary local history [press cuttings and ephemera], dialect and place-names (under controlled conditions), and if possible folk-songs.' Progress, he believed, would be possible only with Recording being standardised (in form and quality), centralised and proceeding with expert advice and help. (The current post of Folk Tradition Officer is clearly designed to cover a wider remit than the former offices of Folk Songs & Music Recorder and, before that,

Folk-Songs Recorder, so one of Thomas's points is still being addressed, and in pursuing the task of systematically recording 'primary local history,' the availability of searchable online newspaper files is of great benefit.)

Thomas was not setting out to be a prophet, but his ideas are always stimulating and sometimes disconcerting, and they have fed into Old Cornwall thinking with positive results. He concludes:

> I see behind us a record of achievement which … is very probably more impressive than most of us yet realise. The Federation, having lasted half-a-century, is entitled to consider whether or not this is a time for radical change … From this point onwards, I leave it, as I must, to the Federation.

The FOCS was certainly willing to consider the points raised by this address, and it was decided that they would be discussed at the 1971 AGM. The willingness to face up to challenges realistically but with deeply felt concern for the welfare of Old Cornwall and a conviction of its importance was still alive fifty years later when the Future Group attempted to engage in a focused assessment of the need for change within the movement, in much the same spirit as Charles Thomas, and to take appropriate action. It is interesting that when a collection of his writings was published in 2012, Professor Thomas was happy to accept its editor's choice of title, *Gathering the fragments*.[79]

At the Spring meeting in March 1972 AK Hamilton Jenkin returned to a theme which he had brought up on many occasions without success, 'that the real work for Old Cornwall Societies was to record the names of pathways, stiles and cottages,' i.e. names for which there is often no written record. At the AGM in October that year it was stated that the work 'was particularly important as the Cornish landscape generally was being shattered by new developments and the work had to be done before the names were lost.' Another comment at the meeting was that the movement seemed to be so frequently conducting 'a funeral service over something lost' though it was conceded that

more positive action was often hampered by lack of advance information.

Overwhelming support was expressed at the Winter Festival in January 1973 for the proposition that the six second-tier local authorities then being created should have Cornish names. The Federation would send a request to the Local Government Boundary Commission. (In the event, five of the six *were* given Cornish names.) David Mudd MP paid tribute to the work carried out by the movement: 'In the absence of an official university or polytechnic the Federation had become a non-university of scholarship and wisdom in Cornish matters.' Grand Bard Denis Trevanion considered that one of the great

The rousing conclusion to the Winter Festival at Redruth in 2017 as members sing 'Trelawny'. Courtesy of Tony Mansell.

benefits of the Federation was that it drew to itself not only educated Cornish people but also those who had become Cornish by adoption.[80] This is a far cry from the early days when the feeling was that the movement should be exclusively Cornish. It also, unintentionally but unfortunately, seems to detract from Nance's wish that Old Cornwall should appeal to people from all walks of life.

1974 was the golden jubilee year of the Federation. At the Spring Meeting in March the President, George Pawley White, reviewed the work and growth of the organisation over its first 50 years, touching on familiar themes, including the need for more interest in the Cornish language, the apparent lack of appeal of the organisation to young people and the benefit of closer links with Cornish societies overseas.

The reports from individual Societies concerning their history and activities are sometimes connected with an anniversary. 1976 was the 50th anniversary year for both the Penryn & Falmouth Society and Penzance, and the Spring 1977 issue of *Old Cornwall* carried detailed and interesting accounts of their origins and their jubilee celebrations and exhibitions. In the case of Penryn & Falmouth, speakers at their inaugural meeting in December 1926 had included Henry Jenner, Robert Morton Nance and AK Hamilton Jenkin. A telegram of loyal greetings to Queen Elizabeth II was sent from the Federation Summer Festival in June 1977 for her silver jubilee and birthday. A reply to the Federation was despatched from London the same day.

In the Spring 1980 issue the outgoing Federation President Hugh Miners, in 'Thoughts of the past President', offers his ideas on the current state of the movement, having visited virtually every Society during his standard two-year term of office. While agreeing that a social dimension to the movement was necessary, he had feared that 'a significant number of Societies were content to project a "picnic-and-cream tea" image which was far removed from the hopes and intentions of the great founders of the Movement.' He nonetheless found that the range and quality of the work being done (albeit often by individuals or small groups) was impressive. Aspects of Old Cornwall work which he saw as declining and in need of reinvigorating were the detailed recording of the environment, the preservation of endangered artefacts and attention to the Cornish

language, notwithstanding the Federation's role in establishing the Cornish Language Board in 1967. His approach is different from that of Charles Thomas. Miners felt that the offices of Federation Dialect Recorder and Folk-Songs Recorder had changed in function and were perhaps redundant. His feeling that there were very few dialect words left to record contrasts with Thomas's point that properly designed dialect recording had rarely been carried out systematically and could be one of the most useful tasks for Old Cornwall to undertake. (Interestingly, Alan Pearson, writing as Federation President, stated in 1982 that the natural tendency to feel that some of the aims of Old Cornwall had been realised, 'particularly … in the areas of dialect, place names and folksong' was incorrect.)[81] Miners suggests ways in which the other Recorders could perform their roles to better advantage, including the suggestion that a new office of Photography Recorder might be created, since photographs were so important in proper recording technique.

The Autumn 1983 issue of the journal opens with 'A personal view' which records the occurrence earlier in the year of 'the realisation of one of the aims of the founders of the Old Cornwall Movement, the holding of the first Esethvos Kernow [Cornish Eisteddfod]':

The first woman President of the Federation, Helen Derrington. Courtesy of Gorsedh Kernow.

> *Let us hope it will soon be possible to make this an annual event with more direct involvement of the Old Cornwall Movement. The Gorseth rightly concentrates attention on the Celtic strands in our heritage while Old Cornwall attempts to reflect them all.*

This issue also saw the start of a long-lasting feature originally called 'The 'Mordon' collection of Cornish dialect words' since it originated in manuscript notes among the papers of Robert Morton Nance, whose bardic name was Mordon ('Seawave'). The publication of this material had been discussed as long ago as 1949. While more than just a word-list (it included some derivations and localisation of terms as well as definitions) it never met the criteria for a rigorous dialect survey and was abandoned, having covered just over half the alphabet, after the Spring 1997 issue when a new journal editor took over. (There is, however, a large dialect component of the Federation website, put in place originally by Dialect Recorder Brian Stevens and the first webmaster George Pritchard.)[82]

Helen Derrington, the first woman President of the Federation, in her message to members in the Spring 1984 issue of the journal, declared that 'we have come a wondrously long way with many hopes realised' since Nance's address in the first *Old Cornwall*:

> *Our membership has consistently contributed sound service and scholarly items for this Journal, and this has surely encouraged the spate and variety in the shops of Cornish books and periodicals of high quality.*

She sees an upsurge in many aspects of Cornish culture and advocates the use of technological advance and ease of communication to promote Old Cornwall's original aims, inviting members to 'encourage our young people to share their expertise with us to our mutual advantage.' At the 1984 Spring meeting the President expressed gratification at the good attendance of Recorders at the special Recorders' meeting which had been held very successfully before the main meeting. Sales of *Old Cornwall* had gone down again, and the Federation now had £5,000s' worth of publications in stock.

The outward appearance of the journal had changed subtly over the years. One of the more obvious new features of the change in design with the first number of volume 10 (Autumn 1985), a feature which became permanent, was an illustration on the front cover. Fittingly, this first illustration is a view of St Ives, and the covers of succeeding issues bore illustrations of places where Old Cornwall Societies had been formed, in the order of their formation. The editorial, presumably by Alan Pearson, looked back briefly on the progress and achievements of *Old Cornwall*:

> *We can point to success in recording in easily accessible form a large amount of information about all aspects of Cornwall past, and present, true to our motto ... In the early days folklore and the saints received*

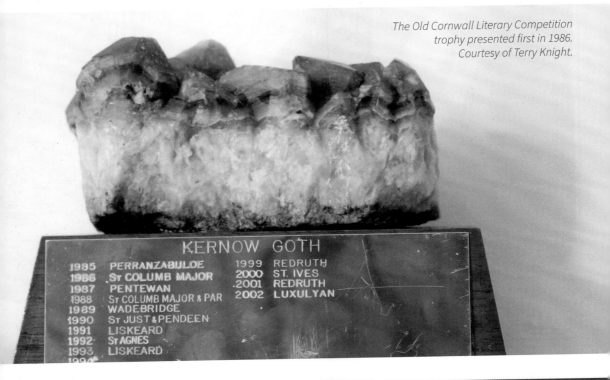

The Old Cornwall Literary Competition trophy presented first in 1986. Courtesy of Terry Knight.

KERNOW GOTH

1985	PERRANZABULOE	1999	REDRUTH
1986	St COLUMB MAJOR	2000	ST. IVES
1987	PENTEWAN	2001	REDRUTH
1988	St COLUMB MAJOR & PAR	2002	LUXULYAN
1989	WADEBRIDGE		
1990	St JUST & PENDEEN		
1991	LISKEARD		
1992	St AGNES		
1993	LISKEARD		
1994			

Bude-Stratton & District OCS collected 40 carols from north Cornwall, published them in 2012, helped to assemble a choir to revive their singing and followed up with a service at Truro Cathedral on December 19th 2016. Courtesy of Bert Biscoe.

much more attention while now the history of buildings and families is more to the fore … Cornish dialect is becoming less used … but we have always provided opportunities for the publication of dialect stories …

Another inspirational message from Denis Trevanion, this time in his role as newly elected President, appears in the following issue. He emphasises the need 'to arouse the interest of children in Cornish matters and channel their energy' and commends the Gorsedh and Esedhvos competitions which 'give opportunities to both young and old to express their love for Cornwall.' He also stresses the importance of keeping in touch with Cornish societies beyond the Tamar and overseas, since Cornishness is not just a matter of geography. Trevanion had close links with the Cornish diaspora in Australia and reported a request from the Cornish Association of South Australia that the Federation arrange the unveiling of a plaque on Plymouth Barbican the following September, commemorating the 19th-century emigration from Cornwall to Australia. The plaque would contain a scroll bearing the names of the emigrants. (The unveiling took place on September 5th 1986, with Trevanion as MC.)[83]

Federation competitions had been held over the years, and the latest series, open to individuals or Societies, was the Literary Competition. The first winner was Perranzabuloe, and they were presented with the first Kernow Goth ('Old Cornwall') trophy at the Spring Meeting in March 1986. There were never great numbers of entries for the different competition series but they produced useful work, the best of which was published in the journal. With reference to a later series, the point was made that the competitions led to the recording of facts about even well-worn topics which would otherwise have been lost, connecting this to the ethos of Old Cornwall, which 'is renowned for its concern with the minutiae as well as the bigger picture. We 'gather the fragments'.'[84]

In 1989 Joan Rendell was elected Federation President. The author of numerous books, she had been and remained a strong force within the movement and a frequent contributor to the journal till her tragic death in May 2010. In her President's Message[85] she expresses great hope for the future of Old Cornwall, seeing in the uncovering of Cornwall's history 'an exciting and never ending quest' for all age groups and looking to unity as the strength of the movement: 'Liaison between Societies, shared knowledge and research, good comradeship.' She served as Federation Secretary from 1981 to 2008, though after her resignation she was made Honorary Life Vice-President and continued as Secretary of Launceston OCS, also retaining her connections with other organisations.[86] She was the driving force behind a series of Federation trips beyond Cornwall in the 1990s and into the 2000s, the first being to the Isle of Man in 1991. Her reports of these trips appeared regularly in the journal. Following her death there was extensive local press coverage of her work and achievements (like Old Cornwall, she was born in 1920), and an appreciation was printed in the 'Old Cornwall remembers' section of the Autumn 2010 issue of the journal.[87]

The most forward-looking Old Cornwall event of 1989 was undoubtedly the Bodmin Society's sealing of a purpose-made casket containing memorabilia of the first 60 years of its history, which was entrusted to Bodmin Museum and would be opened ceremoniously on the Society's centenary in 2027.[88]

At the 1990 AGM Miss Rendell reported that the Recorders' Day organised by her and Michael Tangye had been very rewarding. Most Society Recorders had attended and brought a vast amount of material. A similar Secretaries' Meeting was suggested. The President also gave details of the restructuring of Old Cornwall to give it more general appeal and modernise its approach. An Editorial Board had been formed to replace the Publications Committee (though in 2019 the Board reverted to the previous name). The attempt at modernisation included the use of double columns, but this lasted only for the duration of volume 11 (1991-1997). The redesigned cover appeared with the second number of that volume

but was also abandoned with the start of volume 12. Nonetheless, at the Spring Meeting in 1992 the new-look journal was said to have been well received – perhaps this was more for its content than its layout.

Michael Tangye reported at the 1991 AGM that the Director of the Royal Institution of Cornwall in Truro had agreed to allocate shelf space in the Courtney Library there for any records which the Federation or individual Societies might wish to deposit. The Federation and the Institution had long enjoyed a mutually beneficial relationship, and Societies had been encouraged to use the Institution (or more recently the Cornwall Record Office) as a suitable repository for such material, a place where it would always be available for consultation and research. Members had been encouraged from the start to deposit artefacts as well as documents of value to Cornwall at the RIC to ensure their preservation. A quick return from the agreement with the RIC was achieved in 1992 when, thanks to the vigilance of Terry Knight, the minute book of the now defunct Publications Committee had been 'rescued' and deposited with other Federation records in the Courtney Library.[89] Michael Tangye, formerly the Federation President and Archaeology & Local History Recorder, is probably the most diligent and productive worker in the Recording field in the history of the Old Cornwall Movement. He has contributed numerous articles to Old Cornwall but they represent only a small fraction of the projects he has undertaken, using his own extensive fieldwork (including oral history recording) as well as primary and secondary written sources. His supplementary research in newspapers and other records has been second to none. While much of his work has been focused on his home patch of Redruth it has frequently extended to other areas of Cornwall and the Isles of Scilly. Active Old Cornwall members in general have, throughout the movement's history, done huge amounts of work beyond what is reflected in the journal or other Old Cornwall records, though the results frequently appear in publications not issued by the Federation. Regrettably, readers of Cornish books may often be unaware that many notable publications have been written by Old Cornwall members, who may well also be Cornish bards. It would benefit both Old Cornwall and the Gorsedh if authors made these allegiances known within their publications.

As well as relationships of affiliation or associateship, Old Cornwall support for other organisations has included membership subscriptions, donations and grants, cooperative projects, publicity, and attendance at meetings and symposia. Some of the organisations themselves have already been mentioned. Others have included the Cornwall Buildings Preservation Trust, the Institute of Cornish Studies, the Cornwall Heritage Trust, the Cairo Cornish Association, Homecomers, the National Trust and the Women's Institute. Affiliated bodies have included New York Cornish and 'Westward Television (Research)' in addition to Cornish associations in other UK towns. (At the AGM in September 1984, and again in 1988, the Treasurer had pointed out that though the Federation donated to various organisations it received no donations itself, despite some of the organisations in question being at least as well off as the Federation. Since it relied solely on affiliation fees and sale of publications for its income it should be prudent in its donations. This was agreed to be a valid point, and amendments were subsequently made.) Individual Societies naturally operate on a more local level. The St Ives Society, for example, had invited some particularly interesting groups to help with their Midsummer Bonfire programme at different times and to provide entertainment, including the Catholic Irish Society, Scottish dancers, the Commando Society and groups of Swedish students, one of whom was Lady of the Flowers in 1965.

Richard Jenkin, in his Chairman's Remarks at the 1992 AGM, expressed the hope that all Old Cornwall Societies would fight to ensure that Cornwall existed as an entity in the future as it had always done in the past. In similar vein, at the Spring Meeting on March 5th 1994, St Piran's Day, he spoke in favour of Cornwall becoming a unitary authority – 'One voice for Cornwall' – and a large majority at the meeting supported the proposition. Richard Jenkin was one who used his considerable influence in different forums to carry on the Nance tradition in numerous ways, including his unwavering practical support for inter-Celtic links and for the Unified form of Cornish. His appeal for a Federation donation of £100 towards the Celtic Congress to be held in Falmouth a few weeks after the Spring Meeting was successful. Another proposal carried at the same meeting was that the County Council should be sent a letter advocating a school holiday in Cornwall for St Piran's Day.

In March 1995, to mark the 25th anniversary of its formation, St Columb Old Cornwall Society presented a banner for the Federation to the President, Michael Tangye. It had been made by the Society's Recorder, Kathleen Mary ('Bill') Glanville, who was to take over from Tangye as President. A photograph of the banner formed the cover illustration for the Autumn 1995 issue of the journal.

With the start of *Old Cornwall* volume 12 (Autumn 1997) came a new editor, Terry Knight, and another new look for the journal which, with a few adjustments, became its standard house style. The most obvious change was that the front cover – and sometimes the back cover too – was mostly taken up with illustrative matter, usually photographic, and in full colour from the seventh number (which was also longer than previous issues). In his first editorial the incoming editor praised his long-serving predecessor Alan Pearson for the new features and the evolution of the journal under his editorship[90] and outlined its special place among Cornish history publications:

> *The articles it contains should be appealing and accessible to keen amateurs, and if possible encourage them to become involved in "gathering the fragments". It is not primarily a learned journal, but can accommodate well-researched, properly-referenced short papers, as well as those written from personal knowledge and oral history. On the other hand it is not a magazine, and too infrequent to carry*

transient social news items.

A discussion at the Federation Meeting in March 1998 led, in the Autumn issue that year, to the first of the editor's many thought-provoking editorials, under the heading 'The Old Cornwall Society – the original Cornish pressure group?' He indicates that the origins of the movement lay with those who recognised (as few others did at that time) the dangers of 'the potential obliteration of Cornwall's past, its antiquities, its language and dialect, its traditions, customs and unique culture.' He continues:

> Later generations have re-invented the wheel, setting up all manner of pressure groups, conservation societies, study groups … many of which could have sat happily under the broad Old Cornwall banner.[91]

The 'image problem' of Old Cornwall, he suggests, has little to do with its name, since anyone who gave it a thought would realise that it indicates the movement's concern with Cornwall of earlier times rather than an age requirement for membership. The name issue is a distraction from the need to attract fresh blood to the cause. Ways in which to address this need could include making Old Cornwall activities more user-friendly for young and active individuals, and expanding activities in which local history is interpreted imaginatively for schoolchildren. Better publicity for this and other Old Cornwall work should be sought. Federation Festivals could be more 'open days' to attract wider involvement than 'members only' occasions. The eternal vigilance required to preserve our heritage should involve contributions from all members to help in the Society Recorders' role. 'Until we members ask a little more of ourselves, all those non-members who have the potential for enthusiastic participation – that is, the young at heart – will not be attracted to "Old Cornwall".'

In the same year Amy Hale's academic dissertation *Gathering the fragments* was published. It included reflections on the perceived shift in emphasis within the *Old Cornwall* journal and the movement as a whole, specifically with respect to Cornwall's Celtic roots:

> [O]ver the decades this emphasis on Celticity … seems to have decreased somewhat, perhaps because other, more overtly "pan-Celtic" organizations were started. Or is it possible that these organizations arose to fill the needs that the Old Cornwall Movement failed to fulfill? … Eventually the mandate to promote Cornwall's Celtic heritage was dropped from the … mission statement. Today the Journal … is a forum for local history, Cornish fiction, poetry, archaeology, folklore, and Society news. It barely retains the flavor of the original project set forth by Nance in 1920 … Today there is no emphasis on reviving traditions … [F]rom the beginning the … movement had to fight competing impulses: to serve a growing Cornish ethnonationalist movement … or to provide a forum for more passive cultural pursuits. The two may have been incompatible.[92]

Bernard Deacon has a similar historical perspective:

> The Old Cornwall movement was not just intended to preserve the fragments of Cornwall's heritage. It was also based on the belief that only by keeping alive these 'Celtic' fragments could 'Cornwall be kept Cornish still' … The growth of the Old Cornwall movement … reflected the strength of the Cornish identity. But Nance's hopes for a New Cornwall soon became submerged in a flood tide of local history. Nonetheless, the Old Cornwall Societies did provide a bridge between the revivalists and popular culture.[93]

From the 1920s up to Nance's death it was very clear that maintaining links with the wider Celtic world was seen as a vital strand of Old Cornwall work. Largely thanks to Henry Jenner, Cornwall had been accepted into the Celtic Congress in 1904, its application to join having previously been rejected, and Jenner, Nance and in due course others such as Ashley and Kathleen Rowe were particularly keen in their advocacy and active cultivation of Celtic links within Old Cornwall, not least in the movement's key role in Celtic Congresses held in Cornwall. Federation minutes and newspaper reports repeatedly emphasise the point. To give just one example, at the Federation AGM in 1953 Nance 'remarked that, although he did not think many people realised it, the Federation of Old Cornwall Societies was founded with the idea of getting Cornish people to realise that they were Celts and that they had a nationality and language of their own. It was very much the business of Old Cornwall Societies to help the Celtic Congress and to make all friendly contacts possible with other Celts.'[94] He had also described *Old Cornwall* as 'the first definitely Celtic journal to be issued in Cornwall.'[95] The pan-Celtic side to Old Cornwall has not quite disappeared since Nance's death, but the wider Celtic links which thrive within Cornwall do so principally outside the Old Cornwall Movement. The feeling of being *Cornish*, however, is still strong within the movement – it is worth noting that Dr Hale felt it right to recount her reaction when attending an Old Cornwall meeting (at Probus in 1997):

> When the presenter of that evening's lecture asked us to stand and sing "Trelawny (the Cornish "national" anthem)," the room shook ... These people were making a statement about who they are.[96]

The news in 2005 that the OCSs at Newquay and St Austell had created their own websites led to the creation of the Federation website the following year 'to tell the world what the Old Cornwall movement is really about, what our aims are, and what we do.'[97] George Pritchard of Redruth OCS was the first webmaster, as announced enthusiastically in the Autumn 2006 *Old Cornwall* with an appeal for all Societies to provide material for this 'excellent vehicle for 'marketing' our unique organisation.' Several individual Societies now have their own websites. Terry Knight saw the website as one aspect of improved publicity for the movement:

> The Federation of Old Cornwall Societies is advancing its ambition to reaffirm its status as the principal guardian of 'Cornwall-of-Old' through more consistent media coverage, and by its now extensive presence on the world-wide web. Reports of Federation general meetings regularly feature in the major local newspapers, as do items about this journal.[98]

This resurgence of good publicity was largely due to Barrie Bennetts, then St Agnes OCS Secretary, whose father Redvers Bennetts had also served the movement well as a newspaper reporter. Thanks were also due to those Society officers who regularly, though not always successfully, provided the press with copy. The website ('the most important new Old Cornwall activity') had been remarkably successful, having grown to over 80 pages within 18 months, and included, as well as very informative pages for every Society, a variety of articles and features, an online calendar as a checkpoint for Cornish cultural and historical events, and an online shop. By early 2008 it had been consulted by people in 47 countries[99] and new features were introduced regularly. The twice-yearly Federation Newsletter was also posted on the website (from where it could be downloaded), as well as being sent to Societies. It came to accommodate some of the Society news which had always appeared in the journal.[100] Online journal subscriptions became possible in 2010, and when Tony Mansell took over as webmaster in 2013 the site underwent a fundamental makeover, was relaunched and has continued to grow.[101] The wealth of information it contains is of course augmented by links to other relevant sources.

It should also be said that the website has assisted a dedicated group of enthusiastic members in keeping the flame of Cornish dialect burning. A major result of the groundwork they have put in is the extensive database of words and sayings, freely available to anyone interested in the dialect but also potentially useful for more advanced research.[102] Some of those who have expended considerable time and effort in recent years to ensure that dialect work is not overlooked are Paul Phillips, George Pritchard, Mary Quick, Brian

Cornish dance demonstration at Lowender Peran. Courtesy of Perran Tremewan.

Stevens, Joy Stevenson and Michael Tangye.

Among the subjects covered in the Spring 2011 *Old Cornwall* editorial are two which had surfaced before. The first concerned the problems of Societies which were not thriving. In order to help with such problems the Federation had sent each Society a questionnaire with the intention of using the data so obtained to offer help as needed. This led to the other recurring theme, the concern that some members were not fully aware of the movement's aims. The real role of Old Cornwall 'is left for the few to follow':

> It does not actually say in the Constitution that we are to hold meetings for members' enjoyment, and yet that element of our activities has become paramount for most members. That is not to suggest that this extremely enjoyable part of our existence is not important, as for many of us, the social side is one of the great bonuses of belonging to Old Cornwall. However, it is not for everyone. I suspect it is not for some of the more active people in our community. So I wonder if we are not 'missing a trick' by 'marketing' Old Cornwall almost exclusively in a way that emphasises the cosy indoor entertainment and we draw comparatively little public attention to all the other concerns we have.[103]

The editor also mentions the Federation's 'furtherance powers' with respect to guiding and enabling the work of member Societies, bringing the point back to the purpose of the questionnaire.[104]

The vital importance of Recorders is summed up in a 2013 editorial:

> Recording is ... the number one reason for our existence as an organisation: "gathering up the fragments that remain," as our motto states. It follows that the appointment of Recorders is vital to the purpose of establishing and continuing as a genuine 'Old Cornwall' Society. Societies

should at least appoint a general Recorder, but some add a Dialect Recorder, and/or a Photographic Recorder, and there is no reason not to consider other 'specialists' ...

At that point nearly half of the Societies appeared to have no Recorder, though successful Recorders' meetings had become a regular occurrence.[105] It was unfortunately not unknown for material collected and kept at home by Recorders or other officials to have been unthinkingly destroyed by their family or others, and similar disasters could occur if a Society folded up. One of the Federation's functions is to be available to mitigate just such a contingency or preferably to prevent the demise of a Society in danger.

In the same issue attention was drawn to the need for Old Cornwall vigilance in the matter of naming new streets and developments, since it was all too easy for inappropriate names, sometimes in incorrect Cornish, to slip past unnoticed.[106] The Autumn 2014 issue addresses the question of the developments themselves, looking for resistance to the 'Philistinism concerning our culture and heritage' which 'is alive and well and thriving in Cornwall.' It points up the duty of care required from Old Cornwall members and Societies in view of the barbarous 'developments' being inflicted on the land, and the movement's aims of supporting 'the preservation of Cornish antiquities and relics' and protecting 'the natural beauty and culture of Cornwall,' not a new phenomenon but no less pressing for that. Another editorial strand has a further saddening message, reporting the closure of three of the smaller Societies within a year. They were not the last to founder. These losses once again indicate the need for people who are willing to take on the fairly light duties of office rather than merely benefit from the efforts of others. On a brighter note, the editor (and now also Publicity Officer)[107] reports that he has set up a Facebook account for the Federation. This news is followed up in the subsequent issue with the report that most readers of the Federation postings are not Old Cornwall members, indicating that many people are evidently interested in Old Cornwall objectives without joining the movement.

Societies should therefore send regular news and updates on projects to the Federation to keep such people informed and thereby encourage them to join.

Over the century there have been many recurring problems, low points, close calls and fallow periods in the history of the *Old Cornwall* journal and the movement as a whole. Old Cornwall has also produced its heroes, however, not all of whom have been mentioned in this chapter, and the sheer number of talks and lectures which have been given to Societies at their countless regular meetings, festivals and pilgrimages is enormous, a significant (and preferably also entertaining) contribution to the education of their hearers. As to the work which has been done:

Over the decades [Old Cornwall's] members have refurbished holy wells, stone crosses, instigated archaeological investigations, community improvements of historic features, resisted destructive development schemes, recorded and published hundreds of articles, numerous books, and recorded folk lore and songs, Cornish dialect, disappearing industries. It has effectively raised awareness generally of the need for action to protect what is Cornish and part of Cornwall's identity.[108]

The Old Cornwall centenary year was just over the horizon, signalling something of a new approach to its work by the Federation. Karin Easton, who became Federation President in 2018, used the journal[109] to express the hope that members would embrace the changes that were being proposed by the Future Group, set up that year.

The Future

The Autumn 2019 issue of *Old Cornwall* reprints an important message to all members from the President. She outlines 'New benefits of Federation membership', reinforcing the umbrella organisation's function of helping the independently run local Societies to achieve the movement's aim of 'gathering the fragments' and reflecting the Federation Executive's awareness of the need to keep the movement relevant by working towards a more focused and dynamic profile. She first puts forward some of the benefits which already exist: insurance, advice, support and mentoring, communication (journal, email, website), Summer and Winter Festivals.

The new benefits are: regular workshops on topics such as publicity, finance and fundraising (following the success of the Recorder workshops); an award scheme for Societies actively pursuing the preservation of Cornwall's heritage and culture; a grant scheme for suitable Society projects; Festival guidelines for Societies hosting such events; access to the Publicity Officer for promotional purposes; publication of an annual calendar of forthcoming events and activities; a streamlined Executive Committee leading to shorter general meetings with opportunities for feedback and questions from Society delegates; a special conference with keynote speakers, OCS activities and interactive workshops for exchanging ideas and information. This rethink followed wide consultation to find ways of improving the relationship between the Federation and Societies. After many meetings, the proposals had been accepted at the Federation Spring Meeting in February 2019, reflecting the expressed determination to use all available means in a campaign to demonstrate the benefit to Societies of being participating members of the Federation.

The streamlined Executive would be tasked primarily with decision-making and strategic planning, while sub-committees with specific responsibilities or interests would deal with more specialist aspects of Old Cornwall work, using more targeted lines of communication. The prime motive for the changes was to secure the future for Societies and the movement as a whole. Another initiative from the Publicity wing of the Federation was *Newodhow a Gernow* ('News from Cornwall'), an email bulletin intended to complement other FOCS publicity and publications by bringing to the attention of OC members and the general public 'a variety of historic, cultural and environmental topics,' not only events with Old Cornwall input but any events with a broadly cultural slant initiated by any Cornish organisation, to be shared on the Old Cornwall website or social media.

The members of the Future Group had also written *A best-practice guide for Old Cornwall Societies* which was 'intended to be helpful rather than prescriptive' and which offered advice on all aspects of running a Society and promoting the movement, the most important part of which comprised ideas on the basic and vital activity of Recording (or 'gathering'). The President also mentioned the special events that were being planned by the Federation for the centenary year and ways in which each Society could commemorate the anniversary.

In the event, the 2020 Covid-19 pandemic meant that Old Cornwall, like the rest of the world, was forced to curtail its activities in its special year. Even in this situation of widespread self-isolation, however, Federation Publicity Officer Len Sheppard announced Old Cornwall's Positive Outcomes Project (POP) to share items relevant to Cornwall online, from and for interested parties within and outside the movement. As a tireless advocate of the exploitation of social media as a means of promoting Old Cornwall to non-members, Len Sheppard had taken the Federation Facebook presence to a new level and used modern media skilfully and determinedly to promote the movement, as well as helping individual Societies to create their own Facebook profile. His energy, dedication and sheer hard work also led to the launch, in November 2020, of a completely revamped Old Cornwall website, with a change of name to Kernow Goth and a newly framed statement of purpose:

'Safeguarding Cornwall's unique soul and identity through a sound knowledge of its past.'

This major overhaul – another of the 'New 'Old Cornwall' initiatives' – was undertaken with a view to improving the website's functionality, broadening its appeal and increasing its use.

Despite the movement's long-standing policy of cooperation with other organisations there was an awareness that a lack of communication with local history and heritage societies had sometimes led to loss of cohesion and perhaps failure to achieve worthwhile aims. The FOCS was therefore intending to refresh its willingness to be inclusive by approaching other societies with a view to their becoming Affiliated to the Federation (if within Cornwall) or Associated (if outside). Another project was the establishment of 'Kernow Goth Interest Groups' which would have a forum on the website, the two initial groups being Brass Bands and Soccer.

The journal had been available to members at a reduced rate, but with the Autumn 2019 issue it became free to members as part of their subscription – its cover price of £1.95 in any case represented better value, page for page, than the first issue of 1925, with virtually double the content. (A suggestion to include the journal in the subscription fee had been suggested at the Federation AGM in 1947 but had sunk without trace for over 70 years.)

Again looking to the future while being inspired by the past, the new Federation Heritage and Culture team reflected the recognition of a need for increased emphasis on the movement's fundamental ethos of collecting, preserving and sharing Cornish heritage and culture. The need arose because few members seemed aware of this role and fewer involved themselves in the work, though a shared effort by as many members as possible is required to achieve the movement's stated aims in this area. The Honorary Heritage and Culture Officer's role is one of leadership and motivation and is crucial to the achievement of these aims. The emphasis lies where it has always lain, on Recording, which should be a Cornwall-wide cooperative activity, within and beyond Old Cornwall circles. The Officer's responsibilities include liaison with and assistance for the specialist FOCS Recording Officers, the Publicity Officer, the webmaster and the journal editor; identifying members who are in a position to work with other bodies whose aims are compatible with those of Old Cornwall, and delegating responsibility to those members for cooperation and feedback regarding care for Cornwall's historic landscape and built heritage; reporting to the Executive, and advising on, threats and opportunities with respect to Cornwall's historic environment; reporting on the activities of Society Recorders as conveyed by them to Federation Recording Officers; disseminating enquiries to the most appropriate source of information. Members of the Heritage and Culture team would each be given oversight of a specific area of activity, such as outdoor projects, training in Recording, plaques and interpretation panels, or use of technology.

Input from the Federation continues to be sought by relevant bodies, and its published output is used by researchers, who do not necessarily acknowledge the debt or reciprocate by contributing to Old Cornwall, or *Old Cornwall*.[110] The movement has been described as 'probably the most misunderstood of all our societies' but at the same time 'a movement with a mission' which can claim an extraordinary record of achievement.[111]

Over the years, through a dedicated minority of its members, the movement has done a staggering amount of varied work – though again, its contribution to individual projects has not always been recognised or acknowledged – and it is currently engaging in new ways to fulfil its vital role in Cornwall's life. Cornwall and the world have changed dramatically since 1920 and the Old Cornwall movement has had to change with them, though the core imperative of its activities remains the same. The best interests of everyone concerned for Cornwall's future will be served by ensuring that this movement 'of remarkable and lasting significance to all of Cornwall's people'[112] should thrive:

We do not have ownership of or singular rights to any elements of Cornwall's cultural past or present and ... we must be outward-looking. We are in a position to offer guardianship, guidance, stimulus – and quite possibly leadership at times – in order to help to ensure that the prospects for our culture and heritage remain bright as it passes into the care of future generations.[113]

Old Cornwall and the Cornish language

Peter W Thomas

Cornish Language Fair at Falmouth in 2014. Courtesy of Terry Knight.

One of the stated aims of the Old Cornwall Movement has always been to 'encourage the study and use of the Cornish language.' The subject has been touched on already, but this section aims to provide a more connected account. It will concentrate mainly on Federation publications and activities, though individual OC Societies have made their own contributions to the promulgation of Cornish.

AK Hamilton Jenkin wrote in 1970 that when the first Old Cornwall Society was founded 'the majority of Cornish people ... had only the vaguest notion that Cornwall had ever been a separate Celtic nation with a language of its own, despite the fact that many of the older folk daily used words directly inherited from the latter.'[1] Jenner and Nance wished to redress this situation, seeing the acquisition of the language as one of the most effective ways of preserving the Cornishness of Cornwall. At the March 1920 meeting of the St Ives Society Nance announced that Jenner was willing to hold a Cornish class, for which ten people had already signed up, and Nance himself soon started classes at St Ives and Penzance, following the formation of OC Societies there.

As well as writing Cornish material of his own for *Old Cornwall*, Nance made a point of printing, translating and analysing every scrap of unpublished traditional Cornish he could find. This is apparent from the first issue. A recurring feature called 'Cornel Kernuak' ('Cornish Corner')[2] made its initial appearance in the second issue of the journal. This was the first item to be written entirely in Cornish, and this first example was a translation by Nance's daughter Phoebe of one of Aesop's Fables, comprising a mere six lines, followed by an appeal in Cornish by Nance to those who could read it, encouraging more such items to be submitted. The Cornish language has a part in several articles in the following issue (April 1926), in which the longer 'Cornel Kernuak' is written by Nance himself. The average *Old Cornwall* of today would contain little or no Cornish. Nance is easily the most prolific writer of material in Cornish for the journal in its history as well as the most frequent contributor overall. The definitive bibliography of his published works[3] reveals that 68 of his 240 contributions to *Old Cornwall* were entirely in Cornish, and many others, some in multiple parts, include elements in Cornish.

The 1927 leaflet *Old Cornwall Societies: what they are and what they are doing* made the claim for *Old*

AN

ENGLISH - CORNISH

DICTIONARY

BY

R. MORTON NANCE & A. S. D. SMITH, M.A.

Printed For

THE FEDERATION OF OLD CORNWALL SOCIETIES

By

James Lanham Ltd., St. Ives, Cornwall.

1934

Nance and Smith's "An English-Cornish Dictionary", which first appeared in 1934.
Courtesy of Exeter Cathedral Library and Toby Nicholson.

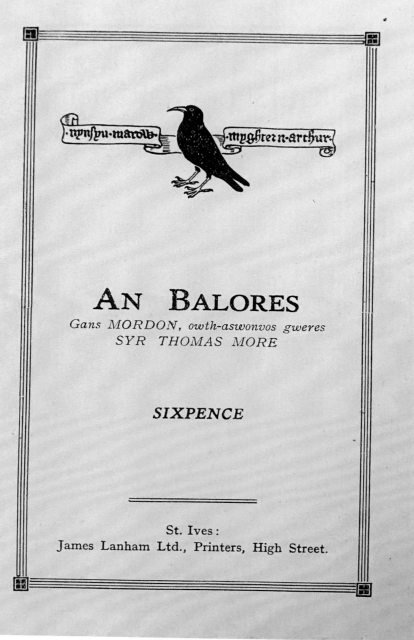

Nance's play "An Balores". Courtesy of Toby Nicholson.

Cornwall that it was 'the only journal in the world that prints as a matter of course a certain amount … of the Cornish language … in every issue,' so it could be said that the journal paved the way for the all-Cornish periodicals which appeared in later years and in some cases continue in publication. *Old Cornwall* was a pathfinder once again.

In 1929 the Federation of Old Cornwall Societies published Nance's *Cornish for all*,[4] initiating the author's Unified Cornish (UC), which attempted to normalise Cornish spelling and became the form of the language which remained standard for over 50 years. It is still the preferred form of some users of Cornish today. One immediate effect on the journal was that the 'Cornel Kernuak' feature became 'Cornel Kernewak' in the first issue that year, and subsequently 'Cornel Kernewek'. (Nance was still making amendments to UC at this early stage.) WD Watson's conversation booklet *First steps in Cornish* was published in 1931, as was the first edition of ASD Smith's *Lessons in spoken Cornish*.[5] It was in that year that AA Clinnick took over briefly as editor of *Old Cornwall*, but Nance retained responsibility for the Cornish language section of the publication despite his workload. Nance's play *An Balores*[6] ('The Chough') was published by the Federation and performed at the Celtic Congress held in Truro in 1932, and at the AGM in October that year it was decided that the Federation should meet the cost of printing an English-Cornish dictionary which had been prepared by Nance and Smith. The Societies were asked to interest their members in becoming subscribers. (In 1933, during the brief period when he was living at Perranporth, Smith held Cornish classes in connection with several Old Cornwall Societies.)[7] The dictionary was published in 1934,[8] the first dictionary under the Federation's auspices and its most important Cornish-language publication to that point. (Nance's Cornish-English companion volume, compiled solely 'for the love of the cause,' appeared in 1938 and brought about renewed interest in Old Cornwall. Revised editions of both dictionaries were issued by the Federation, in 1952 and 1955 respectively.) For Nance in 1936 'the vital thing of the movement was the restoration of the Cornish language.' One of his

helpers in this effort was Edwin Chirgwin, whose *Say it in Cornish*[9] was published in 1937. Nance even sought to draw something positive from national adversity, feeling in 1939 that 'a study of Cornish would give people an opportunity to take their minds off the miseries of the war.'

At the 1941 Federation AGM a recent attack by AL Rowse on the place of Cornish was countered. It was felt necessary to deny that proponents of Cornish wanted the language to be taught compulsorily in schools. FJB MacDowall considered that Cornish 'was a very tender plant … and often had a very inadequate place in the proceedings of the Old Cornwall Societies. He considered that was wrong.' He moved a resolution that 'this meeting …, so far from agreeing that the popular study of the Cornish language is either "useless or unprofitable", contends that proficiency in Cornish should be encouraged, not only for the high educative and recreational values of the study, but as the intimate duty of every lover of Cornwall.' The resolution was carried unanimously. Nance said that Rowse 'whom they all liked and respected personally, had a bee in his bonnet that they wished to introduce Cornish into the schools. Nevertheless, he would be sorry if this gentleman ceased to speak about it as he did, for people disliked being told what they should like, and every time he made one of these attacks, the sales of Cornish books went up.'[10] Nance stated that his 'reason for not wanting Cornish taught in schools is that I want people to learn it because they love it.'

It was clear at the 1947 Federation AGM that Nance had lost none of his forthrightness, remarking that 'any Old Cornwall Society that took no interest in [the Cornish] language was rather a stupid sort of society.' (He was to make a similar comment at the 1951 Spring Conference.)[11] By 1948 the Cornish-English dictionary was out of print, and Nance went as far as to say that 'the world was crying out' for a reprint.

In 1949 the Federation issued a revised edition of Nance's *Cornish for all* and the first in the series *Extracts from the Cornish texts in unified spelling with amended translation*. Over the next 20 years six further booklets were published in the series, all prepared by Nance and Smith, comprising extracts from three medieval texts: the saint's play *Beunans Meriasek* and the first and third in the *Ordinalia* cycle of three plays. (An enlarged edition of the first extract was published in 1966 and most of the others were reissued as reprints.) Also in 1949 a hitherto unknown 16th-century Cornish manuscript came to light, the so-called *Tregear Homilies*. The first of Nance's articles on this substantial discovery (brief introduction, extract converted from Tudor Cornish to Unified Cornish and glossary) appeared in *Old Cornwall* in 1950.[12]

At the 1950 Federation AGM there was a proposal to set up a Publications Fund. Nance adduced the large amount of Cornish material which was available for publication but lacked funding: 'These things are alive. They are treasures to Cornwall, and yet they are not appreciated in the least ... Perhaps the greatest difficulty is that the demand for the Cornish language is so small still. By this time every Old Cornwall Society ought to have its Cornish class. We ought to have thousands of people reading Cornish, and why not? It is only common sense.' He also regretted that more people were not interested in Cornish place-names, 'the essence of Cornwall.' (His own *Guide to Cornish place-names* first appeared in 1951.)[13] Nance also felt that the Fund should be used to enable the publication of the English-Cornish dictionary, the many works by Smith, Chirgwin and himself which were out of print and the *Old Cornwall* index. The proposal for the Fund was carried unanimously, and it was set up in 1951. Appeals for donations to it recurred on a regular basis in subsequent years.

At Perran Round during the Summer Pilgrimage in July 1951 Nance announced that the plays of the *Ordinalia* were being performed in various parts of Cornwall in celebration of the Festival of Britain. *Beunans Meriasek* was staged at Perran Round itself, Nance expressing a wish that it could be repeated every year to help the Old Cornwall Movement. There was an appeal for each Society to hold at least one fund-raising event for the

Publications Fund every year. A sub-committee was appointed to superintend the publication of useful Cornish books, most importantly to enable the enormous amount of scholarship devoted by Nance and ASD Smith to studying the medieval Cornish texts to be published for the benefit of Cornish people in the future, the work being 'vital to Cornwall if she is to remain Cornish.' A revival of interest in the Cornish language was reported at the October AGM. Letters of enquiry had been received from all over the UK, and language classes were being held in several towns. Five of the six 'language bards' initiated at that year's Gorsedh had been members of Nance's St Ives Cornish class. Nance reported that at least £500 would be required to publish the proposed new English-Cornish dictionary, but '[w]hen a delegate suggested that an appeal might be made to the London-Cornish Association ... for a grant for something which was essentially Cornish, the President retorted: "Old Cornwall is not only belonging to an organisation, but is a state of mind, which to us seems perfectly normal, but to them would probably appear crazy." (Laughter).' Sales of Nance's booklet on Cornish place-names had helped to subsidise the Federation publication that year of *An tyr Marya*, part of the third play of the *Ordinalia*, the latest of the extracts from Cornish texts prepared by Nance and Smith.[14]

In 1952 the St Ives Old Cornwall Society held its AGM three days after the Federation, and Nance, as President of both organisations, made his case for Cornish in both forums. At the St Ives meeting he 'emphasised that the society did not exist primarily to hear lectures and make pilgrimages. It was an association that, while doing everything in their power to preserve what remained of Cornwall of the past, should strive to build up a new Cornwall which maintained the integrity of the Cornish race. The Cornish language was the skeletal foundation of this movement, and he urged members to study their ancient tongue, and so help in the fight against its extinction.'[15] Cornish classes would be held in the town each week, and every month members would meet those from other parts of Cornwall to converse in Cornish. 1952 also saw the awaited publication of the revised edition of the *English-Cornish Dictionary*, a greatly expanded and improved version of the 1934 dictionary with much preparatory work by Richard Gendall and with extra data supplied from the *Tregear Homilies*.

It was at this stage that Retallack Hooper's An Lef Kernewek entered the field as a Cornish-language publisher, adding to the stock of material available. Though not the only other publisher of such material, for the next 15 years it was the only one to produce it with a regularity comparable to that of the Federation. In 1953 the Federation published the booklet *Cornish in song and ceremony*, the ceremonies in question including the Midsummer Bonfire and Crying the Neck.

Nance returned to his theme of the fundamental importance of Cornish at the 1954 Federation AGM: 'The object of the movement was to find out everything possible about Cornwall and to preserve as far as possible all that was being so rapidly swept away. The whole root of the matter was the study of the Cornish language.' A new venture was announced in the 1954 issue of *Old Cornwall*: 'three Gramophone Recordings in Cornish made by Mr. Nance.' (With the Federation's permission, these were reissued by Agan Tavas as a tape cassette in 1992 under the title *Lef Mordon* ('The Voice of Mordon').)

The outstanding feature of 1955 was the publication of Nance's improved *Cornish-English Dictionary*, which sold well though more orders had initially come from outside Cornwall than within. At the Federation AGM reference was also made to framed copies of the Lord's Prayer in Cornish which they had presented to over 50 churches. Parish churches had welcomed the gesture but Methodist churches 'just couldn't care less.' Nance ascribed this difference to the fact that the established Church had held services in Cornish in the past. It was recommended that the practice of distributing the Prayer should be continued. Nance also stressed the need once again for the study of Cornish place-names, about which 'frightful ignorance' prevailed.

In 1959 the Federation published Nance and Smith's version of the 16th-century Cornish play *Gwryans an Bys / The Creation of the World* (Unified Cornish with English translation), but after Nance's death that year the presence of Cornish in *Old Cornwall* declined.

In his 1963 address Charles Thomas suggested that issuing scholarly editions of the medieval Cornish literary manuscripts would be a worthy task for the Old Cornwall Societies, and that for the Federation to continue to issue Unified Cornish versions of the texts with no critical apparatus would be to stall the Revival:

> It is no real answer ... to say, as the Old Cornwall movement does, that the neo-Cornish literature is for the benefit of those who wish to learn Cornish, not for scholars. To do so is to admit to producing the second-best as an end in itself.

This matter was not resolved by the Federation, and in 1967 'all functions relating to the Language now undertaken by the Federation or by the Gorsedd,' including the business of publishing books in Cornish, were devolved to the Joint Language Board (as it was originally known, now the Cornish Language Board / Kesva an Taves [formerly Tavas] Kernewek).[16] The two founding bodies originally established the Board by providing it with loans and maintained a strong presence within its organisation, but the question of publishing in Cornish was now largely out of Federation hands. (The need to produce definitive editions of the original texts, however, has still not been systematically tackled. Individual scholarly editions have appeared, but not necessarily under the aegis of the Board. As to learning Cornish, since the 1980s the question has involved a decision as to which version of Cornish one decides to learn, with Nance's Unified Cornish being only one option.)

One of the first acts of the CLB, in 1969, was to produce a long-playing record of Cornish-language readings.[17] All readers were bards, and one, George Pawley White, was Grand Bard at the time and would become Federation President. Others included EG Retallack Hooper, a Federation Vice-President and past Grand Bard, and Richard Jenkin, who was later to become President and Grand Bard.[18]

Between its foundation and 1985, when it was granted autonomy by its founders ('with hindsight most unwisely' according to PAS Pool), the CLB published reprints of Federation publications as well as new books and pamphlets. A few of its more important publications during this period were the complete texts of Nance and Smith's versions of the second and third plays of the *Ordinalia* cycle; their version of the Cornish medieval Passion Poem *Passyon agan Arluth*; the seventh and last in their 'Extracts' series, *An venen ha'y map* (from *Beunans Meriasek*); Nance's version of *John of Chyannor*, the 17th-century folktale by Nicholas Boson; a corrected reprint of the Cornish-English and English-Cornish dictionaries in one volume; translations into Cornish of parts of the Christian liturgy; Smith's translation from Welsh of parts of the *Mabinogion*; and the grammars *Cornish for beginners*, 3rd edition (PAS Pool), *Kernewek Bew* (Richard Gendall) and *A grammar of modern Cornish* (Wella Brown).

Shortly after it became autonomous, the Cornish Language Board made the decision to adopt Ken George's Common Cornish (Kernewek Kemmyn), a much revised form of Nance's Unified Cornish, and to abandon the Unified form. This became a principal cause of disagreement and schism within the language movement. In 1989 these opposing schools of thought were well defended by two of their main proponents, Pool himself (Unified) and Wella Brown, Secretary of the CLB (Kemmyn), in *Old Cornwall*,[19] and in 1990 Richard Gendall, again very ably, promoted his Modern Cornish, based on the most recent survivals of the vernacular language.[20] The Federation was still represented on the CLB, and at the Spring Meeting in March 1991 the question of its representation was discussed in connection with the differences which had arisen over the various forms of Cornish. There was a unanimous vote in favour of the proposition that the Federation, and its representative on the

Language Board, should support Unified Cornish, and in 1994 support was expressed for Agan Tavas, the language organisation committed to retaining UC. The Gorsedh continued to use Unified for its ceremonies until it adopted the Standard Written Form of Cornish in 2009. Richard Jenkin proved a steadying hand at a difficult time in his support for Unified Cornish within both the CLB and the Gorsedh.

In 1963 Charles Thomas had estimated that perhaps a tenth of *Old Cornwall* was in Cornish, most of it written by Nance.[21] Between 2003 and 2017 only three pieces in Cornish appeared, all written by Rod Lyon. Ironically, though the proportion of Cornish in the journal is now much

Dew Vardh (Two Bards, i.e. Bert Biscoe and Pol Hodge) performing bilingual poetry at Lowender Peran. Courtesy of Perran Tremewan.

reduced from what it was during the Nance era, the Autumn 2011 issue was the first to carry a bilingual title, with *Kernow Goth* added to *Old Cornwall*. From the Autumn 2019 issue other details also appeared in Cornish (Standard Written Form) as well as English, with Volume 15, Number 9, Autumn 2019 given the additional designation Kevrol XV, Niver 9, Kynnyav 2019. There is no bar to journal articles in any form of Cornish.

Though dialect has done rather better within the journal, the situation regarding both language and dialect in the Old Cornwall Movement falls short of Nance's dream. Within other Cornish publications and organisations, however, Cornish is doing much better. Interest in the language, and the resources available to it, are probably greater than they have ever been. This situation, and the official recognition of the Cornish as a national minority by the UK government in 2014, are positive points to set against the disturbingly negative forces active in present-day Cornwall. The determination of the Old Cornwall Movement to continue to play its part in defending and promoting the welfare of Cornwall in all its aspects is one of the most positive points of all.

Newquay OCS Archaeology Group members, Richard Prestige, Sheila Harper, Rachel Parry and Hilary Borkett at the St Eval Longstone in 2011. Courtesy of Steve Hebdige.

Practical work undertaken by Old Cornwall Societies

Andrew Langdon

Ever since its inception in 1920 the Old Cornwall Movement has taken an active role in the preservation of Cornwall's ancient sites. In the first issue of the *Old Cornwall* journal in 1925 Henry Jenner, later to be the first Grand Bard, wrote a short article on 'The preservation of ancient monuments in Cornwall'.[1] In it he noted the different types of monuments, with numbers, and implied that there were many more to discover, although we now know that his estimate was rather conservative.

Jenner suggested that 'Old Cornwall Societies have a great opportunity of making themselves useful … It would be a good idea for each Society to take informal charge of the ancient monuments in its district, make lists of them, inspect them periodically, and report on them to the Federation of Old Cornwall Societies, and in case of any danger of destruction or damage write direct to the Ancient Monument Department, H.M. Office of Works, Storey's Gate, Westminster, S.W. 1.'

The Societies' motto 'Kyntelleugh an brewyon es gesys na vo kellys travyth,' 'Gather up the fragments that remain, that nothing be lost,' which appeared on the cover of the first issue of *Old Cornwall*, has proved an apt description for the 100 years of practical work in rescuing, recording and preserving sites, as described below. The motto is a Cornish translation of part of a verse from the

Mr Albert de Castro Glubb, first president of Liskeard OCS. Courtesy of Liskeard OCS.

account of the Feeding of the Five Thousand (the Miracle of the Five Loaves and Two Fishes) in St John's Gospel in the Bible.[2]

In 1934 the Federation of Old Cornwall Societies (FOCS) proposed that individual Societies should adopt a scheme devised by Lieut. Col. FC Hirst, the Archaeological Secretary to the Federation.[3] Through this scheme, each Society would agree a group of parishes which they would look after. Using a list published by Dr Hencken as a basis,[4] they would appoint a Reporter (later to be called a Recorder) for each parish containing one or more monuments, who would visit and report to the Archaeological Secretary twice a year on any damage affecting them. The hope was to have a Reporter for every ancient site in Cornwall. This proposal was reiterated by Charles Kenneth Croft Andrew, Specialist Recorder for Archaeology and Palaeography to the Federation, in a letter to Wadebridge OCS in October 1936.[5] Following on from this, in a letter dated April 1st 1938, the Wadebridge OCS Recorder asked the Bodmin Society if they could agree a boundary between them, as the Wadebridge members wished to restore a cross at St Mabyn and did not want to encroach on Bodmin OCS's parishes.[6]

For 100 years Old Cornwall Societies have helped to repair, fund and preserve a wide range of ancient sites and monuments of all periods, although there has been a particular focus on medieval stone crosses and holy wells, which are two of Cornwall's notable features. Societies have also promoted and highlighted these sites and monuments for the wider public through talks, reports, fixing plaques and rededication ceremonies. Clearing sites and monuments of vegetation is another area where many of our Societies and individual members have been able to play an active role.

The Old Cornwall Societies can be seen as pioneers in the protection of monuments in Cornwall, although other specialist organisations were founded later in the 20th century. One such group was the West Cornwall Field Club, founded in 1933 by Lieut. Col. Hirst himself. In 1961 the Club was renamed the Cornwall Archaeological Society,[7] and many Old Cornwall Society members are also members of the CAS. Cornwall's professional body, the Cornwall Archaeological Unit (originally the Cornwall Committee for Rescue Archaeology), was established by the County Council in the 1970s, partly to meet changes in planning rules. Nonetheless, local Societies still have an important role in monitoring and safeguarding sites within their areas.

Certain Societies have undertaken many practical projects over the years. Opportunity, geographical location and enthusiastic leadership have all helped to generate and tackle these projects. A few of the leading personalities in the field of Old Cornwall Societies' preservation work are described below.

Leaders and personalities

By far the most influential person in the early days of the Old Cornwall Societies was Albert de Castro Glubb, President of Liskeard Old Cornwall Society between 1928 and 1947. He was a keen amateur archaeologist and as a solicitor was very well connected with landowners in the area. He was able to rescue several important ancient sites and monuments by purchasing them from landowners and giving them to the nation or to appropriate public bodies. Glubb dealt with all the legal work himself. As a result, Liskeard OCS can claim the credit for more practical projects than any other Society. Significant achievements included the purchase of land in 1933 to enclose the King Doniert Stone, which was then conveyed to the Ministry of Public Works, and the purchase of the Hurlers stone circles, which were transferred to the Ministry in 1935, as well as Trethevy Quoit (1931) and Dupath Well Chapel (1936). St Lallu's (Lalluwy's) Holy Well at Menheniot was purchased by Liskeard OCS and conveyed to the Revd Canon Edward Spry Leverton and his successors of Menheniot parish, while St Keyne's Holy Well was completely rebuilt and given to the Revd Canon Frank Rupert Mills and his successors in office at St Keyne parish.

Another leading protagonist was CK Croft Andrew, who lived at Darite, St Cleer, during the 1930s. He was a professional archaeologist who advised and assisted in many of Glubb's and Liskeard OCS's projects. Andrew was CA Ralegh Radford's main assistant during the 1930s when archaeological investigations at the Hurlers and Castle Dore Iron Age hillfort took place. He also excavated on Trevelgue Head near Newquay in 1939.[8] Andrew became the Federation's Specialist Recorder for Archaeology and advised on many Old Cornwall Society projects throughout the Duchy during his years in Cornwall. Andrew's photographic collection, which is held by Historic England, includes many photographs of projects undertaken by Old Cornwall Societies.

Nicholas Bray, President of Wadebridge OCS between 1939 and 1949, was another keen individual. He was an active collector of ancient carved stones and artefacts who organised a 'Stone Cross Sub-Committee' at Wadebridge OCS to help restore and re-erect the medieval crosses at Three Holes Cross, Egloshayle, Penwine Cross, St Mabyn, Job's Cross and Trequite Cross, St Kew. His local knowledge, practical understanding and connections assured that these projects were a huge success, while the monuments he helped to restore are still in good condition today.

More recently, Newquay Old Cornwall Society's Archaeological Group under the guidance of Sheila Harper, the Society's Warden of Ancient Monuments and Archaeology Recorder, sets a fine example of what Societies could be doing today and what can be achieved. Sheila and the Group at Newquay OCS have taken on the maintenance of the early medieval village site at Mawgan Porth, liaising with Historic England and the landowners. They regularly clear scrub from the site and cut the grass. The group has a programme of regular visits to ancient sites in the Newquay area, which they record, monitor and clear of vegetation, following the principles first laid out by Henry Jenner and

Neville Meek, Recorder of St Gerrans & Porthscatho OCS scrub clearing at Dingerein Castle. Courtesy of Ann Preston-Jones

Lieut. Col. Hirst. These sites include the St Eval Longstone, Trevemper Old Bridge, Trevornick Holy Well and the crosses at Doublestiles, Penrose, Treloy Hill, St Columb Minor, Crantock and Colan.

Collaboration with other organisations

From the very beginning there has been collaboration with other organisations such as town and parish councils and like-minded societies. In the past, Society members have also been supportive of larger practical projects, even if they have not necessarily taken a leading role. For example, in 1936 and 1937 at least nine Old Cornwall Societies gave financial support towards the professional excavation of Castle Dore Iron Age hillfort by CA Ralegh Radford and the Cornwall Excavations Committee.[9] Since CK Croft Andrew was Dr Radford's assistant during the first year of work at Castle Dore, it was perhaps through Andrew's involvement with the Old Cornwall Societies that so many contributed to

the work.[10] Today, many Old Cornwall Society members are also actively involved with similar organisations. In February 2020, for example, St Gerrans & Porthscatho OCS were liaising with Historic England and the Cornwall Area of Outstanding Natural Beauty's (AONB's) Monumental Improvement Project to help improve the condition of and maintain Dingerein Castle, a multivallate hillfort in their area.

Below is a summary of some of the practical work and other related projects that Societies have promoted and achieved over the last hundred years. The work is reported here by monument type. A fuller list has been added as an appendix, giving, where possible, dates and references.

Prehistoric sites

Liskeard OCS not only instigated the purchase of the Hurlers stone circles for the nation in 1935 but also helped with their restoration in 1935/36. Newquay OCS members were involved with the Trevelgue Head excavation in 1939, and members Ruth Hirst and George White are frequently mentioned in the excavation report.[11] In 1932 Dr WJ Stephens of Newquay OCS was instrumental in arranging to have the fallen St Eval Longstone re-erected at a cost of £2 10s.[12] This Neolithic or Bronze Age menhir, which stands at SW 8713 6802, marks the boundary between St Mawgan and St Eval parishes and is marked on the 1840 tithe map for St Eval as 'Boundary Rock'. At Wadebridge, the Society likewise re-erected part of the Bronze Age menhir known as the Longstone in June 1975 at the hamlet of Longstone (SX 0607 7337) in the parish of St Mabyn.[13]

Early medieval inscribed stones

In 1754 Dr William Borlase recorded an inscribed stone standing 'about four miles East of Michel [Mitchell],' near the inn at Indian Queens.[14] The monument marked the parish boundary between St Enoder and St Columb Major. In 1930 the road was widened and the stone left standing in the pavement where it caused an obstruction to pedestrians and was vulnerable to damage. In

Long Cross, St Endellion rescued by Bodmin OCS in 1932. Courtesy of Ann Preston-Jones.

1939 Newquay OCS facilitated the removal of the stone, for its preservation, to the churchyard of St Francis in St Francis Road, Indian Queens.[15] The stone remains there to this day and is easily accessible. The inscription is very worn and has been debated by archaeologists and historians. Borlase read RVANI HIC IACIT, while Charles Thomas suggested CRVARIGI HIC IA(CIT), 'Here lies [the body] of Cruarigus'.[16]

In 1931 two inscribed stones in Cardinham parish were re-sited by Liskeard OCS. One was located at the top of a lane to Lower Tawna Farm and was being used as a gatepost, while the other at nearby Welltown was fixed against the wall of a pigs' house; both were owned by local farmer Henry Runnalls. The Society agreed to purchase two new gateposts in exchange for the inscribed stones and once they had been removed the stones were set up together on a grass bank at a crossroads above the farms at SX 1361 6785. The inscription on the Tawna stone is highly eroded but has been read by RAS Macalister as OR P EPS TITUS, although Thomas regards the text as uncertain.[17] The Welltown stone inscription is clearer, and according to Elisabeth Okasha it reads VAILATHI FILI VROCHANI, '[The memorial] of Vailathus, son of Urochanus'.[18]

Another inscribed stone, the Long Cross in the parish of St Endellion, first illustrated by John Watts Trevan in 1834,[19] stands at Higher Town Gate, Roscarrock (SW 9898 7973). During the 19th century the inscribed cross was knocked over and for several years lay on the ground, prone and neglected. At this time the monument was taken by Samuel Symons of Gonvena and set up on cliffs on the western side of Doyden Head as a landscape feature, close to his Gothic summerhouse of Doyden Castle – by all accounts the scene of much revelry, gambling and drunken parties.[20] Here it stood, exposed to the Atlantic weather, until 1932, when it was rescued by Bodmin OCS with the support of the then landowner, returned to its former site and set up again on its original base-stone at the gateway to Roscarrock.[21] The Long Cross is a square pillar of granite, 1.5m high, with a stylised chi-rho monogram above the inscription and a very worn relief cross on the reverse.[22] (The Greek letters chi (X) and rho (P) represent the first two letters of the name of Christ (Χριστος / Christos) and together form an early symbol of Christianity.) The inscription reads: BROCAGNI HIC IACIT / NADOTTI FILIVS, 'Here lies [the body] of Brocagnus, son of Nadottus'.[23]

Another small granite stone bearing the chi-rho monogram was discovered at the site of St Helen's Oratory on Cape Cornwall in St Just in Penwith during the early 19th century.[24] The Cape Cornwall stone is said to date from the 5th century.[25] It was discovered by the Revd John Buller, Vicar of St Just, in a watercourse beside the oratory and subsequently removed to the chancel of the parish church. Here a brass plaque was affixed, giving the place of its discovery.[26] The following incumbent, the Revd George C Gorham, who hated religious relics, threw the ancient stone down a well in the vicarage garden, along with a wheel-headed cross, which was later retrieved.[27] On April 24th 1970, the *Western Morning News*, under the headline 'Search for old cross in St Just well', reported that St Just & Pendeen OCS, searching for the stone with the assistance of miners from Geevor tin mine, were going to inspect the well in the vicarage garden. Two wells in the vicinity of the vicarage were checked, but the chi-rho stone has never been found.[28]

Medieval stone crosses

Most of the crosses which Societies have re-erected or repaired have been wayside or boundary crosses out in the countryside. These date from the 12th century and marked ancient trackways to the parish church or the boundaries of the glebe or parish. Some were discovered during the 19th century but not restored until Societies were formed in the 20th century. Others were repaired after being damaged by vehicles or road alterations. At least 19 of the cross restorations by OCSs were completely new discoveries in the 20th century.

Some of the restorations were undertaken by individual members of Old Cornwall Societies, like

George Trethewey and Brian Bawden of Liskeard OCS, who with help from local farmers the Ford family of Hendra Farm, Menheniot, drilled, pinned and glued the broken shaft of the newly-discovered Hendra Cross and re-erected it.[29] Other members such as Stanley Cock from St Ives OCS and Cyril Orchard from Penzance also repaired and re-erected crosses in their respective areas.[30] Many more Societies organised, funded and commissioned repairs to crosses, enlisting local contractors and stonemasons to help fulfil their projects. The following are a few examples of the types of projects that Societies have undertaken.

In 1936 a small wheel-headed wayside cross was discovered face down beside a stile at Polmennor in the parish of Gwinear. The monument had been badly damaged over the years. A segment of the head was missing and there were drill-holes in the shaft, indicating that at one time it had been used as a gatepost. In 1937 the cross was rescued by William E Wallace and H White, members of Camborne OCS, who set it up on a new base-stone in the hedge beside the stile where it was first discovered.[31] It remained there until September 1984, when Gwinear and District Footpath and Bridleway Association, with the cooperation of Tom Clemens, President of Camborne OCS, moved the cross to the parish churchyard for better protection.[32]

A late medieval Latin cross was discovered in 1906, built horizontally into the external wall of an old stable at Tregoad Farm in the parish of St Martin by Looe. The cross is carved from quartz-porphyry, has chamfered corners, displays an incised crucifix figure and lacks one of its horizontal arms. In 1931 members of Looe OCS approached the owner of the stable, Mr Tamblyn, for permission to remove the cross from the wall, which he granted. The cross was set up on a plinth made of local stone and re-erected close to the entrance of the farm. By 1972 the cross had come under threat due to road widening, at exactly the time that a museum was being set up in the old guildhall. It was agreed that the cross should be removed to the lower floor of the museum, where it has been on display since 1973.[33]

Rededication of Hendra Cross, Menheniot by Liskeard OCS in 1991. Courtesy of John Rapson, Liskeard OCS.

The Middle Moor Cross at Camperdown, St Breward, was first recorded by Sir John Maclean in 1873. It stands beside a track from St Breward to Davidstow parish, skirting the high tors of Roughtor and Brown Willy. The cross, which was often used as a rubbing post by moorland animals, was knocked over in 1938, breaking the mortice-and-tenon joint in the base-stone. The following year Bodmin OCS, under the direction of their Honorary Secretary Mr J Clemo, contacted Messrs Nankivell, stonemasons of Tor Down Quarry, St Breward, and commissioned them to re-erect the cross to recommendations made by MHN Cuthbert Atchley, the Federation's Honorary Consulting Architect. He recommended the cutting of a new tenon on the bottom of the cross-shaft. The work was completed in June 1939.[34] In the same year, the Nankivells also restored the Three Holes Cross, Egloshayle, for Wadebridge OCS, following road widening at a crossroads one mile north-east of Wadebridge.[35]

Beside the A30 near Launceston, at a road junction leading to the village of Polyphant, stands the Holyway (Holloway) Cross. This wheel-headed wayside cross was first recorded by Langdon in 1896 when it was partially buried in the corner of a cottage garden.[36] On February 6th 1945 an army bus which was used for transporting prisoners of war hit and demolished one wall of the cottage, which was eventually pulled down. Later the road junction was improved and in 1950 Launceston OCS took the initiative to restore the cross and in conjunction with Cornwall County Council had the

Above: Cyril Orchard, member of Penzance OCS cutting a mortice for the Mayon Cross at Sennen. Photograph from the late Margaret Orchard.

a local builder, fixed the cross to a new granite base-stone and repositioned it in the hedge.[40] In 2010 the cross on its base-stone started to slip down the hedge due to subsidence, and concern for the monument was raised by St Ives OCS. In October that year, after Scheduled Monument Consent had been granted, the Society commissioned local builders Mark and Justin Tooley to remove the monument, rebuild the hedge and provide concrete beams, discreetly set in the hedge to support the weight of the cross and base-stone. This work, carried out on December 4th 2010, was organised by Brian Stevens of St Ives OCS, and the Society funded the work.[41]

When hedges were removed and drainage work undertaken at Mayon Farm, Sennen parish, in 1973, a wheel-headed cross was discovered. Cyril Orchard, a member of Penzance OCS, erected the cross on a granite boulder in the middle of a field, with the help of his son Robert and CH Jewell.[42] In the neighbouring parish of St Buryan in 1943, the Pendrea Cross was discovered, built into the foot of a hedge near the entrance to Pendrea Farm. The farmer, Mr Gwennap, set up the cross on top of the hedge close to the farmhouse. In 1959, Peter Pool of Penzance OCS organised a project to re-erect the monument on a modern base-stone beside the B3283 road 300 metres to the south-west of the parish church. The work was carried out by Arnold Snell of Newlyn. It was later rededicated, on Tuesday May 5th 1959, by the Revd DR Evans, rector of St Buryan, in a service conducted in both Cornish and English, with members of Penzance OCS and St Buryan Parish Council in attendance.[43]

In 1908 Dr William Stephens, later President of Newquay OCS (1929-1932), discovered an old cross in use as a fence post in the parish of Colan near Newquay. Six iron bolts had been let into the monument for fixing the wires of a fence. Arthur Langdon, author of *Old Cornish crosses*, inspected the cross in 1909 and suggested that it should be

monument dug up and mounted at its full height on a new base-stone provided by St Breward stonemasons. Here in June 1950 the Bishop of Truro, the Rt Revd Dr Joseph Wellington Hunkin, rededicated the cross, after being introduced by Stuart L Peter, Chairman of Launceston OCS.[37]

On Lelant Lane, by the road to St Uny's Church, Lelant, is a small Latin cross displaying a crucifix figure, which is set up in the hedge close to the boundary of the West Cornwall Golf Club. The cross was first noted in 1896[38] but was lost in the hedgerows for many years. It was rediscovered in 1956 by Mary Henderson and Joanna Pemberton-Longman, who reported their find to St Ives Old Cornwall Society.[39] In 1964 St Ives OCS, with the assistance of their member Stanley Cock,

Holyway (Holloway) Cross restored by Launceston OCS and rededicated by the Rt Revd JW Hunkin, bishop of Truro in 1950. Courtesy of Launceston OCS.

rescued and removed to the churchyard for its protection. This was due to take place until, at the last moment, the landowners stipulated that they wished the cross to be set up above a family grave in Colan churchyard, and the idea was abandoned.[44] Eventually, 60 years later, Newquay OCS gained permission to remove and re-site the cross in the churchyard, beside the south porch. This rescue project was used to commemorate the 50th anniversary of the Old Cornwall Movement. The work was completed in May 1970 and the cross was later rededicated by the Revd DG Stafford, curate of Colan, on Trinity Sunday, May 24th 1970, in the presence of the vicar, the Revd James Holland, the churchwardens, members of the Parochial Church Council and Newquay OCS.[45]

In 1930 SA Opie, Recorder for Redruth OCS, reported on the discovery of a wheel-headed cross built horizontally into the foot of a hedge at Whitcross Hill, Illogan. The name Whitcross Hill suggests that at one time the cross may have been painted white.[46] Because the Second World War intervened, the cross was not finally lifted out of the hedge and set up on top until 1947. Help with the project came from Camborne OCS (the neighbouring Society) and Redruth.[47] More recently, in 2019, the cross in relief on this monument was painted white by Carn Brea Parish Council after Scheduled Monument Consent had been obtained. In the village of Whitecross, beside the A39 and close to the Royal Cornwall agricultural showground in St Breock, stands

covers for stone coffins. Only about 50 medieval grave slabs survive in Cornwall, and the best examples are carved from freestone, with at least 20 having been imported during the medieval period from the Isle of Purbeck in Dorset. Being freestone, Purbeck stone is much easier to carve than most Cornish stones. At Purbeck these grave slabs were produced in large numbers throughout the medieval period and exported to many parts of the country.[49] They are often not very attractive and in many cases damaged or incomplete, so they are frequently relegated to the darkest corner of the church or churchyard, where despite their age their significance is easily overlooked.

In 2011 concern was raised about part of a medieval grave slab at St Martin by Looe, which had previously been stored in the church but had recently been discarded in the churchyard. It is one of those Cornish slabs carved from Purbeck stone, a limestone which does not survive well in the damp Cornish weather and, if left outside, the layers of decoration can quickly delaminate. The Looe example is a typical product of the Purbeck quarries, consisting of the upper part of a slab decorated with a relief cross with cross-arms terminating in trefoil-shaped ends. Around the edge of the slab is a double concave rebated moulding. On July 31st 2012 Peter King of Looe OCS, with help from Duncan Matthews of Liskeard OCS and the churchwarden Brian Beddoes, arranged for the grave slab fragment to be returned to the church. It was decided to store the monument at the bottom of the church tower until arrangements could be made to set up the stone within the church itself. To make room for the upper part of the grave slab a loose stone in the tower was moved, and it was found to be the lower section of the same monument, the two fitting together exactly.[50]

another 'white cross'. The cross gives its name to the village, which is marked on Thomas Martyn's map of 1748. Traditionally, the relief cross on each face of the monument has been whitewashed, and for the last 25 years this tradition has been maintained by members of Wadebridge OCS.[48]

Medieval grave slabs and sarcophagi

Medieval grave slabs or coffin covers date to the 12th and 13th centuries. Although they are common in other parts of the UK they are rare in Cornwall, and there are many fewer of them than there are stone crosses. These monuments are recumbent stones, which were either laid directly above a grave, set into the paving of a church or used as

A granite grave slab with a St Andrew's cross was set up on the south side of Lostwithiel church tower and spire by Lostwithiel OCS in 1958. The slab was set vertically on a new granite plinth with a slate plaque noting its discovery close to its present site. It might once have been the cover for a stone coffin or sarcophagus which is

Cross on Whitcross Hill, Illogan, restored by Redruth OCS, with help from neighbouring Camborne OCS in 1947. Courtesy of AG Langdon.

preserved in the north porch of the church. At St Anthony in Roseland an old granite sarcophagus was discovered during the 1850 restoration of the church. For a brief period the sarcophagus was removed by a local farmer for use as a cattle trough but was later dumped back in the churchyard. In 2001, through the efforts of Hilary Thompson, Chair of St Gerrans & Porthscatho OCS, the stone coffin was repositioned near the entrance to the churchyard with a plaque recording its restoration.[51]

Medieval chapels

It is estimated that by the 15th century, as well as the 212 medieval parish churches in Cornwall,[52] there were twice as many chapels, some dating to the early medieval period.[53] Although some of these chapels were built beside holy wells, in secluded valleys, on hill tops or cliff tops or even on islands, the majority functioned as manorial chapels, linked to or associated with manor houses. Today, very few complete medieval chapels survive although some still exist as ruins. One ruined chapel at Lammana in West Looe was first brought to the attention of Looe OCS by archaeologist and founder member of the Society CK Croft Andrew, the Federation's Archaeology Recorder. According to PO and DV Leggat, Andrew was looking for volunteers to dig the ruined site as early as 1929, although it took another six years before an official excavation of the chapel took place. During the period from 1935 to 1937 Looe OCS members (Andrew himself with the Revd HA Lewis and Mr Wilcocks) excavated the chapel site. Painted plaster and whitewash were found on the chancel walls, three burials were discovered near the chancel and many artefacts were uncovered, including unglazed ridge tiles and roofing slates.[54] Over the years, the clearance of vegetation at the chapel site has been undertaken by the Society. Further west, in Wendron parish, Merther Uny chapel and enclosure were excavated in 1968, by Professor Charles Thomas and Leicester University, and Helston OCS donated funds towards the excavation.[55]

Holy wells

Many of Cornwall's medieval holy wells are associated with former chapel sites, and the site of a holy well can be found near the enclosure at Merther Uny. Sometimes holy wells and their water were incorporated into chapel buildings as at St Clether or Tregenna in Blisland. Most (but not all) Cornish holy wells have well-houses over them, some of which date from the medieval period. Others are post-medieval or Victorian. Several Societies have been responsible for the restoration of holy wells in their areas, and this is the second most popular type of restoration project undertaken by the OCSs, after stone crosses.

The holy well at Towan Farm near Lobb's Shop, Pentewan (SX 0145 4880) was restored by St Austell OCS in 1937 under the direction of MHNC Atchley, Honorary Consulting Architect for the FOCS. It was rededicated by the Bishop of Truro, JW Hunkin, on Thursday June 10th 1937. Atchley stated that no concrete was used in the restoration, only Pentewan stone.[56] In 1992, the well was found to be very overgrown and members of Pentewan OCS cleared the vegetation on and around it.[57] In November 2003 Pentewan OCS members David Stark, Brian Jacob, Valerie Jacob, Mac Waters, Graham Honey and Sam Edyvean undertook further clearance work, including the removal of roots embedded in the roof.[58] This led to the realisation that there was a need for some timely repairs, so with help from Cornwall County Council's Scheduled Monument Management Project, Pentewan members Graham Honey, David Stark and Geoffrey Prettyman were enabled to repoint the roof of the well with a lime-based mortar.[59]

St Austell OCS completed clearance and drainage work at Menacuddle Well in St Austell (1953),[60] while Looe OCS re-roofed St Cuby's Holy Well at Duloe[61] and Madron OCS has helped to restore and maintain Madron Holy Well and Baptistry over the years.[62]

Between 1936 and 1937 the Liskeard OCS, under the leadership of their President Albert de Castro Glubb, actually purchased the well chapel at Dupath, Callington, with an area of land around it, from the landowner James Hicks for £100. Funds were raised by public subscription, with the support of Callington Parish Council and many individual donations, and the site was then conveyed to the Commissioners of His Majesty's Office of Works and Public Buildings as a national monument.[63] The site is now maintained by the Cornwall Heritage Trust on behalf of the English Heritage Trust.

Roche Holy Well stands just to the north of the A30 road at Victoria (SW 9850 6173). According to M and L Quiller-Couch the water from the well was used for curing eye diseases, particularly in children.[64] Concern for the condition of the well building was first noted by St Austell OCS during the 1930s, and by early 2006 it was in a state of near collapse due to a large sycamore tree which was growing in the building, its roots causing the walls to bulge and become unstable. In September and October 2006, Graham Honey, David Stark, Geoffrey Prettyman and Brian Jacob, members of St Austell OCS, spent three days in clearing vegetation at the site. The sycamore tree was removed and the silt cleared from the area in front of the well to try to improve drainage and access. Following this, the building was restored by conservation contractors Darrock and Brown of Bodmin, with a watching brief by the Cornwall Archaeological Unit. Recording work suggested

Sarcophagus repositioned at St Anthony in Roseland by members of St Gerrans & Porthscatho OCS in 2001. Courtesy of AG Langdon.

that although the holy well includes carved stones dating to the Tudor period, they might have been brought from another building and assembled during the 18th century.[65]

In 1936 Newquay OCS undertook the restoration of Trevornick Holy Well at Cubert under the supervision of MHNC Atchley. Part of his report on the restoration work reads:

> The rubble walls … were in one corner up to the full height, but elsewhere standing at only 1 ft. 6 in. to 2 ft. high. Stones from the walls, doorway, and roof lay around and in nearby hedges. These were carefully collected and reinstated. One new granite door-jamb had to be provided to complete

> the doorway, and such as were broken were dowelled together … Within, the seats on either side and the inner arch were carefully repaired. The inner arch was possibly at one time the only covering of the well, and may be very ancient. The well-house itself dates from the middle 15th century. The interior wall-faces were re-plastered in the same manner as the existing remains indicated had been done in mediaeval times. To protect from cattle, a wall was built in front of the well-house … In this wall a 16th-century granite archway, that had been found nearby, was incorporated so as to preserve it.[66]

On completion of the project the well was rededicated by JW Hunkin, Bishop of Truro, on March 31st 1937. The holy well is a Scheduled Ancient Monument as well as Grade II listed. It stands on private land owned and occupied by Holywell Bay Holiday Park at SW 7733 5889. In 1953 the same Society, again with guidance from Mr Atchley, restored the Holy Well of St Pedyr at Treloy in Colan with the help of builder Mr Chynoweth, at a cost of £60.[67] According to the Quiller-Couch sisters the well supplied water to the Arundells at Treloy and to the priors of Bodmin at Rialton.[68] The well is on private ground and there is no public access.

Wadebridge OCS has had a long association with Jesus Well beside the golf course in the parish of St Minver Lowlands at SW 9376 7634. The Society has paid for its restoration on more than one occasion, repairing the roof as well as fencing the site and later funding a Cornish hedge around it and providing a gate.[69] The Quiller-Couch sisters state that near the well an old chapel once stood, which was known as Jesus Chapel and belonged to the manor of Penmayne, but there is no trace of this now.[70]

In 1997 St Ladoca OCS became concerned about the Glebe Holy Well at Ladock, which is situated approximately ¼ mile north of the parish church at SW 8955 5121. After large amounts of mud and silt had been cleared, it became evident that

Above: Glebe Holy Well, Ladock, restored by St Ladoca OCS in 1997. Courtesy of AG Langdon.

Right: Towan Holy Well being cleared of vegetation in 2003 by members of Pentewan OCS. Courtesy of Ann Preston-Jones.

remedial work on the structure of the well-house was needed. After gaining permission from the owners, the Truro Diocesan Glebe Committee, and obtaining Listed Building Consent, the Society commissioned specialist contractors to restore the building.[71]

In 1984 St Columb OCS rebuilt the holy well situated in Ruthvoes village, to the north of the A30 at SW 9252 6056. According to Charles Henderson, a well chapel dedicated to St Columba once stood at Ruthvoes and a spring called Venton Allen once fed the well.[72] No remains of the original medieval well survived and only a water chute marked the site. A new well facade was built, however, by members Nick Glanville and Vercoe Bennallick, who also designed the structure.[73] Another complete reconstruction took place at Scarlett's Well to the west of Bodmin Jail and close to the

old railway line to Wadebridge (now the Camel Trail) at SX 0566 6752. According to the Quiller-Couch sisters no well-house survived, although they thought that there would have been one originally.[74] In 1995 Bodmin OCS in conjunction with Bodmin Town Council rebuilt the well in local stone.[75]

Domestic wells and water-chutes have been restored in addition to holy wells. In 1970 at Ludgvan, a domestic well known as Tregellast Well, situated at a road junction, was damaged by an articulated lorry. During 2000/01 it was restored by Ludgvan OCS with help and support from local parishioners.[76] Helston OCS was instrumental in preserving the last surviving old pump on Cross Street, Helston, while Pentewan OCS erected a plaque to mark the former site of the village pump in 1990.[77] Following research into

Dupath Well chapel purchased for the nation by Liskeard OCS in 1936. Courtesy of AG Langdon.

the water systems at Gerrans by the St Gerrans & Porthscatho OCS, a booklet was published: *The wells, shutes & springs of Gerrans parish* by their Recorder Hilary Thompson in 2009.

Two wells have been maintained and restored at East Looe by Looe OCS over the years, one being the large St Martin's Well. It has no well-house and is now enclosed by railings beside Dawes Lane and incorporated into private grounds at SX 2569 5407. There is no vehicle access, but the well can be viewed from Dawes Lane above, which connects Shutta with Barbican Road. Closer to the town centre there is another well with a small stone well-house covering it, situated on Shutta Road beside a road junction on a steep and narrow section of the road with no vehicle access, at SX 2552 5348. This well is known as St Mary's Well or Lady Well, and the Society has restored the building on two separate occasions, once in 1977 and again in 2006, through a generous legacy from former member Beatrice Rose Whittington. Both wells appear to have been used formerly for a domestic water supply.

Brian Stevens, with Frank and Angela Stevens, members of St Ives OCS, clearing vegetation from Bussow Culverhouse, St Ives. Courtesy of Ann Preston-Jones.

Medieval culverhouses

The construction of medieval culverhouses or dovecotes for the breeding of baby pigeons (squabs) for food was introduced into this country by the Normans.[78] Sometimes known by their Latin name columbaria they were the preserve of the gentry or clergy and are often located on manorial land or at rectories and vicarages. Today only five complete medieval culverhouses survive intact in Cornwall, in the parishes of St Breock, Calstock, St Ives, Sheviock and Tintagel, although there are the ruins of others and documentary and place-name evidence for at least another eighty.[79] In Cornwall

these buildings were usually of circular plan with a domed roof. Inside they had many rows of nesting holes built into the thickness of the walls for the pigeons, and originally they would have had a revolving ladder or *potence* for access to these holes. Furthermore, there would have been an aperture in the roof to allow access for flight, along with a low door set away from the prevailing weather. Two of the five complete buildings have survived partly due to the restoration work initiated by the Wadebridge and St Ives Societies.

In 1937 Mr TW Cleave, a member of Wadebridge OCS, described Trevanion Culverhay at

Members of St Austell OCS helping to restore Roche Holy Well in 2006. Courtesy of Ann Preston-Jones.

explaining the state of the culverhouse, stating that the roof had fallen in and requesting donations towards a project to restore the building. This letter was distributed throughout the area, and the request was also brought to the attention of the FOCS and published in *Old Cornwall* [81] as well as being printed in local newspapers. Eventually the necessary funds were raised and the building was restored by workmen to specifications provided by the Ministry. The culverhouse is now within a housing estate known as the Culvery (SW 9893 7161). It is owned and managed by Cornwall Heritage Trust and has public access.

Further to the west in St Ives parish another culverhouse survives at Lower Bussow. Here in the 1930s the St Ives OCS helped to strengthen and restore the building. It too is circular in section, with a domed roof, but it is built with granite stones and the roof is corbelled. In recent years the building has become very overgrown with brambles and ivy, and during 2016 members of St Ives OCS gained permission from the landowner to clear the vegetation, under the direction of their chairman Brian Stevens. With members Frank and Angela Stevens he visited several times

Wadebridge (SW 9893 7162), publishing a photograph of a very overgrown building which he stated was last used to house pigeons in 1894.[80] By 1962 this building was in a serious state of neglect, with part of its roof fallen in. Members of Wadebridge OCS were naturally concerned about the situation and contacted the Ministry of Public Buildings and Works for their advice. The Ministry estimated that the cost of repairs would be £400, and they were prepared to give a grant of one third of this amount. Cornwall County Council were also prepared to give a grant, and the remainder had to be raised by public donations through the Society. In May 1962 Wadebridge OCS printed a letter,

Trevanion Culverhouse at Wadebridge prior to restoration.
Courtesy of May Garland, Wadebridge OCS.

during the year, removing the vegetation with the aid of long ladders. The building has an external circumference of 17 metres, is 4.95 metres high and contains 157 nesting boxes built within the thickness of the walls.[82] Unfortunately this medieval building is on private ground and there is no public access.

Modern crosses

Helston OCS and Councillor Frank E Strike organised the setting up of a memorial cross on the cliffs above Loe Bar in March 1949 to commemorate 100 officers and crew of HMS Anson who perished when the ship was wrecked on December 29th 1807 and who were buried nearby. On April 30th 1949 the cross was unveiled during a memorial service on the cliff top. Another memorial cross was set up by the Society and Councillor Strike to mark unknown graves in the Wrestling Field at Porthleven.[83] Furthermore, Helston OCS has also helped to fund a Millennium Cross which was set up on Sithney Common Hill, Helston, in April 1999.[84] The project was organised by Old Cornwall member Roland Holton and the cross was funded by the Millennium Commission through the National Lottery, Helston Town Council and Helston OCS. The new cross, which is modelled on the 10th-century Lanhydrock Cross near Bodmin, was dedicated by clergy representing three denominations, the Church of England, the Methodist Church and the Roman Catholic Church, in the presence of Grand Bard Ann Trevenen Jenkin and the President of the Federation of Old Cornwall Societies, Roy Woolcock of Truro.

Miscellaneous projects

Many miscellaneous and unusual projects to preserve Cornwall's heritage have been undertaken by Societies. Perhaps one of the most unusual was taken on by Padstow OCS, when their President created replica terracotta figures for the rooftop of a Padstow house. For centuries two small terracotta men on horseback could be seen moulded into the ridge tiles and facing each other on the roof of an old property which

had formerly been the post office. The property was demolished in the 20th century to make way for a new Barclays Bank, but the horsemen were saved and set on the new roof.[85] These figurative ridge tiles are considered to be late medieval and it has been suggested that their position on the roof was a sign that horses could be exchanged at a coaching inn. The figures were first recorded in 1906 by folklorist and storyteller Nellie Sloggett of Padstow, who, writing under the pen name Enys Tregarthen, told a story about the horsemen. She wrote that when they heard St Petroc's Church clock strike midnight they would come down off the roof and ride around the Market Place and streets before returning to the roof. Tregarthen's tale concerned a young boy called Robin Curgenven who saw the horsemen.[86] This is a folk story which has been passed down through many generations of Padstow children. Daphne Hicks of Padstow OCS takes up the story in 2011, stating that when maintenance work to the roof took place a bank clerk rescued the horsemen for the town museum after discovering that they had been thrown into a skip. The people of Padstow felt the loss of these ridge tiles and Jean Haigh, President of Padstow OCS and a potter, skilfully recreated replica figures with the help of John and Fran Osborne, and permission was gained to fix them on the roof of a listed property nearby.[87] A plaque by Padstow OCS has been fixed to the building to record the history of the figures.

During the 1950s an old cannon which had been dismantled during the Second World War was re-erected by Mullion OCS on the cliff above Mullion harbour;[88] and in Redruth, the local OCS President Arthur Pearse Jenkin purchased Murdoch House in Cross Street, which had been damaged by fire in 1922, and under the direction of WT Martin, a member and local builder, restored the building and later used it for Society meetings.[89] More recently, members of Perranzabuloe OCS repainted the stones which mark the route taken by modern-day pilgrims across Penhale Sands to St Piran's Oratory, while at Wadebridge, the lettering on a commemorative stone on Egloshayle Road to mark the silver jubilee of Queen Victoria was painted by Wadebridge OCS Recorder David

Bartlett. Saltash OCS in conjunction with Saltash Town Council and Saltash Heritage was awarded a lottery grant of £6,750 to restore the old animal pound in the village of Trematon, as the walls of the pound had become unstable and needed to be rebuilt. This work was completed in 2007.[90] More recently still, a Harvey's of Hayle boundary stone marking the extent of their land was found to be right on the edge of an eroding cliff at Harvey's Towans. Linda King of Hayle OCS campaigned to have the stone rescued before it toppled over the edge of the cliff. Despite calls for help to several organisations, in the end members of Hayle OCS themselves managed to secure the boundary stone, drag it back from the cliff and re-erect it 20 feet inland on February 27th 2020.[91]

Plaques, tablets and information boards

One of the aims of the Old Cornwall Movement is to promote education and inform local people and visitors about Cornish monuments, historic sites, famous people and events in history. Over the last 100 years Societies have set up many plaques, tablets and information boards to commemorate some of Cornwall's famous sons and daughters, including authors, academics, philanthropists, sculptors and Cornish-language speakers. Some of these plaques were set up at their birthplace or at a property they lived in or were associated with, others as headstones in churchyards and cemeteries.

At Newquay a plaque was set up in honour of Sir William Golding (1911-1993), Nobel Laureate and author of *Lord of the Flies* among other books. The plaque was fixed to his birthplace at 47 Mount Wise, Newquay, on July 26th 2001 by Newquay OCS in the presence of members of his family, the mayor of Newquay and Old Cornwall members.[92] A plaque was also set up at the birthplace of author and academic Dr Alfred Leslie Rowse by St Austell OCS at 45 Tregonissey Road, St Austell. Dr Rowse was formerly patron of the Society and had been its guest of honour on several occasions. The plaque reads: 'The birthplace & early home of A L Rowse CH, 1903-1997, Historian, Poet, Cornish Scholar & Author'. It was unveiled in a ceremony on October

21st 2000.[93] At Blackwater, philanthropist John Passmore Edwards (1823-1911) is commemorated on a plaque at his birthplace in Impsey Lane. It was erected by St Agnes OCS and unveiled on July 16th 1966. The slate plaque reads: 'John Passmore Edwards was born here 24th March, 1823'. He was known as the 'Fairy Godfather of Libraries' and caused over 20 public institutes, libraries and other buildings to be built in Cornwall and at least a further 50 elsewhere in the country.[94]

A number of plaques celebrate the Cornish language or Cornish speakers. The renovation of the inscription on the tomb of Dolly Pentreath (1692?-1777) at Paul churchyard was undertaken by Penzance OCS around 1930, as it had become

illegible.[95] Nearly 50 years later, at Mousehole, a plaque was set up on the wall of a cottage where Dolly once lived. It was unveiled by Peter Pool, an active Old Cornwall supporter and Past President of the Royal Institution of Cornwall. This was arranged by Mousehole OCS to commemorate the bicentenary of her death.[96] St Ives OCS commemorated John Davey of Boswednack (1812-1891), said to be the last to possess any traditional knowledge of the Cornish language, with a slate tablet erected on the church tower at Zennor in 1930.[97]

In 1970 Truro OCS affixed a plaque to the wall of Bishop Benson's Library, which reads: 'Adjoining this building stood the Fighting Cocks Inn where Richard Lander the Cornish explorer was born on 8th February 1804.'[98] Richard Lander (1804-1834) was one of the first Europeans to follow the course of the river Niger. A monument at the top of Lemon Street carved by sculptor Neville Northey Burnard (1818-1878) commemorates his life. In the moorland village of Altarnun, Burnard himself is commemorated with a plaque organised by Launceston OCS. (A sculptured bust of John Wesley carved by Burnard is fixed to the Old Sunday School next door.)[99] Tragically, the talented Burnard fell on hard times later in life and died a pauper in Redruth. He was buried in an unmarked grave in Camborne churchyard, but in 1954 Camborne OCS commissioned a slate headstone to mark his grave.[100]

The unveiling of a plaque to philanthropist John Passmore Edwards at Blackwater in 1966 by St Agnes OCS. Photograph from the late Ken Young.

Plaque on Zennor church tower to commemorate Cornish speaker John Davey of Boswednack by St Ives OCS. Courtesy of AG Langdon.

Thomas Bond (1765-1837), the author of *Topographical and historical sketches of the boroughs of East and West Looe, in the county of Cornwall* (1823), is buried in St Martin by Looe churchyard. A plaque was set up on his former home in Looe by the local Society.[101] In 2007 Looe OCS also set up four plaques around the town to commemorate civil engineer Joseph Thomas (1838-1901), who designed Banjo Pier at Looe.[102] Penzance OCS set up a plaque to their famous son Sir Humphry Davy (1778-1829), chemist and inventor, at his birthplace on Market Jew Street, Penzance,[103] while another Cornish inventor, Sir Goldsworthy Gurney (1793-1875), is

commemorated with a slate plaque at Bude Castle commissioned by Bude-Stratton & District OCS. It was unveiled in 1977 by SG Howlett, President of the Federation of Old Cornwall Societies.

One of the artists commemorated by an Old Cornwall Society is Reuben Chappell (1870-1940), who was originally from Goole in Yorkshire but later made his home in Par. He was known as the 'Pierhead Painter' and is celebrated for his portraits of sailing ships. A plaque was set up on the wall of his former home by Par OCS in 2010.[104] In 2019 Hayle OCS erected a plaque at Penpol Terrace, Hayle, the birthplace of Cornish hero Rick

(Cyril Richard) Rescorla (1939-2001). In 2001 Rick was the chief security officer for Morgan Stanley, who occupied 22 floors of the World Trade Center's south tower in New York. On the day of the 9/11 attack, Rick's quick action saved thousands of lives when he ordered the evacuation of the building.

Historic buildings, sites and monuments have also been provided with plaques about their history. Penryn & Falmouth OCS set up several plaques between 1933 and 1936 to mark historic sites and buildings in their towns. These included Upton Slip, the Old Prison, Winchester Buildings, Arwenack Manor and the King's Pipe.[105] The wall of the old lock-up at Callington was provided with a plaque by Callington OCS, with the wording: 'The Old Clink. The ancient Prison of Callington Court Leet'.[106] At St Austell and Pentewan the old railway line is commemorated with three plaques set up jointly by the two local Societies in 2018. These were sited at the railway terminus at West Hill, St Austell, in London Apprentice and at the harbour in Pentewan.[107] At Launceston the site of the first hospital at Western Road is recorded by a plaque erected by Launceston OCS.[108]

Two historical sites have plaques commemorating engagements of the Civil War, one erected by Bude-Stratton & District OCS and the other by Tywardreath OCS. The former, set up in 1971, is on Stamford Hill at Stratton and is a copy of an earlier notice set up by Lord Lansdown in 1713, reading: 'In this place ye army of ye rebells under ye command of ye Earl of Stamford receiv'd a signall over-throu by ye valor of Sᵣ Bevill Granville & ye Corniſh army on Tueſday ye 16ᵗʰ of May 1643.' The replacement tablet was placed on an arch surmounted by a late 15ᵗʰ-century pinnacle at the entrance to the battle site.[109]

Another reference to the Civil War can be found on a plaque erected at the Iron Age hillfort of Castle Dore near Fowey. The site was held by the Parliamentary army but taken by the Royalists on August 31ˢᵗ 1644. On Saturday June 13ᵗʰ 1964, Tywardreath OCS hosted the Federation's Summer Festival at Castle Dore, on which day a plaque about its history was unveiled by Ashley Rowe, a Vice-President of the Federation of Old Cornwall Societies.[110] The plaque also records the earthworks and the legendary history of King Mark of Cornwall and his connection with Tristan and Iseult. The 6ᵗʰ-century inscribed stone near Fowey, known as the Tristan Stone, also has an information plaque set up beside it to explain its inscription and history. The monument has been re-sited on several occasions and once stood near the earthwork, hence the alternative name Castle Dore Stone. The plaque was unveiled by Foy Quiller-Couch, President of Fowey OCS, on August 31ˢᵗ 1960.[111]

More recently, in August 2019, a plaque was erected by Bodmin OCS to commemorate the 75ᵗʰ anniversary of the bombing of Mill Street in Bodmin on August 7ᵗʰ 1942. Nine people were killed in the bombing, eight from the same family, and another 18 were injured. The names of the victims have now been recorded on the plaque near the site.

As well as commemorating people, historical sites and events, Societies have also erected plaques beside many ancient monuments, particularly stone crosses and holy wells. In these cases, they often simply state that the monuments were re-erected, restored or repaired by an Old Cornwall Society. Examples include Gwealavellan Cross (Camborne OCS) and St Mary's Well (Looe OCS).

Gravestone memorials

In 2016 a slate memorial tablet was erected in Camborne churchyard by Camborne OCS in commemoration of Richard Trevithick (1735-1797) and Anne Teague (1736-1810), the parents of the great inventor Richard Trevithick (1771-1833), who is also commemorated, as is another engineer, John Budge (1731-1823). All four of them are buried in unmarked graves. The memorial was dedicated on Trevithick Day, April 30ᵗʰ.[112] In 2013 Madron OCS visited Gulval churchyard where their Chairman Roy Matthews showed the members the unmarked grave of a young bal maiden, Eliza Jane Hall (1857-1873), who tragically died in a mining accident at Ding Dong mine. Members of the Society considered that she should be provided with a headstone and immediately set about raising funds. The money was quickly found, and on the evening of July 12th 2013 the headstone was placed on her grave and dedicated to her memory.[113] Many years earlier, in 1957, Par OCS had refurbished the grave of Colonel John Whitehead Peard (1811-1880) at Fowey cemetery with the help of Mr Coggin of De Lank Granite Quarry at St Breward. Peard was a British soldier who in 1860 joined Garibaldi, fighting in the wars for Italian unification.[114]

Donations to practical projects

As well as funding their own practical projects, many Societies have subscribed towards or helped fund larger projects. For example, nine Societies donated funds towards the Castle Dore excavations of 1936, and when Liskeard OCS rebuilt St Keyne's Holy Well in 1936, they received donations from the Federation of Old Cornwall Societies, the Societies in St Austell, Bodmin, St Ives, Looe, North Hill and Penzance, and from the London Cornish Association. In 1938 St Ives OCS funded the restoration of a stone cross at Youlstone in the parish of Warbstow on the edge of Bodmin Moor, 75 miles to the east. The cross had been built into the bank of a tributary of the River Ottery, where it was used as a support for a wooden footbridge. How St Ives OCS came to fund the project to re-erect Youlstone Cross is unknown, but a stainless-steel plaque on the site records their involvement.

Generosity of stonemasons

Stonemasons and craftsmen have often been both sympathetic and generous towards Old Cornwall Society projects, sometimes giving their time or materials free or at a nominal rate. The memorial plaques which commemorate the birthplace at Blackwater of John Passmore Edwards and that of Neville Northey Burnard at Altarnun were created and given free of charge by Mr J Setchell of the Delabole Slate Company. In the minute books of Wadebridge OCS is a note that a letter of thanks was to be sent to Mr Coggin of De Lank Granite

Quarry at St Breward 'for his gift of a suitable base and shaft for the Trequite Cross in the parish of St Kew and the labour for its erection.'[115] This suggests that the quarry carried out the restoration of the cross without charge. Letters relating to the Three Holes Cross at Egloshayle indicate that William Nankivell of Tor Down Quarry, St Breward supplied the three-ton base-stone required for its restoration free of charge.[116]

Controversy

Some OCS projects have proved controversial. In 1939, after the Newquay Society had moved the Indian Queens inscribed stone from beside the A30 to the churchyard at St Francis Church, objections were raised by St Enoder Parochial Church Council. They complained that the stone belonged to Queens' Ebenezer Chapel and had been removed without their consent. The Council also noted that since the stone marked the boundary between the parishes of St Enoder and St Columb Major, both parish councils should have been consulted. In 1946 and 1947 Newquay OCS received further requests from St Enoder PCC for the return of the stone.[117] Nonetheless, it still stands in the churchyard at St Francis where it remains freely accessible. During the 1930s the Federation, with help from Helston OCS, planned to erect a tablet at Landewednack Church on the Lizard, to commemorate the last sermon preached in Cornish in 1678 by the Revd Francis Robinson.[118] This proposal, however, was thwarted by the rector, who objected to the proposed tablet, giving dates from the parish registers that cast doubt on the supposed facts.[119] In 1947 Wadebridge OCS restored the cross on the Green at Trequite near St Kew, but their minute books betray the fact that not everyone in the village was happy with the result.[120] Again, Trequite Cross remains in the centre of the village and the controversy has long been forgotten. One of the most controversial schemes was perhaps the restoration of St Keyne's Holy Well in 1936 by Liskeard OCS. The well was in a state of collapse due to a large tree which was growing on the bank above, but the 'restoration' turned into a complete rebuild of the well-house, with little if any of the old fabric saved. This gave

Cast-iron fingerpost restored by Mullion OCS and Mullion Parish Council.
Courtesy of Colin Roberts, Mullion OCS.

rise to letters of complaint from Helston OCS, Canon GH Doble and others who felt strongly that the existing well should have been repaired, not rebuilt. Letters were sent to the *Cornish Times* and *Western Morning News*.[121] Later newspaper reports, however, state that the restoration of the holy well was commended by County authorities.[122] The Federation of Old Cornwall Societies supported the rebuild, which they concluded was to a very high standard.

Rededications

Some Old Cornwall Societies have involved local clergy and occasionally the Bishop of Truro or St Germans in rededication ceremonies for restored religious sites and monuments such as crosses, holy wells and chapels. The ceremony can help to raise the profile of the monument with the local community and promote the work of the Society as well as provide an opportunity for celebration and a blessing for the monument.

Local Societies have been involved in rededication ceremonies even when sites have been restored without Old Cornwall input. In 1991 the Revd Brian Coombes, a member of Bodmin OCS who would later become President of the Federation of Old Cornwall Societies, rededicated the Lamorrick Cross at Lanivet following its discovery and preservation by a local parishioner.[123] On Ascension Day (20th May) 1993, in the neighbouring parish of Luxulyan, the Luxulyan OCS organised the rededication of the Tregonning Cross by Captain Robin Grigg of the Church Army. This cross had been discovered in 1988 and set up beside a stile on the Saints' Way footpath.[124] Two years later Captain Grigg and Canon Desmond Proberts rededicated the St Cyors Holy Well, below the church at Luxulyan, in the presence of the Mayor of Restormel, Councillor Olive Irons. At the same time, a plaque organised by Luxulyan OCS was unveiled.[125] The Fursnewth Cross, St Cleer, which was restored and re-sited in a joint project by Caradon Hill Area Heritage Project and the Historic Environment Service at Cornwall Council was later rededicated by Liskeard OCS.

Hayle OCS rescuing a boundary stone from cliff edge in February 2020'. Courtesy of Linda King.

Joint projects

In 2009 and 2010 Societies were united in a combined project led by the Federation Archaeology Recorder to record post-boxes. Twenty-two Societies took part in this survey, recording local post-boxes, their types, styles, date (from Victoria to Elizabeth II) and manufacturer. Each box was photographed.[126] Following on from this survey, another project was set up to record the cast-iron fingerposts which survive beside Cornish roads. This project saw 33 members

representing 14 Societies engaged in recording and photographing the fingerposts and noting their condition, along with the legend on each arm, the different styles and the manufacturer's name. The information was collated and passed to Cornwall Council's highways staff as well as the Milestone Society. The project, together with recording work done by Ian Thompson of the Milestone Society, led to the repair and restoration of many local fingerposts. Thanks to parish councils and other local groups and individuals as well as Societies, fingerposts have been repaired,

lost arms replaced and some signs simply given a facelift by cleaning and painting.[127] In 2010 Par OCS restored a fingerpost in their area, while at Bridgend, Wadebridge, the local OCS arranged the casting of a replacement arm which points the way to Bodmin, Liskeard and Plymouth via the A389. This project was part-funded by Cornwall Councillor Steve Knightley with a substantial donation from the Council. The arm was cast by the local Irons Brothers Foundry and was fixed in place by construction company Cormac.[128] The only surviving cast-iron fingerpost in Mullion parish was in a very poor condition: one finger was broken off and lost, and the sign was covered in rust. In 2017 Mullion OCS, with help from Mullion Parish Council and funding from Goonhilly Wind Farm Community Fund, organised its repair. The fingers were removed and used as a model by Irons Brothers Foundry at Wadebridge to create a new finger. The post was dug up and re-sited further back from the busy road and the signpost repainted.

Conclusions

In the 21st century all Old Cornwall Societies need to be even more vigilant, as our sites and monuments are often under much greater risk. Faster and much larger vehicles pose a greater threat to our roadside crosses, milestones and other roadside furniture, while increasing agricultural pressures and the perceived need for more development all impact on Cornwall's sites and monuments.

All Societies still have a vital role to play. Even if they are not able to complete practical projects they can help other like-minded organisations or act as 'eyes and ears', monitoring, recording and notifying the relevant authority when a monument or site is in need of repair.[129]

Gwealavellan Cross unveiled by Rod Lyon, Grand Bard on Saturday May 22ⁿᵈ 2004, in a ceremony organised by Camborne OCS. Courtesy of AG Langdon.

Folk tradition and the Old Cornwall Societies

Merv Davey

Folk tradition is understood quite differently today than it was in the early 20th century, the formative years of the Old Cornwall Movement. In the 1920s it was something static, the heritage of a bygone cultural golden age, for some a curiosity for academic study, for others a bastion against undesirable changes in the established social structure. Today we would see folk tradition as a living thing, informed and shaped by continuity with the past but something dynamic that we engage with, bring new things to and, importantly, use to express our identity.[1]

The early Old Cornwall Societies and their founder, Robert Morton Nance, took a quite different approach to folk traditions from their peers and anticipated our modern thinking. For them, the folk traditions of Cornwall belonged to the Cornish people, not the academic world. They saw these traditions as something to record, nurture and build upon in order to create a new and self-confident Cornwall, and they embraced the changes it promised.[2]

The impact of the Old Cornwall Societies on folk traditions in Cornwall cannot be overstated. The motto of 'Gathering the fragments so that none may be lost' was particularly effective in capturing the living folk traditions of Cornwall. As well as recording them for posterity the Societies put their shoulder behind customs that were at risk of dying out and revived those that had been all but forgotten. They recorded the singing and dancing traditions, together with the customs that marked the turning of the year and the folklore that went with them. In this chapter we will explore the work of the Old Cornwall Societies in recording, supporting and reviving Cornish folk traditions so that they became part of the distinctive modern Cornish identity.

The Cledry Plays

The genesis of the Old Cornwall Societies occurred with the arrival of Nance to live in a small cottage in the village of Nancledra in the early 1900s. Through contributions as an illustrator for the *Cornish Magazine* of the late 19th century he already had some engagement with Cornish folk traditions[3] but at Nancledra he became immersed in the subject. He was inspired by the stories of the early 19th-century Droll Tellers and the Guise / Geeze Dancers. Droll Tellers were itinerant entertainers and vendors of local gossip and news who also carried with them the stories and lore of the old Celtic world.[4] The Guise Dancers were seen as successors to the actors in the Cornish medieval mystery plays, with their exotic costumes, dragons, hobby horses and general anarchy.[5] Nance wrote a series of plays which captured the atmosphere of the traditional stories, songs, dances and folklore of West Cornwall. Initially these were aimed at performances by schoolchildren, but they were easily adapted for adults. In recognition of their origins he called them Guise Dance Drolls. The story goes that in the winter of 1919/20 a performance of one such Guise Dance Droll, 'Duffy and the Devil', captured the public imagination in St Ives and led to the formation of the first Old Cornwall Society.

Nance's illustration of Duffy from the **Cledry Plays,** *published by the Federation of Old Cornwall Societies in 1956.*

The *Cledry Plays*, as they became called, were not published as a collection until 1956[6] and even then, not all the plays were included. A number of unpublished drafts, with extensive notes, remain among the Nance papers in the Courtney Library at the Royal Institution of Cornwall. Individual snippets and songs were occasionally published in the *Old Cornwall* journal and elsewhere, notably *Tom Bawcock's Eve* and *Morvah Fair*, both of which were brought to a wide audience by Cornwall's 'First Lady of Song' Brenda Wootton. The song *Tom Bawcock's Eve* has since become an integral part of Mousehole's celebration of Tom Bawcock and his Star-Gazey Pie on December 23rd each year.

The Celtic Revivalists

The 19th- and early 20th-century antiquarians and folklorists in Cornwall were trophy hunters. They saw the traditions and customs around them as dying embers of a lost past to be captured on record for academic study and scholarly interpretation. There was a sense in which they had a vested interest in the passing of these traditions and often mistook change for decline.[7] Against this background it can be seen just how radical Nance and the early Old Cornwall Societies were in seeking to build a new Cornwall from the fragments rather than collecting folkloric curios.

Robert Morton Nance was first and foremost a creative person rather than a systematic folklore researcher. He perceived Cornish folk tradition as fragmentary and ripe for creative interpretation. As we shall see, this sometimes blinded him to the extent of living tradition in Cornwall but what he did do was inspire a community to explore and record their folk traditions with a detail he himself never captured. Importantly, ownership of these traditions remained with the Cornish community whence they came rather than becoming part of a scholarly collection.[8] By using this approach the Old Cornwall Movement anticipated the development of 'Oral History' as a research discipline by half a century.

Henry Jenner is celebrated as the father of the Cornish language, and the Celtic Revival was rooted in his campaign for recognition of the Cornish language and identity nearly 20 years before the first Old Cornwall Society. It was the formation of the Old Cornwall Societies that gave substance to the Celtic Revival by integrating it with other aspects of Cornish cultural identity. Initially this comprised dialect, folklore and customs but was quickly joined by history and archaeology. Within a decade the number of Old Cornwall Societies had risen to 18, spread across the length and breadth of the Duchy, plus an association in London. With the burgeoning number of Societies came key players who enthusiastically recorded Cornish folk traditions and were instrumental in their revival and promotion. Not only did they contribute to the pages of the *Old Cornwall* journal, they published articles, pamphlets and books as well as informing other research, all of which has served to underpin our modern understanding of Cornish folk tradition and identity.

It is impossible to do justice to all Old Cornwall Society Recorders, contributors and activists but touching on the lives and work of a few of the early pioneers does show how the scene was set for the future and how far their activities reached. Some names spring immediately out of the pages of *Old Cornwall* in the 1920s and 1930s. Jim Thomas and his daughter Bessie Wallace, Tom Miners and William D Watson[9] were immersed in folk song and the Guise Dance traditions and recorded a large amount of material from their own experiences. William Paynter and Barbara Spooner focused on the stories and folkways still remembered in Cornwall during the inter-war years and showed the continuity with traditions recorded by folklorists like William Bottrell a century earlier.[10] They were researchers rather than participants but nevertheless part of their own immediate community and had strong links elsewhere in the Duchy through their involvement with the Old Cornwall Societies.

At the age of 79, Jim Thomas was the first person to be made a Bard of Gorsedh Kernow in the inaugural ceremony of 1928. He took the Bardic name *Tas Cambron*, Father of Camborne, which hints at the reverence in which he was held. True to Nance's aspiration to wrest Cornwall's cultural heritage from the world of academia Thomas's formal education was limited. He worked as a miner abroad in his younger years and returned to Camborne to spend 30 years as a postman before retirement. Our interest here is in his contribution to folk tradition but for the Old Cornwall Societies of the time he was also renowned for his knowledge of antiquities.

Jim Thomas had been a point of contact for folk song and dance collector Cecil Sharp when he visited Cornwall in 1913 and 1914. Although only acknowledged by Sharp as 'one of his singers,' Thomas was also a folklore researcher in his own right. He introduced Sharp to traditional singers from Camborne, Redruth and Helston and personally provided him with 15 of the 66 songs taken down in Cornwall. Three of Thomas's songs were arranged and published in the *Old Cornwall* journal[11] and eight were included in Ralph Dunstan's *Cornish dialect and folk songs.*[12] He contributed a further 14 articles to the journal on games, rhymes and folklore and was often cited by other contributors.

Tom Miners was a younger contemporary of Jim Thomas and also one of the sources for the songs collected by Cecil Sharp in Cornwall. He lived in Penponds near Camborne, was a schoolmaster, established folk song collector and one of the founders of the Old Cornwall Movement.[13] In 1915 he prepared a paper for the Royal Institution of Cornwall on folk carols from Camborne and contributed an article on Cornish carols for the *Journal of the Folk-Song Society* in 1929.[14] In many ways Miners' detailed recording balanced Nance's somewhat creative approach to folk tradition in the developing Old Cornwall Movement. Tom Miners was a popular speaker at Old Cornwall Society meetings and wrote a number of articles for *Old Cornwall* covering topics from folklore to Guise Dancing as well as folksongs and carols.[15]

William D Watson worked closely with Nance in collecting dialect words for use in a revived form of the Cornish language. Watson left school at

13, worked as a gardener and was entirely self-educated, which reputedly resulted in his being ignored by Jenner for academic and class reasons.[16] Watson's claim of still finding Cornish expressions and vocabulary in use within the Cornish community was inevitably going to irk Jenner, who felt that it was he who had interviewed the last people with traditional knowledge of Cornish some 50 years earlier. They shared platforms at Old Cornwall Society meetings, however, and Watson was praised for his work on folk tradition, so tensions were probably not terribly high. William D Watson nevertheless embodies Nance's mantra that Cornish cultural heritage should be owned by the people of Cornwall rather than the academic community. Watson contributed regularly to the journal on topics linked to folk tradition and the Cornish language.[17] Some of his songs in Cornish were captured on wax cylinder by the American folklorist James Madison Carpenter.[18]

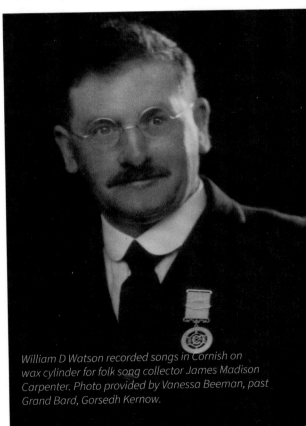

William D Watson recorded songs in Cornish on wax cylinder for folk song collector James Madison Carpenter. Photo provided by Vanessa Beeman, past Grand Bard, Gorsedh Kernow.

Carpenter was a Harvard-trained folk song researcher. He visited Cornwall at least twice between 1929 and 1934 and contacted members of the Old Cornwall Societies, probably following up Tom Miners' article on carols published in 1929. Using a wax cylinder, supported by notes on a portable typewriter, Carpenter recorded 44 folk songs and plays from Cornwall including three from Miners, five from Wallace and 11 from Watson. There are several sources named Thomas amongst Carpenter's notes, and though none is identifiable with Jim Thomas he was clearly there in spirit if not person. The wax cylinder recordings of Watson, which include his version of the St Day Carol, are some of the earliest audio recordings in Cornish. Nance also supplied Carpenter with information about the original Padstow Mummers' Play from the recollections of his his father, WE Nance, who grew up in the town in the 1840s.[19]

Singing was not the only tradition that Bessie Wallace inherited from her father. She was a popular dialect reader and storyteller within the early Old Cornwall Movement, and her stories were published in the journal as well as the local press. These stories capture the dialect and folkways of Cornwall as well as setting the songs and Guise Dance customs in context.[20] Importantly, Bessie Wallace set the example and encouraged future generations of Cornish dialect readers. Jim Thomas was born in the mid-19th century, and he and his daughter between them provide a link between the Droll Tellers of Bottrell's Celtic world and the dialect readers and storytellers of modern Cornwall.

True to its philosophy of gathering the fragments, the Old Cornwall journal created a medium for recording the smallest snippets of information through its section entitled 'The Crowdy Crawn'. This was inspired by the Cornish tradition of hanging up a skin sieve in the kitchen to store odds and ends. This was called a 'crowdy crawn', derived from the Cornish kroder / sieve, kroghen / skin, hide. Many people supplied contributions to 'The Crowdy Crawn' and indeed larger articles on Cornish folk traditions. These extended beyond the singing traditions, storytelling, and Guise

Dances to include the lore of beliefs, superstitions and charms. Here, two people stand out with their research: Barbara Spooner and William Paynter. Both were part of the early Celtic Revival and active Old Cornwall Society members, and both were made Bards of Gorsedh Kernow during the ceremony held at the Hurlers, St Cleer in 1930.

Barbara Spooner was born in Richmond. Her family had strong Cornish links and in 1923, at the age of 30, she returned to live at North Hill.[21] She was a founder member of the North Hill Old Cornwall Society in 1930 and when she moved to Wadebridge in 1948 became an active member of that Society. She wrote two books on Cornish folklore[22] and a series of articles for both *Folklore* and *Old Cornwall* journals. Occasionally she gives a source as 'oral' in the footnotes but provides no names, dates or contexts. She nevertheless describes Cornwall as her 'hunting ground' and alludes to friends and people she meets who add to her collection of tales or supply local variants of them. What Spooner does meticulously is cross-reference and extrapolate stories and meanings across a wide range of written sources. For example, by drawing on stories from both Robert Stephen Hawker and William Bottrell and cross-referencing them with newspaper reports she paints a vivid picture of the lore of Cornish phantom ships.[23]

Spooner reaches back to a quite different seam of Cornish storytelling from that of Bessie Wallace and the dialect tales of Jim Thomas. Her interest was in the mythology of Cornwall, the giants, the little people, the buccas, King Arthur and so on. She captures the way in which legends weave these figures into the story of Cornwall to explain geological and historical features as well as folklore. In one piece of research she traces the various stories around the 'Dons Meyn', the Dancing Stones of Cornwall and the pipers standing sentinel over the dancers who turned to stone for dancing on the Sabbath.[24] In another she explores the stories of haunted stiles and the ghosts and the Bucca Du that made people wary of crossing them.[25] Barbara Spooner's work represents a move away from the pisky-led fakelore of early 20th-century tourist promotion towards the recognition of a significant body of Cornish Celtic mythology.[26]

William Paynter, the wonderfully nicknamed 'Cornish Witch-finder' was born in Callington in 1901. His biographer Jason Semmens explains that Paynter's fascination with Cornish history and folk tradition was kindled by his childhood explorations of the industrial remains around Kit Hill. He was inspired by an Old Cornwall Society meeting in the late 1920s in Penzance and went on systematically to record the charms, cures and superstitions which were fast being forgotten. It was his aspiration to collect from every parish in Cornwall and he travelled the length and breadth of the Duchy to achieve this.[27]

As a correspondent for the *Cornish Times* William Paynter took the opportunity to publish a series of articles on what he had discovered. He also wrote items on folklore for other local newspapers and was a regular contributor to the pages of *Old Cornwall*. He collated these articles together with additional material and prepared them for publication as a book but was unsuccessful in finding a publisher. The manuscripts were loaned to a friend and eventually found their way to the Cornish Studies Library in Redruth in 2009.[28] It was eventually published privately printed in 2016 as a companion volume to his biography, *The Cornish Witch-finder*.[29] He was a founder member of the Liskeard Old Cornwall Society and involved with the Midsummer Tansys Golowan (bonfire) ceremonies in the east of Cornwall. He set up a Cornish Museum in Looe in 1961 which housed the artefacts he had collected over his lifetime.

From an immediate practical perspective, the charms, cures and beliefs collected by William Paynter have not impacted upon modern Cornwall or Cornish identity in the way that other Old Cornwall Society activities have, but they do provide us with a wonderful window into the world of pre-National Health Service society!

The Living Traditions

Jim Thomas, Tom Miners and William Watson were regular speakers at early Old Cornwall Society meetings along with Robert Morton Nance and Henry Jenner. The focus was often on folk customs, games and singing traditions such as carols. At the February meeting of the St Ives Old Cornwall Society in 1921 Nance talked about the Cornish custom of hurling which had been popular throughout the 19th century but had become limited to St Ives and St Columb.[30] During the ensuing discussion concern was expressed that the hurling at St Ives Feast Day was at risk of dying out.[31] It was felt that the Society should support the St Ives hurling and passed a resolution to sponsor a new silver ball. This was

Raising the silver ball at St Columb. Hurling was popular throughout Cornwall in the 19th century. Author's photo.

duly done, inscribed with a Cornish motto, and formally presented to the mayor of St Ives as part of the promotion in the lead up to the Feast Day in 1922. The intervention of the Old Cornwall Society placed the tradition on a firmer footing, and it is now an integral part of St Ives Feast Day celebrations in the 21st Century.

The Revd Robert Stephen Hawker was inspired by the Cornish traditions surrounding the Guldhize (Cornish: *gool* / feast, *dheys* / hay ricks) to create a service celebrating the harvest at Morwenstow Church in 1843. This quickly became adopted into the Church calendar as the Harvest Festival. One of the traditions associated with the Guldhize was 'Crying the Neck'. Celebrating the harvest with the ceremonial cutting of the last sheaf was once a widespread tradition.[32] In Cornwall this last sheaf

was called a 'neck' and held aloft with a cry and response varying along the lines of:

'I 'ave 'n! I 'ave 'n! I 'ave 'n!'

'What 'ave 'ee? What 'ave 'ee? What 'ave 'ee?'

'A neck! A neck! A neck!'

'Hourah! Hourah! Hourah!'

The neck, sometimes woven into a corn dolly, was then hung up in the farm kitchen until Christmas, when it was fed to the best cow to ensure a good harvest for the ensuing year.

It is difficult to know the extent to which 'Crying the Neck' was still being practised in the 1920s

Below: Traditional neck from Withiel. After the ceremony, the neck is sometimes woven into a corn dolly. Author's photo.

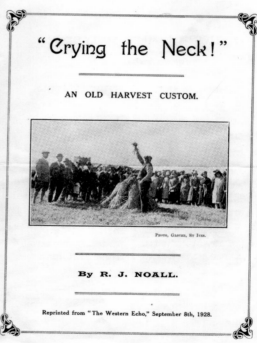

Above: On August 28th 1928 the St Ives Old Cornwall Society staged their own 'Crying the Neck' ceremony.

as it was by nature an intimate local event that attracted no more than occasional attention in the correspondence column of the local press. It was clearly well remembered by Old Cornwall Society members and was a popular topic in talks and discussions on Cornish folk traditions. On August 28th 1928 the St Ives Old Cornwall Society created their own ceremony on a farm at Towednack at the invitation of farmer Hugh Dunstan.[33] This event did raise press interest and encouraged discussion of the ritual and its origin in the correspondence pages. As well as inspiring other Old Cornwall Societies to stage their own 'Crying the Neck' ceremonies this event encouraged Society Recorders across Cornwall to take note of their own local traditions, the result being that over the years the journal has secured a detailed account of this tradition across Cornwall.[34]

On the evening of Golowan, Midsummer's Day, in 1929 a chain of bonfires was lit from Chapel Carn Brea at St Just to Kit Hill on the Cornish border.[35] As well as reinvigorating an age-old tradition this represented the coming of age of the Old Cornwall

Liskeard Old Cornwall Society.

Kyntelleugh an brewyon es gesys, na vo kellys trawyth.
(Gather ye up the fragments that are left, that nothing be lost).

St. John's Eve Celebrations, St. Cleer Downs,
Near Liskeard, Cornwall.   23rd June, 1948.

PROGRAMME

8 p.m. to 9 p.m.	Flora Dance through the village of St. Cleer.
9 p.m.	Maypole and Folk Dancing by the School Children.
9 p.m. to 10 p.m.	Welcome to ONE AND ALL by Mr. A. H. Philp, President of Liskeard Old Cornwall Society.
	Reading of the COLLECT for the Benediction of the Fire of St. John from the "Ritual of Montauban" in France (printed in 1785) and a short address by Rev. A. Lane-Davies, Vicar of St. Cleer.
	A Short Description of the ancient Customs and Superstitions connected with St. John's Eve by Mr. William H. Paynter.
	Songs in Cornish.
	BRO GOTH AGAN TASOW (*Land of our Fathers*)
	ARTA EF A-DHE (*He shall come again*) School Children.
10 p.m.	The Bonfire will be lighted by Mrs. W. H. H. Huddy, President of Liskeard Women's Institute
	When the fire is well alight, Mr. Edwin Chirgwin will throw on the flames a garland of emblematic plants and weeds with the cry in Cornish: "Ny a-wra kepar del o gwres gans agan kendasow yn dedhyow solabrys", meaning "We do as our fathers did in the days that are long past".
10.30 p.m.	Hand-in-hand Dance round the Bonfire.
11 p.m.	Singing of the National Anthem.

The Hon. Secretary, Mr. Kenneth Oates, will be happy to give any information as to membership of the Society.

The programme for the Liskeard Midsummer Bonfire in 1948 included the 'Hand in Hand' dance around the fire at the end of the evening.

Tansys Golowan – the Midsummer Bonfire Ceremony. The speeches made at these ceremonies by the Old Cornwall Societies could be 'fiery'. Midsummer Bonfire, Kit Hill, June 23rd 1975, © Charles Woolf Slide Collection, University of Exeter Penryn Campus. ICS12-15470.

Society movement which had now spread across, and represented all of, Cornwall. Tansys Golowan, the Midsummer Bonfire Ceremony, celebrates the turning of the season at Midsummer. A bonfire is lit on high ground and part of the ritual involves casting a scythe-shaped bunch of herbs into the flames. The herbs are specially chosen for their folkloric significance and are intended to invoke mother nature into protecting that year's harvest and promoting productivity in the next.[36]

The Tansys Golowan ceremony in 1929 was set out in Cornish and English and included a prayer as well as an introduction to the custom and its origins. The introductory speech was used by the Societies to explain both the history of the custom and the revival of Cornish Celtic identity that it represented. Some of these speeches can only be described as, well, 'fiery'! In 1931, at Castle An Dinas in West Cornwall, Walter Eva, President of Penzance Old Cornwall Society, proclaimed the death of Cornish with Dolly Pentreath to be a fallacy and introduced William Watson as one of the modern speakers. He went on to encourage the study of Cornish as it 'will enable you to understand the meaning of our place names which are such a stumbling block to the foreigner from England.'[37] These were popular events with literally thousands attending throughout Cornwall. They certainly placed both the Old Cornwall Societies and a sense of a distinctive Cornish identity firmly within the fabric of modern Cornish society.

The Guise Dance is an enigmatic Cornish tradition. Early in the 19th century the Cornish historian Richard Polwhele described it as answering 'to the 'mummers' of Devon, and the morrice dancers of Oxfordshire.'[38] In 1882 the antiquarian Fred WP Jago refers to it variously as 'Giz' or 'Geez' Dancing, derived from the Cornish *ges* meaning mockery or jest, a 'kind of carnival or *bal-masqué* at Christmas.'[39] The Cornish word *ges* for jest seems to be conflated with 'giz' here, meaning disguise. In Cornish dialect this became written as 'Guize' or 'Guise' but pronounced 'Geeze'. The Guise Dancers adopted a variety of costume so that they would not be recognised and processed from house to house or pub to pub. At each stop they would enact a piece of 'folk business' which might be a song, a wassail, a folk play, a dance or a combination of all these things. Typically, the folk play would be a combat / death / resurrection ritual with characters ranging from St George and the Turkish Knight to Father Christmas[40] but could also involve Cornish folk tales, a mock trial or the election of a mock mayor. The narrative of the song or drama was adapted to topical or local circumstances, often at the expense of the audience, hence the value of disguise. Several examples of Guise Dance plays were recorded from oral tradition in the early *Old Cornwall* journals.[41]

The Guise Dancers of St Ives have a long history. In the 1850s the custom was to travel from house to house, providing entertainment in return for refreshments in the fashion described above, but by 1900 popularity had overtaken the custom so that it became a large, rowdy procession through the town.[42] This earned criticism for unseemly behaviour in the local press, especially with regard to the tradition of cross-dressing:

> *… but what seems to create the greatest fun, and is the most enjoyed by the crowd, are men dressed as women and women dressed as men, girls as boys and boys as girls, some of whom under the influence of drink, perform sundry antics which, for vulgarity, would be hard to beat.*[43]

Despite, or perhaps because of, official disapproval the Guise Dancing was clearly still going strong in 1923 when a Police Superintendent reported triumphantly that there had been only one incident during the revelry that year![44]

The St Ives Guise Dancers seem to have burned themselves out by 1926 and the town's Old Cornwall Society became concerned about dwindling interest in the tradition. The Society responded by organising a more structured procession between the Drill Hall and the Palais de Danse where the Guise Dance costumes were judged. An element of fancy dress inevitably

Guising in St Ives circa 1970. Courtesy of Dave Lobb Archive.

competed with the traditional themes of mock posh, veils and cross-dressing, and this did not pass without comment:

> But there was just a point that one could not help noticing. The tradition of guise-dancing is that the costumes should be essentially grotesque, and such as to totally disguise the dancer … the second qualification was loyally fulfilled on Thursday, for few of the dancers were recognisable. But there was less – much less – of the grotesque than there should have been; "guise" disguises seem to have become the fancy-dresses associated with fancy-dress balls.[45]

Watering down tradition with joke-shop masks and fancy dress is a problem not unknown to Guise Dancing in the 21st century and the border between the two is a fine one. What the St Ives Old Cornwall Society did was ensure that the custom had official approval, which helped it thrive between the wars.[46]

The custom continued after the World War of 1939-45 and children were encouraged to take part, but much of the enthusiasm had been lost,

as OCS member William Barber explains:

> It was all changed after the War, some people did not like the guising because it made it obvious where the gaps were in the family photograph albums, the people who were known for certain songs or parts did not come back so it upset people to be reminded.[47]

It was nevertheless well remembered by the St Ives community when Dave Lobb, son of one of the original Guise Dancers revived the tradition again in the 1970s.[48] It has undergone several changes since then but the Guisers can still be seen over the Christmas period and during St Ives Feast thanks to Dave and Dee Brotherton of the St Ives Old Cornwall Society.

At the Federation of Old Cornwall Societies Winter Festival in Penzance in 1929 AK Hamilton Jenkin praised St Ives OCS for the revival of the town's Guise Dance and urged Helston OCS to consider doing the same for the Hal An Tow.[49] The Hal An Tow is a Guise Dance with a song and a combat ritual resplendent with knights and dragons. It takes place during Flora Day at Helston on May

8th each year. It was a recognised part of the day in the 1800s but had ceased to be performed by the end of the 19th century. Helston OCS used information provided by older Helstonians and an observational trip to the Padstow May Day celebrations in 1929 to reconstruct the Hal An Tow, and it was performed by boys from Helston Grammar School at Flora Day 1930. The tradition was inherited by Helston Community School in the 1960s and opened out to involve the wider community in 2000.[50]

On January 4th 1937 on the BBC's Western Regional Service AK Hamilton Jenkin introduced a broadcast of the Madron Guise Dancers' 'Twelfthtide'. He warns listeners to look out for strangely garbed people roaming the streets on these dark nights, taking part in an ancient Cornish tradition. Inspired by the success of the St Ives Guise Dancers and the Hal An Tow the Madron OCS revived the village's own Guise Dance with players using costumes that had traditionally remained within their families. The Guise Dancers included a 'Miss Phyllis Trevorrow, who did the ancient broom dance, [and] wore a costume which is nearly 150 years old. She learned the dance from her great grandfather.'[51] The revival was well received and enjoyed another broadcast the following year when the Guise Dancers were augmented by Jack Collings the famous 'Port Isaac Bass' singing Pasties and Cream and the Mabe Male Voice Choir singing Cornish carols from the Warmington collection.[52] The Madron Guise Dancers were popular performers for Old Cornwall Society events and took part in the Breton-Cornish solidarity demonstration in 1942, supporting the Breton fishing community exiled to Cornwall during the War. One of the dances from the Madron Guise Dance was 'Turkey Rhubarb' and the 'Turkey Rhubarb Band' carries on the Guise Dance tradition today.

Guise Dancing in general has enjoyed a revival of interest in the 21st century and is a feature of events like the Golowan and Montol festivals in Penzance, the Bodmin Riding and Heritage Day, and the Polperro Festival. This is due in no small part to the enthusiastic recording and support of the tradition by OCS members in the 1920s and 1930s.

Cornish singing tradition was in no need of revival or revitalisation when the Old Cornwall Societies were first formed and continues to go from strength to strength today. Singing, whether carols at Christmas time or robust renderings of Trelawny, automatically became part of the culture of the Societies, just as it was, and is, for gatherings of Cornish people worldwide. The definition of folk tradition that introduces this chapter is no better demonstrated than it is with singing in Cornwall. Here we have a continuity that goes far into the past with medieval carols that traced the ancient mysteries of the Cornish Miracle Plays[53] and blossomed into the 19th-century chapel carol culture of Thomas Merritt. Songs like the Sweet Nightingale with 17th-century origins appear comfortably alongside songs adapted from American music hall such as Little Eyes and songs with overt expressions of Cornish identity like Trelawny.

There was an interesting discussion at the FOCS Winter Festival held at Redruth in 1926 as to whether a song like Robert Morton Nance's Three Men on a Horse could ever become a folk song.[54] The conclusion was that it could, and of course as Morvah Fair it was popularised by Brenda Wootton in the 1970s. The report on the Winter Festival also gives us a window into the 1920s and the way in which Cornish identity was being expressed through song. Some of the songs cited have intriguing titles, like Joseph Thomas's Come all ye jolly tinners, who to Camborne town belong; Herbert Thomas's Cornish Wrestler's Song, Loveday Tregambo and With Candle and Lantern; and the Zennor Mermaid Song. Many of the songs mentioned did not remain in the popular repertoire but two will be known to Cornish singers today, Tryphena Trenerry and Pasties and Cream.

The inclusion of Cornish songs in Alfred P Graves's publication of 'songs of the six Celtic nations' in 1928 was a clear endorsement of Cornwall's Celtic identity,[55] and the Federation of Old Cornwall

Societies recognised the need for a specifically Cornish songbook 'suitable for community singing wherever Cornishmen (and Cornish women) foregather the world over.'[56] Dr Ralph Dunstan was an obvious choice to lead on this project. He had just retired to Cornwall after a successful musical career in London but had spent his early years steeped in the musical traditions of Cornwall as a bandsman playing for tea treats and regattas. With encouragement from the FOCS and other Cornish societies *The Cornish Song Book (Lyver Canow Kernewek)* was published in 1929 and a sequel, *Cornish Dialect and Folk Songs*, in 1932.[57] The sources Dunstan gives for his songs are OCS 'activists' like Arthur L Mata, RJ Noall and Ethel Jewell, as well as Robert Morton Nance and Jim Thomas.

In addition to contemporary compositions expressing Cornish identity these two collections contain 73 traditional songs and tunes which continue to underpin Cornish tradition to this day. They were followed up by Inglis Gundry's *Canow Kernow* in 1966 and a plethora of Cornish song collections in the latter part of the 20th century. Cornish singing tradition continues to be supported in print today with Hilary Coleman and Sally Burley's *Shout Kernow* and *Hark!* together with the FOCS Cornish Carols series and *Kenewgh! Sing!*

Like the singing, Cornish dance tradition was in no need of revival in the formative years of the Old Cornwall Societies. Just as Guise Dancing had provided a medium for Cornish folk dances, so did the parish feast days, tea treats and coastal regattas. As early as 1808 a newspaper correspondent records what appears to be a scoot[58] / step dance competition held during Illogan's Whitsuntide Feast,[59] and we see similar reports throughout the 19th century, sometimes listing the winners. Step dancing at Boscastle was reported at social events in the village in the early 1900s.[60] It was recorded for the BBC by Richard Dimbleby in 1943[61] and was a popular entertainment on the moorland farms in the inter-war years.[62] Margaret Courtney described feast-day dances and dance games in her *Cornish Feasts and folk-lore*[63] and Charles Lee portrayed the Cornish tea treat dances in the early 1900s in his notebook as he researched the novel *Dorinda's birthday*.[64] Cornish tea treats remained popular events during the inter-war years,[65] with

The Molinnis Fife and Drum Band, who played for the Snail Creep at Rescorla tea treats. Courtesy of Rescorla Festival.

dances like *The Serpent*, *The Snail Creep* and *The Miller's Dance* as well as broom dances.[66] Robert Morton Nance paid tribute to the scoot dance tradition in his 'Guise Dance Drolls' with dances like the *The Cobbler's Hornepipe*,[67] but provides only outline instructions for the dances and leaves it to players to improvise.

Both Nance and Jenner had a flirtation with the English Folk Dance Society in Cornwall during the 1920s, which seems strange in view of their well-publicised position on Cornwall as a Celtic country rather than an English county. The story is a complex one but in short, Cecil Sharp, founder of the English Folk Dance Society, had influential friends and was able to impose an idiosyncratic view of 'proper' English folk dances upon the education system. He set up special training for dance tutors who taught in schools and organised clubs and dance events. One of his protégées was Lady Mary Trefusis, who was a popular figure in the Cornish community and a great friend of Henry Jenner. Neither Jenner nor Nance had a deep knowledge of Cornish dance traditions and when Lady Mary organised an EFDS branch in Cornwall it was inevitable that they would be drawn in. The culture of Recording that Nance had put in place within the Old Cornwall Societies was gathering momentum, however, and taking note of the native dance traditions of Cornwall.

Elizabeth S Shapcott was one of the founder members of Looe Old Cornwall Society in 1927. She came from an established Looe family and spent much of her childhood in the town but moved away in her late teens when her father found work as a shipwright in Greenwich. She retired to Looe sometime after 1911 but had probably spent her summers in the town before then.[68] She took up writing on her retirement and had several articles published. In 1929 she gave a talk to the Looe OCS on feast-day customs in the area, which was subsequently published as an article in the *Old Cornwall* journal.[69] She describes a number of dances and makes the comment that she has not seen any of these performed at recent folk-dance displays, which is a reflection on the influence of the English Folk Dance Society described above.

Shapcott talks of dancing to a fiddler in a barn or a field and even the highway if fine, and describes a clog dance providing a percussive accompaniment to singing. The dances mentioned by name are the *Four-hand, Six-hand* and *Eight-hand Reel*, *The Triumph* and *The Cushion Dance*, which was described by Davies Gilbert in his collection of carols and dances in 1823[70] and was clearly still popular in East Cornwall nearly 100 years later. She explains that *The Four-hand Reel* is the *Furry Dance*, but we do not know if this is from her own observation or an assumption based on another's recollection. *The Four-hand Reel* was the name for a popular scoot dance in the moorland communities nearby.

The Looe OCS Recorder notes that in the discussion following Shapcott's talk members reported that *The Triumph* was still being danced at Morval and that all the dances named were done in the district down to about 25 years previously. *The Triumph* is another dance with a long pedigree in Cornwall. It was in the repertoire of a dancing master called John Old who taught country dancing to the families of wealthy Cornish industrialists in the early 1800s.[71] The adaptation of genteel country house dances to the more exuberant reels of the ordinary folk is a well-worn path. The version of *The Triumph* described by a Mrs Baker from Rilla Mill in 1981 was danced to a hornpipe, which makes it quite distinct from variations found elsewhere in Britain and America.[72] Over the next few decades other Recorders and contributors provided information about dances, dance games and the music that went with them – sometimes descriptions and sometimes just snippets for the 'Crowdy Crawn' pages of *Old Cornwall*, all of which provided an invaluable legacy for succeeding generations of Cornish dancers.

In 1961 the Newquay Old Cornwall Society played a quite different role in promoting Cornish dance tradition. The town had historically used the *North Cornwall Furry* to process from Crantock Street School out to the bonfire at Pentire Head on Midsummer's Eve and had adapted it as a weekly event during the summer tourist season. It was felt that Newquay needed a Furry Dance of its own

TOLCARNE BEACH
Wednesday, 12th July, 1961

10.30 a.m. to 12 noon BAND CONCERT
by **THE CENTRAL BAND OF THE WOMEN'S ROYAL AIR FORCE**
by permission of the Air Council.   Conducted by Flight Lieutenant J. E. WAGNER, L.R.A.M., A.R.C.M., Director of Music Royal Air Force.

3 p.m.

NEWQUAY
HEVA DANCE

Music by H. WHIPPS, A.R.C.M. and Words by NIGEL TANGYE, Esq.

Special Performance by Newquay C.P. Junior Mixed School.   PROGRAMMES 1/- obtainable on the beach.

Group Capt. CHESHIRE V.C., D.S.O., D.F.C.
will attend, supported by
Alderman JACK STEPHENS, Penzance, Secretary of the Cornish Home.
R. ALLDRITT, Esq., J.P., Chairman Newquay U.D.C.   GEOFFREY BRIGGS, Esq., O.B.E., C.C. Chairman Newquay Hotels Assoc.
ARTHUR CROSBY, Esq. Vice Chairman N.H.A.   S. P. COLLINGS, Esq., Chairman, Newquay Chamber of Commerce.   NIGEL TANGYE, Esq., Glendorgal.
Representing the Royal Air Force : Group Capt. E. F. J. O'DOIRE, D.F.C., A.F.C. Officer Commanding St. Mawgan.
Television Cameras in attendance.

3.30 p.m., FLORA DANCE
Teams taking part :— Crantock St. School, Treviglas School, and a special team from Goonhavern.
Hotel Visitors welcomed.   Conditions of Dance : Every Set to wear Flowers.
PRIZES and CUPS given by firms in England.
Prizes presented by MRS. JACK STEPHENS.
Judge of Dancing : MAISIE WALKER (Star of Television Dancing Club, Devon & Cornwall Champion).

8.10 p.m., COMMANDO RAID
A Spectacular Display of Cliff Assault by the
ST. IVES & BRISTOL UNITS ROYAL MARINE VOLUNTEER RESERVE.
The Cheshire Homes Organiser F. HYDON, 6, Atlantic Road wishes to thank RALPH OSBORNE, Central Garage and MR. DANIELS for Tolcarne Beach.
COLLECTORS ARE URGENTLY REQUIRED.

JOHN CHUGG, Printer, Bank Street, Newquay   Phone 2637

In 1961 Newquay created the Heva Dance with help from Newquay Old Cornwall Society members.

Cornish fish jousters, courtesy of Morrab Library, Penzance, ref. M0116. At the Old Cornwall Societies' Winter Festival in 1929 tea was served by ladies attired as fish jousters.

and the *Heva Dance* was written together with a song informed by OCS members that captured the history of the town. The song started with the lyrics 'Heva, Heva now the catch is in, let the singing, dancing and the troyl begin.' 'Heva!' was the cry that went out to launch the seine boats when a shoal of pilchards was seen in the bay. 'Troyl' is a dialect word for a barn dance, or in this case a fish-cellar dance as that was where they held the parties at the end of the pilchard season. Whilst Furry Dances continued as a living tradition in Cornwall throughout the early part of the 19th century they were not as widespread in the 1960s as they had once been. Newquay set an example for other towns to follow in reviving or creating their own Furry Dance tradition.

A folk tradition that features less strongly in the pages of the *Old Cornwall* journal but nevertheless deserves special mention is Cornish costume. The traditional industries of Cornwall evolved their own distinctive dress such as the cloaks and bonnets of the 'fish jousters', the 'gooks' of the 'bal maidens' and the knit frocks of the fishermen. The fish jousters were women fish vendors who carried the fish in baskets on their backs, supported by a strap held in place on their foreheads by specially shaped bonnets. They also wore striking scarlet or tartan shawls. The gook was a protective bonnet worn by the women surface workers of the mining industry ('bal maidens').[73] The tradition here was that each mining company or mining area had its own special pattern for a gook. The knit frocks were Guernsey pullovers with patterns unique to different fishing villages in Cornwall and the families involved. Members of the Societies were clearly aware of this heritage and from time to time the opportunity was taken to wear traditional costume. At the Winter Festival in 1929, for example, tea was served by ladies dressed as fish jousters.[74] Gooks also make an appearance from time to time, although the baton of wearing traditional costume in the 21st century has really been picked up by the Cornish dance display teams.

The pageantry of the Federation of Old Cornwall Societies is marked by two things, the parade of individual Society banners and the proud display of Cornish tartans, the latter of which has an interesting story in its own right. The first of our modern tartans was designed by Robert Morton Nance's nephew Ernest Morton Nance and was registered in 1963 as the *Cornish National Tartan*.[75] He made no reference to the tartan shawls of the Cornish fish jousters in the background story he gave for this tartan. He focused instead on the Celtic lore that the tribes of ancient Britain were noted by the Greeks and Romans for the tartan weave of their dress. In the Brythonic language this was called *brith* and so they were called *Brithens* and the story goes that this gave rise to the name Britannia,[76] the point being that all the Celtic lands from Scotland down to Brittany therefore have a claim on tartan dress. The Celtic Revival has also seen the advent of specifically Welsh, Manx and Breton designs in addition to the established Scottish ones, but it is Cornwall where tartan has really taken off and is now confidently used as an expression of Cornish identity.

The Legacy

As far as folk tradition is concerned the Old Cornwall Societies did considerably more than gather a few fragments. In the first 25 years of the journal there were 64 references from oral sources and a further 52 from other texts. Later journals continue to record folk traditions, but the tendency is towards further information and discussion on those recorded earlier, which is to be expected. If you add these to the work of Ralph Dunstan and Inglis Gundry, then we have upwards of 200 folk customs, dances and songs captured by the Old Cornwall Movement. Number crunching provides a sense of scale, but the real legacy of the Societies is the way in which folk songs, dances and associated customs have remained a living tradition in Cornwall.

The bonfires of Tansys Golowan, the ceremonies of Crying the Neck, the Hal An Tow and the ubiquitous Furry Dances continue to be highlights of the Cornish calendar. The Guise Dances have spread far beyond St Ives, returning to their traditional homes across Cornwall, and they provide a Cornish equivalent to the English Morris in the 21st century just as Polwhele described them two centuries ago. The OCS festivals and events provide a natural home for Cornish singing tradition and an opportunity to celebrate our cultural heritage.

The Celtic Revival in Cornwall and elsewhere has gone from strength to strength, and although the Old Cornwall Movement's contribution to this in the first half of the 20th century is a matter of record its contribution more recently is less visible, but it is still an important legacy. The advent of the 'Celtic Festival' in the 1970s created a demand for Cornish musicians, drama and dance groups who could deliver traditional and original material relating to Cornwall in their performances. It was the work of the Old Cornwall Societies that was 'quarried' for both traditional material and creative inspiration, from the stories of Barbara Spooner to Elizabeth Shapcott's dancing at Looe. The author of this chapter has had the privilege of being FOCS Recorder of Folk Tradition for a little over ten years, and there continues to be a steady stream of enquiries on the subject.

In 2014 the UK Government announced that the 'proud history, unique culture, and distinctive language of Cornwall will be fully recognised under European rules for the protection of national minorities.'[77] In many respects this was a realisation of the aspiration to build a new and self-confident Cornwall outlined in the opening words of the first edition of the *Old Cornwall* journal in 1925. In the 21st century there are organisations engaged across the spectrum of Cornish heritage and cultural identity but there is a sense in which they are all heir to the activities of a group of far-sighted enthusiasts who formed the first Old Cornwall Societies. The challenge for the Old Cornwall Societies today is to maintain the foresight of their predecessors in securing Cornwall's cultural heritage as a living tradition. The range of projects in hand as we celebrate the 100th anniversary of the Old Cornwall Societies would encourage a certain optimism in this respect.

Cornish dance demonstration at Lowender Peran. Courtesy of Perran Tremewan.

The 'Young Cornwall' Movement at Helston

Priscilla Oates

In 1960 Richard Gendall, a Cornish Bard (*Gelvynak*) and a French teacher at the County Grammar School Helston, was joined on the staff by Richard Jenkin, a chemistry teacher. He was also a Cornish Bard (*Map Dyvroeth*). Both ardent Cornishmen, they decided to start a 'Young Cornwall' group during the lunch hour once a month.

Invitations were given to a number of students who were identified as having shown an interest in their homeland and were natural dialect speakers. These would be the guinea pig cohort. They avidly absorbed information on their heritage, the meaning of place names, Cornish customs and traditions, the landscape with its stone circles and quoits, as well as other interesting bits and pieces. They were introduced to the Cornish language and, encouraged to 'gather up the fragments', they set about jotting down sayings and words used at home, which were then discussed at the next meeting. At the end of each summer term they went on a Pilgrimage, a notable one being to Bodmin Moor when Miss D Taylor, the geography teacher, came along to explain the underlying geology.

Later on they were introduced to the Cornish Gorsedh and the bards, discovering for the first time that both 'Sirs' were bards. No pressure was brought to bear, but the students did get a regular copy of *New Cornwall* magazine. They were also encouraged to join their local Old Cornwall Society, with the warning that homework came first!

When the guinea pig cohort finally left school most of them would go up country for work or further education, but they were so excited and enthused by those lunchtime meetings that many would go on to become enthusiastic members of their local Old Cornwall Society or to play their part in the up-country Cornish Associations.

'Thank you, Sirs,' you did a proper job.

Richard Jenkin. Courtesy of Mebyon Kernow.

In Praise of the Banners of the Old Cornwall Societies

David Stark

A banner can be described as a flag of cloth, usually rectangular in shape, of distinctive colour and design, used as a standard, emblem, signal, logo or slogan. Banners have been used as visual symbols in warfare for thousands of years to identify allies and enemies and to reinforce morale, and in peacetime to promote pride and spectacle in regimental pageantry, ceremonial and religious observances and inspiration in nationalism, sporting events, advertising and in political, trades union and other demonstration marches.

The colourful banners of the Old Cornwall Societies, designed and painstakingly made by dedicated embroiderers, are occasionally shield-shape but generally rectangular, often with a pointed lower edge, much the same shape as the *vexillum* standard carried by the ancient Roman armies, where a flag was suspended from a horizontal crossbar attached to a vertical pole. Some banners are adorned with full-length cords and tassels suspended from each end of the crossbar or with cordless tassels on the ends of the crossbar.

The Old Cornwall Society banners fulfil several roles: they unite like-minded members of the Old Cornwall Movement, they identify the different Societies and the geographical areas which they represent and they often highlight the traditional occupations of the residents of an

area. Consequently, the designs of the banners incorporate a variety of icons which include the arms of the Duke of Cornwall, Cornish saints, civic insignia, churches, local landmarks, mining equipment, legends and the chough, Cornwall's national bird.

The banners are paraded by proud banner-bearers at the Summer and Winter Festivals of the Federation of Old Cornwall Societies and at the open Gorsedh Kernow ceremony in September each year, where they provide a much-applauded spectacle.

The Banners of the Old Cornwall Societies, published in 2007 by the Federation, gives details of the individual Societies' banners in alphabetical order and describes their origins with accompanying colour photographs.

Courtesy of David & Carole Stark (St Austell OCS) for the images from 'Banners of the Old Cornwall Societies' (2007). Also, Terry Knight (St Agnes, 2014) and Priscilla Oates (Cury & Gunwalloe, 2020).

Old Cornwall Societies

The names of the 42 current Societies (shown in bold below) are listed in the form indicated on the inside back cover of *Old Cornwall*, vol. 15, no. 10, Spring 2020. Several Societies have used different forms of name during their history, and some have restarted years after falling into abeyance. The number of Societies in existence at any one time has never quite reached 50. Affiliated organisations in Cornwall, places from which individual affiliated Recorders have worked, and associated organisations outside Cornwall are not listed.

1. **Bodmin**
2. **Bude-Stratton & District**
3. **Callington**
4. **Camborne**
5. **Camelford & District**
6. Carharrack
7. **Carnon Downs**
8. Chacewater
9. **Cury & Gunwalloe**

   Falmouth see

   Penryn & Falmouth
10. Fowey

    Gerrans see St Gerrans &

    Porthscatho
11. **Goonhavern & District**

    Gorran see St Goran

    Gunwalloe see Cury & Gunwalloe
12. **Hayle**
13. **Helston**

14. **Kea**

    Ladock see St Ladoca

    Landewednack see The Lizard

    (Landewednack)
15. **Launceston**
16. **Liskeard**
17. The Lizard

    (Landewednack)
18. **Looe**
19. **Lostwithiel**
20. Ludgvan
21. **Luxulyan & District**
22. **Madron**
23. Mawnan
24. Mount Hawke
25. **Mousehole**
26. **Mullion**
27. Newlyn East
28. **Newquay**
29. North Hill
30. **Padstow**

31. **Par**

    Pendeen see St Just & Pendeen
32. **Penryn & Falmouth**
33. **Pentewan**
34. **Penzance**
35. **Perranzabuloe**
36. **Porthleven**
37. Port Isaac

    Portscatho see

    St Gerrans & Porthscatho
38. **Probus**
39. **Redruth**
40. **St Agnes**
41. **St Austell**
42. **St Buryan**
43. **St Columb**
44. **St Denys & District**
45. St Gennys
46. **St Gerrans & Porthscatho**
47. **St Goran**

48. **St Ives**
49. **St Just & Pendeen**
50. St Ladoca
51. **Saltash**

    Stratton see Bude-Stratton & District
52. Tintagel
53. **Torpoint**
54. **Truro**
55. Tywardreath
56. **Wadebridge**

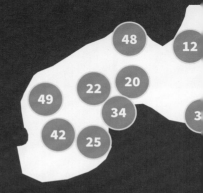

Presidents of the Federation of Old Cornwall Societies

Henry Jenner	1924-1934	Denis Archibald Trevanion	1985-1987
Robert Morton Nance	1934-1959	William John Rowe	1987-1989
Alfred Kenneth Hamilton Jenkin	1959-1961	Barbara Joan Rendell	1989-1991
John Andrew Shearme	1961-1963	Richard Garfield Jenkin	1991-1993
William Mitchell Symons	1963-1965	Michael Tangye	1993-1995
Arthur Jeffrey Lyne	1965-1967	Kathleen Mary Glanville	1995-1997
Frank Michell	1967-1969	Thomas Roy Harvey Woolcock	1997-1999
John Noel Rosewarne	1969-1971	Anthony Spiller	1999-2001
Edward Blight	1971-1973	Barry William Kinsmen	2001-2003
George Pawley White	1973-1975	Frederick Brian John Coombes	2003-2006
Spencer George Alfred Ames Howlett	1975-1977	Ronald Opie	2006-2009
Hugh John Miners	1977-1979	Graham Terence Knight	2009-2012
Charles William Woolf	1979-1981	Duncan Paul Matthews	2012-2015
Alan Pearson	1981-1983	Emily Priscilla Oates	2015-2018
Mary Helen Derrington	1983-1985	Karin Florence Easton	2018-

Courtesy of Gorsedh Kernow Archive, R Cole,
T Knight, J Neale, and Liskeard, Newquay
and St Ives OCSs.

Old Cornwall Publications

Anne & Terry Knight

These lists are incomplete: they offer examples of items which are known to have been published and of which copies survive in, for example, Kresen Kernow. Doubtless other items which have never been deposited will survive in private hands. Furthermore, it does not include the hundreds of books written and/or published by individual members of Old Cornwall Societies. These omissions will probably include books and booklets printed in the early decades of Old Cornwall at the private expense of its founders.

Publications by the Federation of Old Cornwall Societies

Bro Goth Agan Tasow, Cornish National Anthem. (1 page). *ca.1937*

Calendar of events: celebrating Cornwall's culture & promoting Cornish customs. (Folding leaflet). *2015*

Carols of the Stratton Hundred, published jointly with Bude-Stratton & District Old Cornwall Society. *2011*

Christmas cards. (4 known: Probus Church; Mevagissey Harbour, by Hugh E Ridge, 1964 & 1967 respectively: Quaker Meeting House, Come-to-Good; Altarnun, both by Charles Woolf, 1970s).

Cornish books for people who care about Cornwall from the people who care for Cornwall. (Folding leaflet). *2010*

Cornish dialect in prose and verse: a selection compiled by the Federation of Old Cornwall Societies from the prize winning entries in the Gorsedd competitions 1969-1980. *1982*

Cornish in song and ceremony. *1953*

Cornish stamp. (Green and white postage-style stamp in sheets of 10). *ca. 1959*

Cornish words, with a phonetically spelt guide to the pronunciation and English translations, of Mr Henry Jenner's Cornish versions of the Welsh *Hen Wlad fy Nhadau* and of *God Save the King*. (Leaflet). *1926*

Crying the Neck: a harvest celebration. *2005*

Hobby Horse ballad sheet. (Contains old words of the Padstow May songs). *1925/26*

The Lord's Prayer in the Cornish language. (Leaflet). *ca.1934; 1955?*

Old Cornwall, vol 1, no 1 to date. *1925-*

Old Cornwall, Index to vols I, II, and III, compiled by S W Johns. *1948*

Old Cornwall, Index to vol IV, compiled by S W Johns and E H Oliver. *1954*

Old Cornwall, Index to vol 5, compiled by John J Beckerlegge. *1961*

Old Cornwall, Index to vol 6, compiled by John J Beckerlegge and L R Moir. *1971*

Old Cornwall, Index to vol 7, compiled by Y Langley. *1974*

Old Cornwall, Index to vol 8, compiled by A Pearson. *1980*

Old Cornwall, Index to vol 9, compiled by H A Spiller. *1985?*

Old Cornwall, no 1, April 1925. (Reset by George Pritchard & reissued as e-book for download). *2008*

Old Cornwall, no 2, October 1925. (Reset by George Pritchard & reissued as e-book for download). *2008*

Old Cornwall, no 3, April 1926. (Reset by George Pritchard & reissued as e-book for download). *2008*

Old Cornwall, no 4, October 1926. (Reset by George Pritchard & reissued as e-book for download). *2008*

Old Cornwall Societies. (Information booklets; subtitled: What they are and what they are doing). *1927; 1977 (2nd); 1982 (3rd); 2003 (4th); 2004 (rev)*

(Folding publicity leaflets; titled: Do you love Cornwall?). *2009; 2010 (repr); 2011 (rev)*

(Folding publicity leaflets; subtitled: What are they? What do they do?). *2018; 2019 (rev)*

Reports: 1934-1935. *1935*

Reports: 1936-1937. [No other editions extant or known]. *1937*

Strike Sound!: a collection of Padstow carols. (Originally published in 1971 by Lodenek Press. Re-sequenced). *2017*

Victorian Cornish carols, no 1: Redruth & St Agnes district. (Facsimile of Cornish carols, part 1, published 1889). *2010*

Arthur, M. The autobiography of a china clay worker. *1995*

Attwater, D. Some saints of Cornwall. *1967*

Chirgwin, E. Say it in Cornish: 240 remarks in English-Cornish with a complete guide to pronunciation and mutations. *1937*

Davey, M. Tansys Golowan: the Cornish Midsummer Bonfire ceremonies. *2019*

Davey, M (ed). Kenewgh! Sing!: lever Kanow Kernewek. *2018*

Edyvean, C R. Roche village memories. *1995*

Gundry, I (ed). Canow Kernow: songs and dances from Cornwall. *1966*

Gundry, I (ed). Canow Kernow: songs and dances from Cornwall, 2nd ed. (Published jointly with Soundpost Publications in association with the Dartington Institution of Arts). *1972*

Harris, T R. Sir Goldsworthy Gurney, 1793-1875. (Published jointly with Trevithick Society). *1975*

Herring, I J. 400 years of Tremaynes at Heligan. *1999*

Jenkin, A K H. Mines and miners of Cornwall, part 15, Calstock, Callington and Launceston. *1969*

Jenkin, A K H. Mines and miners of Cornwall, part 16, Wadebridge, Camelford and Bude. *1970*

Jenkin, A K H. Mines and Miners of Cornwall, Index to volumes 1-16. *1978*

Jenner, H. Who are the Celts and what has Cornwall to do with them? *1928*

Jewell, C H. The Crying of the Neck. *1981*

Kendall, B H. The art of Cornish wrestling. (Reissue). *1990*

Kinsmen, B. Good fellowship of Padstow. *1997; 2011 (2nd rev)*

Lane-Davies, A. Holy wells of Cornwall: a guide. *1970*

Langdon, A G. Stone crosses in East Cornwall. *1996; 2005 (2nd rev)*

Langdon, A G. Stone crosses in mid Cornwall. *1994; 2002 (2nd rev)*

Langdon, A G. Stone crosses in North Cornwall. *1992*

Langdon, A G. Stone crosses in West Cornwall. *1999*

Langdon, A G. Stone crosses in West Penwith. *1997*

Langdon, A G. Wade-Bridge: notes on the history of the fifteenth century bridge. *2012*

Lyon, R. Early Newquay: a brief introductory history. (Rev ed of The start of Newquay). *2018*

Lyon, R. The start of Newquay. *1991*

Nance, R M. An Balores. *1932; 1950 (repr)*

Nance, R M. The Cledry plays: drolls of old Cornwall for village acting and home reading. *1956*

Nance, R M. Cornish for all: a first book, containing a précis of Cornish grammar. *1929*

Nance, R M. Cornish for all: a guide to Unified Cornish. (Rev ed of the 1929 publication, with variant subtitle). *1949; 1961 (3rd)*

Nance, R M. A Cornish-English dictionary. (Rev ed of Gerlyver noweth Kernewek ha Sawsnek / A new Cornish-English dictionary). *1955*

Nance, R M. An English-Cornish dictionary. (Rev ed of Nance & Smith's An English-Cornish dictionary). *1952*

Nance, R M. Gerlyver noweth Kernewek ha Sawsnek / A new Cornish-English dictionary. *1938*

Nance, R M. A glossary of Cornish sea-words. *1963*

Nance, R M. A guide to Cornish place-names: with a list of words contained in them. *1951; 1958 (2nd); 1961 (3rd); 1963 (4th); 1967 (5th)*

Nance, R M. Lyver an Pymp Marthus Seleven. *1939*

Nance, R M & Smith, A S D. An English-Cornish dictionary. *1934*

Nance, R M & Smith, A S D (eds). Extracts from the Cornish texts in Unified spelling with amended translation *(1949-58)*:

No 1. Bewnans Meryasek, lines 759-1096. (2nd ed, 1966: St. Meriasek in Cornwall (Bewnans Meryasek, lines 587-1099)).

No 2. An Tyr Marya (R.D., lines 679-834).

No 3. Sylvester ha'n dhragon (B.M., lines 3896-4180).

No 4. Abram hag Ysak (O.M., lines 1259-1394).

No 5. Adam ha Seth (O.M., lines 684-880).

No 6. Davyd hag Urry (O.M., lines 2105-2254).

Nance, R M & Smith, A S D (eds). Gwryans an Bys / The Creation of the World, as written by William Jordan. *1959*

Newall, T. Echoes from carn, cove, & cromlech, by 'Nicky Trevaylor'. *1935*

Noall, C. The Cornish Midsummer Eve bonfire celebrations. *1963; 2003 (rev with additions)*

Palmer, J L. The Cornish chough through the ages. *1953*

Paynter, W H. The Cornish Witch-finder: William Henry Paynter and the witchery, ghosts, charms and folklore of Cornwall, selected and edited by J Semmens. *2008*

Pearson, A .Robert Hunt FRS (1807-1887). *1976*

Pender, N M. A short history of Mousehole with personal recollections. *1970*

Pool, P A S. The place-names of West Penwith. *1973*

Pritchard, G (comp). The 'Old Cornwall' Christmas anthology. *2012*

Pritchard, G (ed). Angletwitch and poppydocks: Cornish dialect words, rhymes and stories. *2010*

Smith, A S D. Lessons in spoken Cornish, part 1. *1931*

Stark, D. The banners of the Old Cornwall Societies. *2007*

Tangye, M. Once 'twas serpentine and fish: Cadgwith and Poltesco. *2007*

Taylor, P. The toll-houses of Cornwall. *2001*

Watson, W D. First steps in Cornish. *1931*

Recording

Gramophone records: 1, Lord's Prayer and Lessons in the Cornish service; 2 & 3, John of Chyannor, and Boorde's Colloquies, read by R Morton Nance. *1954*

Books and pamphlets written and/or published by Old Cornwall Societies

BUDE-STRATTON

Around Bude, compiled by Kenneth Hargrove & Lucille Opie (1st ed published by Chalfont; reprinted by Nonsuch). *1998; 2005*

Carols of the Stratton Hundred, collected by Bude-Stratton & District OCS and published jointly with the Federation. *2011*

Forty years at Stratton Senior School: a teacher's personal view, by Sallie Sweet. *2001*

CAMBORNE

Camborne's great men: a paper read before the Camborne Old Cornwall Society, May 9th, 1930, by the President, J Sims Carah, Vicar of Penponds. *1930*

The parish of Camborne: some notes on its history, its antiquities and its people parts 1 & 2, by J Sims Carah. *1925-27*

CARHARRACK

The book of Carharrack: born of the mines, compiled & written by Eric Rabjohns & Barrie May (published by Halsgrove). *2003*

A Carharrack pilgrimage: a walk around the religious sites in the village, by Barrie S May. *1996*

Carharrack pop works, researched and compiled by Eric Rabjohns. *1996*

Carharrack railway walkabout: the Redruth and Chasewater railway 1824-1915, designed by Eric Rabjohns. *1996*

Carharrack: the growth of the village, researched and compiled by Eric Rabjohns. *1996*

FOWEY

Fowey: a brief history, by I D Spreadbury. *1965; 1972 (2nd); 1978 (3rd); 1981 (4th rev)*

A short history of the town of Fowey, by E W Rashleigh. *(1st ed 1887). 1964*

HELSTON

Helston Furry Day, by James Dryden Hosken. *1931*

LISKEARD

Census index, Liskeard, 1861. *n.d.*

Crying the Neck. (Programme). *2010*

Lanreath's antiquities: the church and Court Barton, statement of responsibility by Liskeard OCS. *n.d.*

LOOE

The Secret Army (a talk given to Looe OCS April 2014 entitled 'Ordinary men and their quiet war') (Tales from the Archives), by John Jolliff. *2017*

Whale ashore (Tales from the Archives), by Bert Middleton. *2017*

NEWQUAY

Local shipbuilding, by E J Ennor. *1943; 2012*

Newquay & Cornwall's heritage at Newquay Heritage Archive & Museum. (Leaflet). *2017*

Newquay Old Cornwall Society / Cowethas Kernow Goth Towan Blystry, 1928-1978: fifty years of events, personalities and records, written and edited by Charles Woolf. *1978*

Newquay's pictorial past, compiled by Newquay OCS. *1983; 1993 (2nd rev)*

Seafaring, by E J Ennor. *1943*

NORTH HILL

A collection of sayings and superstitions from the area, compiled by North Hill OCS (publication uncertain). *1930-1935*

PAR

Cap'n Harry, by H J Purches. *2020*

My story of the Tywardreath Orchestras, by Sybil Harris. *2016*

Par, the little town that came out of the sea, by Diana Osborne & Jill Hore (comps). *2020*

Par excellence: a history of Par, Cornwall, by Derek G Reynolds. *2008*

St Blazey, Par, Tywardreath remembered: 1914-1928, compiled and edited by Barbara Seed. *2016*

PENTEWAN

Pentewan Old Cornwall Society, 1954-2004: 50th anniversary. *2004*

A short history of Pentewan, by K M Batchelor. *n.d. (various rev eds 1960-1989)*

Six circular walks in and around Pentewan village, by Maureen Prettyman. *1995*

PENZANCE

Ceremony of the unveiling of Pendrea Cross, St Buryan, Tuesday May 5th 1959. (Programme). *1959*

Looking at Penzance: from the archive of Penzance Old Cornwall Society, 1926-2006, compiled by Margaret Perry. *2006*

Penzance: a brief history of the town and borough, by P A S Pool. *1965; 1970 (2nd)*

Reminiscences of Penzance, by G C Boase, edited by P A S Pool. *1976*

PERRANZABULOE

Memories of Perranzabuloe in the early 1900s. *2010*

Perran paths. *1972; 1975; 1980*

Perranzabuloe 1900-1985: a study of changes in our locality this century. *1995*

'While Shepherds' [to the tune] 'Bolingey', arranged by Ralph Dunstan. *1968*

PROBUS

A study of changes in the parish of Probus this century, by M Joyce Taylor & Probus OCS. *1985*

REDRUTH

Crying the Neck. (Programme). *198-*

Notable events in the history of Redruth from ancient times to the present day, by Frank Michell, published by the Rector with [Redruth] Old Cornwall Society in aid of Camborne-Redruth Hospital Appeal Fund. *193-*

Old Redruth: original studies of the town's history. *1992*

Redruth Old Cornwall Society: 90th anniversary celebration booklet. *2012*

Redruth Town Museum: at Tolgus Tin Mill, Cornwall Gold. (Leaflet). *ca.2014*

ST AUSTELL

A celebration of the 80th anniversary of St Austell Old Cornwall Society, compiled by David & Carole Stark. *2005*

St Austell Jubilee souvenir 1925-1975 [of St Austell OCS]. *1975*

St Austell Town Museum. (Leaflet). *2012*

ST GERRANS & PORTHSCATHO

Cornish stiles in the Roseland: parish of St Gerrans 1997, compiled by John Coppin & St Gerrans & Portscatho OCS. *1998*

Cornish stiles in the Roseland, vol 2: parishes of Philleigh & St Just in Roseland, 1999-2000, compiled by John Coppin & St Gerrans & Porthscatho OCS. *2000*

Golyow Gerens hag Entenin: Feast of St Gerrans and St Anthony. *2018*

Gwariow Fleghes yn Pluw Erens: children's games in St Gerrans. *2019*

The wells, shutes & springs of Gerrans parish, edited and compiled by Hilary Thompson & St Gerrans & Porthscatho OCS. *2009*

ST IVES

The Cornish jury: a dialect dialogue for 12 characters, by R M Nance. *1926*

Federation of Old Cornwall Societies Summer Pilgrimage, Saturday 16th June 1962. (Programme). *1962*

ST JUST & PENDEEN

The Cornish Hundreds, by Roger Venables. *1980*

The 1851 Census for St Just-in-Penwith, compiled by Peter Joseph & St Just & Pendeen OCS. *2003*

'The man engine' of Levant Mine 1857-1919, by R L Ellis & St Just & Pendeen OCS. *2004*

New bread: North Cornish verses, by Roger Venables. *1981*

A short guide to St Just and Pendeen, by Edith M Nicholas. *1968; 1969 (2nd); 1996 (3rd)*

The stone frigate: verses from West Penwith, by Roger Venables. *1982*

The traders of St Just, 1920 to 1985, by Colin Stephens. (Dedicated to St Just & Pendeen OCS for their 25th anniversary). *1985*

ST LADOCA

Ladock Glebe Holy Well: service of thanksgiving and rededication. *2011*

TRURO

The history of Truro: a reprint and update of Notable events in the history of Truro... from ancient times to the end of Queen Victoria's reign, compiled by A A Clinnick, 1922 (to mark the 90th anniversary of the Society). *2002*

Bibliography of Sources

Peter W Thomas

Beacham, Peter & Pevsner, Nikolaus. *The buildings of England: Cornwall* (New Haven: Yale University Press, 2014).

Blight, JT. *A week at the Land's End* (London: Longman, 1861).

Bond, Thomas. *Topographical and historical sketches of the boroughs of East and West Looe, in the county of Cornwall* (London: J. Nichols and Son, 1823).

Borlase, William. *Observations on the antiquities historical and monumental, of the county of Cornwall* (Oxford: W. Jackson, 1754).

Boson, Nicholas. *John of Chyannor; or, The three points of wisdom* ([St Ives]: Cornish Language Board, 1969) [parallel text: RM Nance's Unified Cornish version and his literal English translation].

Bottrell, William. *Stories and folk-lore of West Cornwall* (Penzance: the author, 1880) [the *Third series* of the following entry].

Bottrell, William. *Traditions and hearthside stories of West Cornwall.* 2 vols. (Penzance: the author, 1870-73).

Brown, Wella. *A grammar of modern Cornish* (Saltash: Kesva an Tavas Kernewek (The Cornish Language Board), 1984).

Carah, J Sims. *Camborne Old Cornwall Society, record book, 1924-30* (Kresen Kernow, Redruth).

Chirgwin, Edwin. *Say it in Cornish* (St Ives: Federation of Old Cornwall Societies, 1937).

Church Monuments Society. *Newsletter* (London: Church Monuments Society, 1985-).

Cole, Richard. *Roche Holy Well, Cornwall: consolidation work and archaeological recording* (Truro: Cornwall County Council, Historic Environment Service, 2007).

Coleman, Hilary & Burley, Sally. *Hark!: the glad sound of Cornish carols* (London: Francis Boutle, 2017).

Coleman, Hilary & Burley, Sally. *Shout Kernow: celebrating Cornwall's pub songs* (London: Francis Boutle, 2015).

Cornish & Devon Post.

Cornish archaeology / Hendhyscans Kernow ([n.p.]: Cornwall Archaeological Society, 1962-).

Cornish Language Board. *Cornish Language* ([n.p.]: Kesva an Tavas Kernewek / Cornish Language Board, [1969]) [vinyl recording: IBC/LP/3624].

Cornish Magazine. 2 vols. (Truro: Joseph Pollard, 1898-99).

Cornish Studies (Pool [etc.]: Institute of Cornish Studies, 1973-).

Cornish Telegraph.

Cornish Times.

Cornishman / Cornishman and Cornish Telegraph.

Council of Europe. *Framework Convention for the Protection of National Minorities* (1998).

Courtney, Margaret A. *Cornish Feasts and folk-lore* (Penzance: Beare and Son, 1890).

Crofts, E Whitfield ('Peter Penn') (ed.) *Cornish Notes & Queries. (First series): reprinted from The Cornish Telegraph* (London: Elliot Stock; Penzance: Cornish Telegraph Office, 1906).

Davey, Merv. *As is the manner and the custom* (Doctoral thesis, Institute of Cornish Studies, University of Exeter, 2011).

Davey, Merv (ed.). *Kenewgh! Sing!: lever kanow Kernewek / the Cornish song book* (St Agnes: Federation of Old Cornwall Societies, 2018).

Davey, Merv. *Tansys Golowan: the Cornish Midsummer Bonfire ceremonies* (St Agnes: Federation of Old Cornwall Societies, 2019).

Davey, Merv & Davey, Alison. *Snail Creeps and Tea Treats: Clay Country customs* (St Austell: Rescorla Project, 2008).

Davey, Merv, Davey, Alison & Davey, Jowdy. *Scoot Dances, Troyls, Furrys and Tea Treats: the Cornish dance tradition* (London: Francis Boutle, 2009).

Deacon, Bernard. *A concise history of Cornwall* (Cardiff: University of Wales Press, 2007).

Devon & Cornwall Notes & Queries (Exeter: James G. Commin, 1901-).

Dimbleby, Richard (presenter). *BBC Sound Archive 6796 and 6918* (1943) [available as vinyl recording: Topic Records 12T240].

Doyden Castle (https://www.atlasobscura.com/places/doyden-castle).

Dunstan, Ralph (ed.). *Cornish dialect and folk songs* (Truro: Jordan's Bookshop, 1932).

Dunstan, Ralph (ed.). *The Cornish Song Book (Lyver Canow Kernewek)* (London: Reid Bros., 1929).

Evans, RE & Prettyman, GW. *Pictorial Pentewan* (Pentewan: Pentewan Publications, 1994).

Falmouth Packet.

Federation of Old Cornwall Societies. *Carols of the Stratton Hundred* (St Agnes:

Federation of Old Cornwall Societies / Bude-Stratton & District Old Cornwall Society, 2011).

Federation of Old Cornwall Societies. *[Christmas cards]* ([n.p.]: Federation of Old Cornwall Societies, [various years]).

Federation of Old Cornwall Societies. *Cornish in song and ceremony* (Marazion: Federation of Old Cornwall Societies / Worden, [1953]).

Federation of Old Cornwall Societies. *[Cornish translation by Henry Jenner of the UK and Welsh national anthems, with ancillary material]* ([n.p.]: Federation of Old Cornwall Societies, [1926]).

Federation of Old Cornwall Societies. *[Lord's Prayer in Cornish]* ([n.p.]: Federation of Old Cornwall Societies, [1955?]).

Federation of Old Cornwall Societies. *Minute books / Records*.

Federation of Old Cornwall Societies. *19ᵗʰ century Cornish carols. Book 1: Redruth & St Agnes district [Victorian Cornish carols. Number 1]* (St Agnes: Federation of Old Cornwall Societies, 2010) [facsimile of publication compiled by Robert H Heath (Redruth, 1889)].

Federation of Old Cornwall Societies. *Old Cornwall Societies: what they are and what they are doing* ([n.p.]: Federation of Old Cornwall Societies, 1927) [2003 and 2004 issues revised by David Stark].

Federation of Old Cornwall Societies. *Reports. 1934-1935* (St Ives: Federation of Old Cornwall Societies / James Lanham, 1935).

Federation of Old Cornwall Societies. *Reports. 1936-1937* (St Ives: Federation of Old Cornwall Societies / James Lanham, 1937).

Federation of Old Cornwall Societies. *Strike sound!: a collection of Padstow carols*. (St Agnes: Federation of Old Cornwall Societies, 2017) [original ed.: (Padstow: Lodenek Press, 1971)].

Federation of Old Cornwall Societies. *[Words of songs performed at the May festivities in Padstow]* ([n.p.]: Federation of Old Cornwall Societies, [1925/26]).

Folklore ([London]: Folklore Society, 1890-).

An Gannas (Liskeard [etc.]: Graham Sandercock / Cowethas [later Kowethas] an Yeth Kernewek, 1976-).

Gendall, Richard. *Kernewek bew* ([n.p.]: Kesva an Tavas Kernewek, 1972).

Gilbert, Davies. *Some ancient Christmas carols* (London: John Nichols and Son, 1823).

Gorsedh Kernow Archives & Publications Committee & St. Ives Archive Study Centre. *Cornish bards of the St Ives area / Berdh Kernow a ranndir Porthia* ([n.p.]: Gorsedh Kernow, 2010).

Gover, JEB. *The place-names of Cornwall* (1948) (typescript, Courtney Library, Royal Institution of Cornwall, Truro).

Graves, Alfred Perceval (ed.). *The Celtic song book: being representative folk songs of the six Celtic nations* (London: Ernest Benn, 1928).

Gundry, Inglis (ed.). *Canow Kernow: songs and dances from Cornwall* (Redruth: Federation of Old Cornwall Societies / Truran, 1966).

Hale, Amy. *Gathering the fragments: performing contemporary Celtic identities in Cornwall* (Doctoral dissertation, University of California Los Angeles, 1998).

Hencken, H O'Neill. *The archaeology of Cornwall and Scilly* (London: Methuen, 1932).

Henderson, Charles. *The Cornish church guide* (Truro: Oscar Blackford, 1925).

Jago, Fred WP. *The ancient language, and the dialect of Cornwall* (Truro: Netherton & Worth, 1882).

James, Ronald M. *The folklore of Cornwall* (Exeter: University of Exeter Press, 2018).

James Madison Carpenter Collection (Archive of Folk Culture, Library of Congress, Washington DC).

Jenner, Henry. *Bards, druids and the Gorsedd* (ca.1929) (manuscript, RM Nance Collection, Courtney Library, Royal Institution of Cornwall, Truro).

Jenner, Henry. *A handbook of the Cornish language* (London: David Nutt, 1904).

Jenner, Henry. *Who are the Celts and what has Cornwall to do with them?* (St Ives: Federation of Old Cornwall Societies, [1928]).

Johns, SW [et al.] *Old Cornwall: the Journal of the Federation of Old Cornwall Societies. Index to vols. I., II. and III [- 9]*. 7 parts (Marazion [etc.]: Federation of Old Cornwall Societies / HA Spiller, [1948-85?]).

Journal of the Folk-Song Society (London: Folk-Song Society, 1899-).

Journal of the Royal Institution of Cornwall (Truro: Royal Institution of Cornwall, 1865-).

Journal of the St Agnes Museum Trust (St Agnes: St Agnes Museum Trust, 1985-).

Knight, Terry. *Do you love Cornwall?* ([n.p.]: Federation of Old Cornwall Societies, 2009) [2018 and 2019 revisions issued as *Old Cornwall Societies. What are they? What do they do?*].

Lane-Davies, Alfred. *Holy wells of Cornwall* (Penzance: Federation of Old Cornwall Societies, 1970).

Langdon, Andrew G. *Cross records*.

Langdon, Andrew G. *Stone crosses in East Cornwall*. 2ⁿᵈ ed. ([n.p.]: Federation of Old Cornwall Societies, 2005).

Langdon, Andrew G. *Stone crosses in mid Cornwall* ([St Austell]: Federation of Old Cornwall Societies, 1994) [2ⁿᵈ ed. 2002].

Langdon, Andrew G. *Stone crosses in North Cornwall* ([n.p.]: Federation of Old Cornwall Societies, 1992).

Langdon, Andrew G. *Stone crosses in West Penwith* ([n.p.]: Federation of Old Cornwall Societies, 1997).

Langdon, Andrew G. *Wade-Bridge* (St Agnes: Federation of Old Cornwall Societies, 2012).

Langdon, Arthur G. *Old Cornish crosses* (Truro: Joseph Pollard, 1896).

Lee, Charles. *The Cornish journal of Charles Lee, 1892-1908* (Padstow: Tabb House, 1995).

Lee, Charles. *Dorinda's birthday: a Cornish idyll* (London: J.M. Dent and Sons, 1911).

Leggat, PO & Leggat, DV. *A tale of two mediaeval chapels in Lammana parish (Looe)* (West Looe: the authors, 1993).

Liskeard Old Cornwall Society. *Records*.

Lyon, Rod. *Gorseth Kernow / The Cornish Gorsedd: what it is and what it does* ([n.p.]: Gorseth Kernow, 2008).

The Mabinogion in Cornish / An Mabinogion yn Kernewek (Falmouth: Kesva 'n Tavas Kernewek / Cornish Language Board, 1975) [translation into Cornish by ASD Smith of two of the stories from the medieval Welsh collection].

Martin, Mary. *A wayward genius: Neville Northy [sic] Burnard* (Padstow: Lodenek Press, 1978).

Martyn, Thomas. *A new and accurate map of the county of Cornwall* (London: Robt. Sayer, 1748).

McCann, John & McCann, Pamela. *The dovecotes of historical Somerset* (Martock: Somerset Vernacular Building Research Group, 2003).

McGrady, Richard. *Traces of ancient mystery: the ballad carols of Davies Gilbert and William Sandys* (Redruth: Institute of Cornish Studies, 1993).

Miners, Hugh & Crago, Treve. *Tolzethan: the life and times of Joseph Hambley Rowe* ([n.p.]: Gorseth Kernow, 2002).

Nance, R Morton. *An Balores* (St Ives: [Federation of Old Cornwall Societies] / James Lanham, [1932]).

Nance, R Morton. *The Cledry plays: drolls of old Cornwall for village acting and home reading* (Marazion / Penzance: Federation of Old Cornwall Societies / Worden, 1956).

Nance, R Morton. *Cornish for all* (St Ives: Federation of Old Cornwall Societies / James Lanham, [1929]) [2nd, revised ed. 1949; 3rd ed. 1961].

Nance, R Morton. *An English-Cornish and Cornish-English dictionary* ([Redruth / Penzance]: Cornish Language Board, 1978) [corrected reprint, in a single volume, of *An English-Cornish dictionary* (1952) and *A Cornish-English dictionary* (1955)].

Nance, R Morton. *Gerlyver noweth Kernewek ha Sawsnek / A new Cornish-English dictionary* (St Ives: Federation of Old Cornwall Societies / J. Lanham, 1938) [2nd, revised ed. 1955: *A Cornish-English dictionary*].

Nance, R Morton. *A glossary of Cornish sea-words* ([Truro / Marazion / St Ives]: Federation of Old Cornwall Societies, 1963).

Nance, R Morton. *A guide to Cornish place-names* (Marazion: Federation of Old Cornwall Societies / Worden, [1951]).

Nance, R Morton. *[Readings of Pader agan Arluth (Lord's Prayer) etc.]* ([n.p.]: Federation of Old Cornwall Societies, [1954] [vinyl recordings, reissued on cassette tape as *Lef Mordon: readings in Cornish* ([Redruth]: Agan Tavas, 1992)].

Nance, R Morton & Smith, ASD. *An English-Cornish dictionary* (St Ives: Federation of Old Cornwall Societies / James Lanham, 1934) [2nd, revised ed. 1952].

Nance, R Morton & Smith, ASD (eds). *Extracts from the Cornish texts in Unified spelling with amended translation*. 7 parts (Camborne [etc]: Federation of Old Cornwall Societies / Cornish Language Board, 1949-69) [1. *Bewnans Meryasek*, lines 759-1096 (2nd, enlarged ed. 1966: *St. Meriasek in Cornwall*); 2. *An tyr Marya*; 3. *Sylvester ha'n dhragon*; 4. *Abram hag Ysak*; 5. *Adam ha Seth*; 6. *Davyd hag Urry*; 7. *An venen ha'y map*].

Nance, R Morton & Smith, ASD (eds). *Gwryans an Bys / The Creation of the World* (St Ives: [Federation of Old Cornwall Societies], 1959).

Nance, R Morton, Smith, ASD & Hooper, EGR (eds). *Passyon agan Arluth / Cornish Poem of the Passion* ([St Ives]: Kesvd [sic] an Tavas Kernewek, 1972).

Nance, R Morton, Smith, ASD & Sandercock, Graham (eds). *The Cornish Ordinalia*. 2 vols ([Saltash / Truro / Penzance]: Cornish Language Board /

Kesva an Tavas Kernewek, 1982-84) [2nd & 3rd plays only; a complete text of the 1st play in the same format did not appear till 2001, published by Agan Tavas].

New Cornwall (Leedstown: Richard and Ann Jenkin, 1952-73).

Newall, Tom ('Nicky Trevaylor'). *Echoes from carn, cove, & cromlech* (St Ives: Federation of Old Cornwall Societies / James Lanham, 1935).

Noall, Cyril. *The Cornish Midsummer Eve bonfire celebrations* (Marazion: Federation of Old Cornwall Societies / Worden, 1963) [2nd, revised & enlarged ed. 2003].

North, David J & Sharpe, Adam. *A word-geography of Cornwall* (Pool: Institute of Cornish Studies, 1980).

Nowakowski, Jacqueline A & Quinnell, Henrietta. *Trevelgue Head, Cornwall* (Truro: Cornwall Archaeological Unit, 2011).

O'Connor, Mike. *No song, no supper: the music of John Old, Dancing Master of Par* (Wadebridge: Lyngham House Music, 2002).

Okasha, Elisabeth. *Corpus of early Christian inscribed stones of South-West Britain* (London: Leicester University Press, 1993).

Old Cornwall (St Ives [etc.]: Federation of Old Cornwall Societies / James Lanham [etc.], 1925-).

Orme, Nicholas. *A history of the County of Cornwall [The Victoria History of the County of Cornwall]. Vol. 2: Religious history to 1560* (London: Institute of Historical Research, 2010).

Oxford Dictionary of National Biography (Oxford: Oxford University Press, 2004-) [online version: www.oxforddnb.com].

Padel, OJ. *Cornish place-name elements* (Nottingham: English Place-Name Society, 1985).

Padstow Museum. *Archive*.

Page, William (ed.). *The Victoria History of the County of Cornwall. Vol. 1* (London: Archibald Constable, 1906).

Paynter, S Winifred. *Old St Ives: the reminiscences of William Paynter* (St Ives: privately published, 1927).

Paynter, William H. *Cornish witchcraft* (Liskeard: privately printed, 2016).

Paynter, William H. *The Cornish Witch-finder: William Henry Paynter and the witchery, ghosts, charms and folklore of Cornwall* (St Agnes: Federation of Old Cornwall Societies, 2008) [ed. Jason Semmens].

Payton, Philip. *Cornwall* (Fowey: Alexander Associates, 1996) [2nd, revised ed.: *Cornwall: a history* (Fowey: Cornwall Editions, 2004); 3rd, revised ed.: *Cornwall: a history* (Exeter: University of Exeter Press, 2017)].

Phillips, David Rhys. *Correspondence* (manuscripts, Llyfrgell Genedlaethol Cymru / National Library of Wales).

Polsue, Joseph. *A complete parochial history of the County of Cornwall. Vol. 2* (Truro: William Lake, 1868).

Polwhele, Richard. *The history of Cornwall*. 3 vols. (London: Cadell and Davies, 1803-08).

Pool, PAS. *Cornish for beginners*. 3rd (revised) ed. ([n.p.]: Cornish Language Board, 1970).

Preston-Jones, Ann. *Towan Holy Well, St Austell, Cornwall: recording and repointing* (Truro: Cornwall County Council, Historic Environment Service, 2005).

Quiller-Couch, M & Quiller-Couch, L. *Ancient and holy wells of Cornwall* (London: Chas. J. Clark, 1894).

Rawe, Donald R & Ingrey, Jack. *Padstow and district* (Padstow: Lodenek Press, 1984).

Robertson, Rosemary & Gilbert, Geoffrey. *Some aspects of the domestic archaeology of Cornwall* (Pool: Institute of Cornish Studies / Cornwall Committee for Rescue Archaeology, 1979).

Royal Cornwall Gazette.

Royal Cornwall Polytechnic Society. *Annual Report* (Falmouth: Royal Cornwall Polytechnic Society / W. Tregaskis, 1833-).

St Ives Old Cornwall Society. *Minute books / Records*.

St Ives Times.

St Ives Weekly Summary.

Sloggett, Nellie ('Enys Tregarthen'). *North Cornwall fairies and legends* (London: Wells Gardner, Darton, 1906).

Smith, ASD. *Lessons in spoken Cornish. Part 1* (St Ives: Federation of Old Cornwall Societies, 1931).

Spooner, Barbara C. *John Tregagle of Trevorder: man and ghost* (Truro: A.W. Jordan, 1935) [reprint: [n.p.]: Blackthorn Press, 1977;

précised version: St Peter Port: Toucan Press, 1979].

Spooner, Barbara C. *Mazed tales* ('Barbara Spooner 1893-1983': http://mazedtales. org/content/barbara-spooner-1893-1983).

Spooner, Barbara C. *Queer tales of the Cheesewring; The Hurlers; The Other Half Stone* ([n.p.]: the author, 1950).

Stark, David. *The banners of the Old Cornwall Societies* ([n.p.]: Federation of Old Cornwall Societies, 2007).

Stark, David & Stark, Carole. *St Austell Old Cornwall Society: a celebration of its 80th anniversary, 1925-2005* (St Austell: St Austell Old Cornwall Society, 2005).

Stevens, Brian J (ed.). *St. Ives Museum* (St Ives: St Ives Museum, 2003).

Tartan Register (www.tartanregister.gov.uk).

Thomas, Charles. *And shall these mute stones speak?* (Cardiff: University of Wales Press, 1994).

Thomas, Charles. *Gathering the fragments* (Sheffield: Cornovia Press, 2012).

Thomas, Peter W & Williams, Derek R (eds). *Setting Cornwall on its feet: Robert Morton Nance, 1873-1959* (London: Francis Boutle, 2007).

Thompson, Hilary. *The wells, shutes & springs of Gerrans parish* ([n.p.]: Gerrans and Porthscatho Old Cornwall Society, 2009).

Trevan, John Watts. *Summary memoirs of the parish of Endellion, prior to the year 1834* (Port Isaac:

Port Isaac Local History Group, 2010).

Wadebridge Old Cornwall Society. *Minute books / Records*.

Wakelin, Martyn F. *Language and history in Cornwall* (Leicester: Leicester University Press, 1975).

Watson, WD. *First steps in Cornish* (St Ives: Federation of Old Cornwall Societies, [1931]).

West Briton.

Western Morning News.

Westland, Ella (ed.). *Cornwall: the cultural construction of place* (Penzance: Patten Press, 1997).

Williams, Derek R (ed.). *Henry and Katharine Jenner: a celebration of Cornwall's culture, language and identity* (London: Francis Boutle, 2004).

Williams, Derek R (ed.). *Richard G. Jenkin: a great son of Cornwall* (London: Francis Boutle, 2013).

Wilton, Brian. *Tartans* (London: Aurum, 2007).

Woolf, Charles. *Newquay Old Cornwall Society / Cowethas Kernow Goth Towan Blystry, 1928-1978: fifty years of events, personalities and records* (Newquay: Newquay Old Cornwall Society, 1978).

Appendix of Practical Work

Andrew Langdon

Date	Society	Project/work undertaken	Source reference
1932	Bodmin	Returned the inscribed Long Cross from the cliffs at Doyden to Long Cross, Trelights, St Endellion.	FOCS Annual report, 1934-35, 3; OC 2, no6, 17-18.
1939	Bodmin	Restoration of the Middle Moor Cross or Mid Moor Post at Camperdown, St Breward.	OC 3, no6, 237-9 & illus.
1982	Bodmin	Cleaning and repositioning carved stones from the Priory Church of St Mary and St Petroc (1138-1539) in the grounds of Priory Park Bodmin in conjuction with Bodmin Town Council.	OC 9, no8, 399.
1984	Bodmin	Re-erecting the Woodley Cross on the old Coach Road at Lanivet.	OC 9, no12, 613-6 & illus.
1991	Bodmin	Rededication of Lamorrick Cross at Lanivet.	AG Langdon (2002) *Stone crosses in mid Cornwall*, 2nd ed., 50.
1995	Bodmin	Restoration and rebuilding of Scarlett's Well near Bodmin.	OC 11, no9, 433-4 & illus.
2019	Bodmin	Plaque to commemorate a family of eight who died in Mill Street Bodmin, along with another man at the dairy next door when bombs fell on their home on August 7th 1942. Funded through public donations.	Information from Stephanie Thomas, President & Secretary Bodmin OCS.
1971	Bude-Stratton	Commemorative Civil War plaque erected at Stamford Hill, Stratton.	OC 7, no10, 449-50 & illus.
1977	Bude-Stratton	Plaque to Sir Goldsworthy Gurney erected at Bude Castle.	Information and photograph from Audrey Aylmer, Bude OCS.
1930	Callington	Protected Dupath Well near Callington from neglect.	OC 1, no12, 34.
?	Callington	Information plaque erected to mark the town's old Clink at Callington.	OC 7, no7, 298-9.
1920s	Camborne	Instigated interest in restoring Trevithick's cottage at Penponds near Camborne.	OC 7, no7, 299-300.
1938	Camborne	Re-erecting the Polmennor Cross at Gwinear.	OC 3, no4, 163.
1939	Camborne	Re-erecting a milestone at Roseworthy, Gwinear.	OC 3, no5, 217.
1954	Camborne	Slate headstone erected to Cornish sculptor Neville Northey Burnard (1818-1878) who was buried in Camborne churchyard.	M Martin (1978) *A wayward genius: Neville Northy Burnard*, pl70.
1998-99	Camborne	Re-erecting newly discovered Reskajeage/Gwealavellan cross on a new base-stone.	OC 12, no7, 18-19 & illus.
2004	Camborne	Rededication of the Reskajeage/Gwealavellan cross at Camborne.	OC 13, no7, 33 & illus.
2011	Camborne	Project to re-erect cross-head on a new base-stone at Crowan churchyard and rededication.	OC 14, no5, 25-28 & illus.
2016	Camborne	Information plaque to commemorate the unmarked graves of Richard Trevithick's parents, Trevithick himself and John Budge in Camborne churchyard.	OC 15, no3, 55-60 & illus.

2009-10	Federation OCS	Joint project to record post-boxes throughout Cornwall.	OC 14, no5, 10-15 & illus.
2011-13	Federation OCS	Joint project to record cast-iron fingerposts throughout Cornwall.	OC 14, no11, 37-44 & illus.
1960	Fowey	Information plaque erected beside the Tristan Stone on the road to Fowey.	OC 6, no1, 35-38 & illus.
2019	Hayle	Plaque set up at the birthplace of Cornish hero Rick Rescorla of New York's 9/11 disaster at Penpol Terrace, Hayle.	Information from Trevor Smitheram, President Hayle OCS.
2020	Hayle	Rescue and repositioning of Harvey's boundary stone at Harvey's Towans, Hayle.	Information and photographs from L King, Hayle OCS.
1949	Helston	Helped with the memorial cross in memory of the victims of the wreck of HMS Anson near Loe Bar, Porthleven.	OC 7, no7, 303.
1949	Helston	Helped with a commemorative cross to unknown graves in the Wrestling Field at Porthleven.	OC 7, no7, 303.
1968	Helston	Donation towards the excavation of Merther Uny chapel at Wendron.	OC 7, no7 304.
?	Helston	Assisted the Cornish Historical Association with restoring the gravestone of Samuel Drew at Helston.	OC 7, no7, 303.
?	Helston	Instrumental in preserving an old pump in Cross Street, Helston.	OC 7, no7, 303.
1999	Helston	Organised, commissioned and erected a large Millennium Cross at St Johns, Helston.	*West Briton* May 6th 1999.
2007	Helston	Memorial plaque to Henry Trengrouse (1772-1854) inventor of the Rocket Life-Saving Equipment, at his former home at 122 Meneage Street, Helston.	Information from Martin Matthews, past President of Helston OCS.
1950	Launceston	Restoration of Holloway (Holyway) Cross at South Petherwin.	OC 7, no7, 304.
1954	Launceston	Restoration and re-erecting of a cross in the churchyard at Laneast.	OC 7, no7, 304.
1954	Launceston	Relocation of granite gateway from Western Road, Launceston.	OC 7, no7, 304.
1958	Launceston	Repair and re-erecting of an old direction post beside the Polyphant to Altarnun Road.	OC 7, no7, 304.
1968	Launceston	Information tablet erected at Altarnun to commemorate Neville Northey Burnard.	OC 7, no4, 153; OC 7, no7, 304.
?	Launceston	Renovated St Stephen's Holy Well and cleaned up its approaches.	OC 7, no.7, 304.
1976	Launceston	Re-erecting the Occazinney Cross at Altarnun.	OC 8, no8, 398-9 & illus.
1979	Launceston	Re-erecting the lantern cross-head on a new plinth on the east side of St Mary Magdalene churchyard.	OC 9, no1, 31 & illus.
1979	Launceston	Relocation of a gravestone carved by 15-year-old Neville Northey Burnard to the church porch at Altarnun.	OC 9, no3, 144.

1981	Launceston	Partial restoration of the Hender memorial drinking fountain at Launceston.	OC 9, no6, 261.
1983	Launceston	Information plaque fixed to the King's Arms to mark Blindhole Lane (old name).	OC 9, no8, 399
?	Launceston	Plaque set up to mark the site of the first hospital at Launceston on Western Road.	Information from J Neale, Recorder Launceston OCS.
?	Launceston	Plaque set up to mark the name Tynewells Lane in High Street, Launceston.	Information from J Neale, Recorder Launceston OCS.
?	Launceston	Donated funds to the repair of St Thomas Church, Launceston.	Information from J Neale, Recorder Launceston OCS.
?	Launceston	Donated funds to St Mary Magdalene Church clock, apparently £250.	Information from J Neale, Recorder Launceston OCS.
2013	Launceston	Donated funds towards the repair to angels in the roof of St Mary Magdalene Church at Launceston.	OC 14, no10, 77.
1928	Liskeard	Funded exploration of tunnel at the rear of an old house at Liskeard.	FOCS Annual report, 1934-35, 7; OC 4, no7, 241.
1930-31	Liskeard	Undertook restoration and maintenance of Old Treverbyn Bridge on the boundary of St Neot and St Cleer.	FOCS Annual report, 1934-35, 7; OC 1, no12, 35; OC 4, no 7, 241.
1931	Liskeard	Trethevy Quoit purchased for the nation.	FOCS Annual report, 1934-35, 7; OC 4, no7, 241.
1931	Liskeard	Discovered a cross at North Trekeive and re-erected it on a new base-stone at Redgate, St Cleer.	FOCS Annual report, 1934-35, 7; OC 4, no7, 241.
1931	Liskeard	Re-erected Wenmouth Cross at St Neot.	FOCS Annual report, 1934-35, 7; OC 4, no7, 241.
1931	Liskeard	Re-sited and re-erected two inscribed stones from Welltown and Tawna at Cardinham.	FOCS Annual report, 1934-35, 7.
1931	Liskeard	Attempted to rescue Upton Cross-shaft at Linkinhorne (unsuccessful).	FOCS Annual report, 1934-35, 7.
1932	Liskeard	Re-erected Polmenna Cross at Polmenna Farm, St Neot.	FOCS Annual report, 1934-35, 7; OC 4, no7, 242.
1932	Liskeard	Discovered Latin cross in the glebe fields and had it re-erected against the south wall of St Ive churchyard.	FOCS Annual report, 1934-35, 7; OC 4, no7, 242.
1932	Liskeard	Re-erected Treslea Cross at Cardinham.	FOCS Annual report, 1934-35, 7.
1933	Liskeard	Purchased land for new enclosure for King Doniert's Stone and the Other Half Stone at St Cleer and gave the site to the Ministry of Works.	FOCS Annual report 1934-35, 7; OC 2, no4, 25-27; OC 4, no7, 242.
1934-36	Liskeard	Purchase and rebuilding of St Keyne's Well, St Keyne.	FOCS Annual report, 1934-35, 7; OC 4, no 7, 242; OC 7, no7, 305.
1935	Liskeard	Instigated restoration of the Hurlers stone circles and purchased the monument for the nation.	FOCS Annual report, 1934-35, 7; OC 4, no7, 242.
1937	Liskeard	Restoration, purchase and conveyance to the vicar and parish, of St Lalluwy's Holy Well at Menheniot.	*Cornish Times* November 12th 1937.
1943	Liskeard	Re-siting of a stone cross at Polscoe Hill, Sheviock on a new base-stone, in conjunction with Cornwall County Council.	OC 4, no7, 242-3.

1960	Liskeard	Re-erecting and rededication of the Tredinnick Cross at St Neot.	OC 5, no12, 538-9 & illus.
1986	Liskeard	Preservation of Tremabe Bridge on the Liskeard & Caradon Railway and setting up an information plaque.	Information from Brian Oldham, President Liskeard OCS.
1991	Liskeard	Restoration and re-erecting a cross at Hendra Farm, Menheniot.	OC 11, no2, 72-74 & illus.
1994	Liskeard	Relocation of the Newton Cross at St Neot.	OC 11, no10, 510.
2004	Liskeard	Joint project to restore architect Henry Rice's tombstone and erect an information plaque.	OC 13, no3, 54-55 & illus.
2013	Liskeard	Rededication of Fursnewth Cross at St Cleer.	OC 14, no10, 47-51 & illus.
1930s & 1983	Liskeard & Callington	Re-erecting St Ive Rectory Cross on a plinth with information plaque.	FOCS Annual report, 1934-35, 7; OC 9, no8, 400-1 & illus.
1930	Looe	Re-erected the Parlooe Cross, West Looe.	FOCS Annual report, 1934-35, 10; OC 1, no12, 13-16 & illus.; OC 7, no7, 305.
1930s	Looe	Opening up of ancient chapel site at Lammana, West Looe.	FOCS Annual report,1934-35, 9; OC7, no7, 305.
1931	Looe	Re-erected Tregoad Cross at the entrance of Tregoad Farm on a new base-stone.	FOCS Annual report, 1934-35, 10; OC 7, no7, 305.
1932	Looe	Provided a donation towards the King Doniert Stone project.	Liskeard OCS records.
1934	Looe	Donation towards the rebuilding of St Keyne's Well, St Keyne.	FOCS Annual report, 1934-35, 10.
c1936	Looe	Re-roofing of the St Cuby Holy Well, Duloe.	FOCS Annual report, 1936-37, 7; OC 7, no7, 305.
?	Looe	Information plaque erected on the house of Thomas Bond (topographer and historian of Looe).	OC 7, no7, 305.
1977 & 2006	Looe	Restoration of St Mary's Well or Lady Well, Shutta, East Looe.	Information from Norma Dobinson, Secretary Looe OCS.
2007	Looe	Raising funds to install information and viewing point to show the work of Joseph Thomas, civil engineer. Four plaques were set up to commemorate his work at Banjo Pier, the Railway Station, Old Vicarage and Hannafore Road.	OC 13, no8, 55-57 & illus.; OC 13, no9, 62-65 & illus.
2012	Looe	Rescue of a medieval sarcophagus cover/grave slab made of Purbeck stone at St Martin by Looe.	OC 14, no9, 45-48 & illus.
?	Looe	Cleaning up and restoration of St Martin's Well at Dawes Lane, East Looe.	Information from Norma Dobinson, Secretary Looe OCS.
?	Looe	Regular painting of the old bridge signs which mark where the original stone bridge across the river Looe stood.	Information from Norma Dobinson, Secretary Looe OCS.
?	Looe	Cleaning Looe Heritage Trail signs in the town.	Information from Norma Dobinson, Secretary Looe OCS.
1958	Lostwithiel	Re-erecting a medieval grave slab in the churchyard at Lostwithiel.	OC 7, no7, 306.
2000-01	Ludgvan	Restoration of Tregellast well and the erection of a plaque at Ludgvan.	OC 12, no9, 56-58 & illus.

1993	Luxulyan	Rededication of the Tregonning Cross on the Saints' Way footpath near Luxulyan.	OC 11, no8, 405-6.
1995	Luxulyan	Rededication and plaque at St Cyors' Holy Well at Luxulyan.	OC 11, no10, 490-1 & illus.
?	Madron	Restoration and maintenance of Madron well and baptistry.	OC 7, no7, 307.
2013	Madron	Erection of a gravestone for the unmarked grave of Eliza Jane Hall in Madron churchyard.	OC 14, no10, 71-73 & illus.
1977	Mousehole	Information plaque erected on Dolly Pentreath's cottage at Paul.	OC 8, no10, 515-6.
1950s	Mullion	Re-erecting a cannon on the cliff overlooking Mullion Cove.	OC 7, no7, 309.
2017	Mullion	Restoration of cast-iron fingerpost, with Mullion Parish Council.	Information from Colin Roberts, Chairman Mullion OCS.
1932	Newquay	Re-erected the prehistoric Longstone at St Eval.	FOCS Annual report, 1934-35, 11; OC 2, no8, 41; OC 4, no 7, 243; OC 7, no7, 309.
1936	Newquay	Rebuilding of the Trevornick Holy Well at Holywell Bay in Cubert.	FOCS Annual report, 1936-37, 11; OC 3, no3, 128; OC 4, no7, 243; OC 7, no7, 309.
1939	Newquay	Re-siting of the Inscribed Stone at Indian Queens in the churchyard of St Francis Chapel.	OC 3, no6, 247; OC 4, no7, 243; OC 7, no7, 310.
1939	Newquay	Labouring for an archaeological excavation on Porth Island, Newquay.	OC 4, no7, 243.
1943	Newquay	A rare portable altar stone restored to St Columb Minor Church.	OC 4, no7, 243; OC 7, no7, 310.
1953	Newquay	Restoration of Treloy Holy Well at St Columb Minor.	OC 7, no7, 310.
1964	Newquay	Assisting at excavation and restoration of Rosecliston Bronze Age urn.	OC 7, no7, 310.
1970	Newquay	Rescue and re-erection of Colan Cross in the churchyard at Colan near Newquay.	OC 7, no7, 310; OC 7, no11, 518-9.
1973	Newquay	Discovery and preservation of a medieval cross-base at Trerew in Crantock.	OC 8, no4, 180.
1978	Newquay	Preservation of Trerew cross-base in Crantock.	C Woolf (1978) Newquay Old Cornwall Society: fifty years of events, personalities and records, 23.
?	Newquay	Preservation of a cross-base at Trevemper in Crantock.	AG Langdon (1994) Stone crosses in mid Cornwall, 69.
2001	Newquay	Information plaque erected at the birthplace of author William Golding at 47 Mount Wise, Newquay.	OC 13, no3, 61 & illus.
2015-20	Newquay	Continuing maintenance of the Mawgan Porth medieval village.	Information from Sheila Harper, Warden Newquay OCS.
2011	Padstow	Rescue of terracotta ridge tiles displaying horsemen at Padstow and the creation of replicas to replace them.	OC 14, no5, 23-24 & illus.

1957	Par	Refurbishment of grave of Colonel John Whitehead Peard (1811-1880) at Fowey.	OC 7, no7, 310-11.
1970	Par	Plaque at the Sloop Inn, Par, unveiled by President of Federation of Old Cornwall Societies, Denis Trevanion.	Information and photograph from Diana Osborne, Chairperson Par OCS.
2010	Par	Information plaque erected on the home of Reuben Chappell, artist at Par.	OC 14, no3, 30-31 & illus.
1930s	Penryn & Falmouth	Tablet erected on the wall of the old Observatory Tower by member AV Baker.	FOCS Annual report, 1934-35, 14.
c1933-36	Penryn & Falmouth	Five plaques erected: at Upton Slip, site of the Old Prison, Winchester Buildings, gateway to Arwenack Manor and the King's Pipe.	FOCS Annual report, 1934-35, 14.
1965	Pentewan	Relocation of memorial slate to George Carew (1595-1661) at Mevagissey.	OC 7, no7, 312.
1990	Pentewan	Information plaque to record the relocation of the village pump.	OC 11, no2, 74.
1990	Pentewan	Construction and installation of a new sluice gate for the harbour at Pentewan.	OC 11, no2, 74-76 & illus.
1992	Pentewan	Clearance project at Towan Holy Well, near Lobb's Shop, Pentewan.	OC 11, no3, 126-7 & illus.
2003-04	Pentewan	Clearance of vegetation and further repairs to Towan Well, near Lobb's Shop.	OC 13, no2, 58-59 & illus.
2016	Pentewan	Clearance of vegetation at Lanhadron inscribed cross-base at St Ewe.	OC 15, no3, 51-52 & illus.
2017-18	Pentewan	Clearance and reconstruction of the weighbridge building at Pentewan Harbour.	OC 15, no8, 3-5 & illus.
2018	Pentewan	Erecting three information plaques about the Pentewan Railway, together with St Austell OCS.	OC 15, no7, 27-29 & illus.
1930	Penzance	Renovation of inscription on Dolly Pentreath's tomb at Paul churchyard.	OC 1, no12, 34.
1931	Penzance	Rediscovered St Levan's Well and cleaned it up.	OC 4, no7, 244.
1939	Penzance	Repairs to the Boskenna Cross at St Buryan.	OC 4, no7, 244.
1959	Penzance	Re-erecting the Pendrea Cross at St Buryan.	OC 5, no11, 477-8; OC 7, no7, 313.
1960s	Penzance	Erecting a slate tablet to mark the birthplace of Sir Humphry Davy on Market Jew Street Penzance.	OC 7, no7, 313.
1968	Penzance	Re-siting of a cross-base at Heamoor, Penzance.	AG Langdon (1997) Stone crosses in West Penwith, 7.
1973	Penzance	Discovery and re-erection of Mayon Cross in Sennen.	AG Langdon (1997) Stone crosses in West Penwith, 7.
1976	Penzance	Plaque set up to mark the Bleu Bridge inscribed stone at Gulval.	Information from Cedric Appleby, Recorder Penzance OCS.

2014	Penzance	Commissioned and set up a replica Borough of Penzance boundary stone in conjunction with Penzance Town Council.	OC 14, no11, 26-35 & illus.
2018	Penzance	Erected explanatory boards at Penzance Harbour in conjunction with Cornwall Council.	Information from Cedric Appleby, Recorder Penzance OCS.
2017	Perranzabuloe	Clearance and repainting of the white marker stones on the path to St Piran's Oratory.	OC 15, no5, 71-72 & illus.
1930	Redruth	Discovery of stone cross at Whitcross Hill Illogan.	OC 1, no12, 17-18 & illus.
c1933-35	Redruth	Murdoch House (fire-damaged since 1922) purchased by the President of the Society as their meeting place.	FOCS Annual report, 1934-35, 15; OC 7, no7, 315.
1934	Redruth	Part of a wheel-headed cross discovered in the rectory hedge and placed in the church on a wooden stand by WT Martin.	OC 4, no7, 245.
1943	Redruth	Roman milestone discovered at Menheer Farm, Gwennap re-erected by Messrs FG Barnett and FJB MacDowall for the Society.	OC 4, no7, 245.
1946	Redruth	St Euny's Holy Well cleaned and preserved.	OC 4, no7, 246.
1947	Redruth	Re-erecting the stone cross on a hedge at the top of Whitcross Hill, Illogan.	OC 4, no7, 244.
1956	Redruth	Information plaque erected at the remains of St Rumon's Chapel at Cross Street, Redruth.	OC 7, no7, 315.
1983	Redruth	Pet cemetery gravestones at Tehidy Mansion, Illogan rescued and re-sited.	OC 15, no8, 63-65 & illus.
2000	Redruth	Rededication of St Rumon's Cross which was re-sited outside Murdoch House, Cross Street, Redruth.	OC 12, no8, 60 & illus.
2004-05	Redruth	Re-siting and re-use of capstones from Tehidy Mansion courtyard, Illogan.	OC 15, no8, 62-63 & illus.
1966	St Agnes	Information tablet erected on a cottage at Blackwater to commemorate John Passmore Edwards.	OC 6, no12, 571.
1972	St Agnes	Information plaque fixed to Harmony Cottage at Trevellas to commemorate the birthplace of artist John Opie, unveiled by Prof. Charles Thomas.	FOCS Minute book March 4th 1972.
1937	St Austell	Clearance and maintenance of Towan Holy Well, Pentewan.	OC 7, no7, 319.
1953	St Austell	Clearance of Menacuddle Holy Well at St Austell.	OC 7, no7, 319.
2000	St Austell	Information plaque erected at the birthplace of writer and historian AL Rowse at 45 Tregonissey Road, St Austell.	OC 12, no8, 58-59 & illus.
2002	St Austell	Rescue of plaques from the demolished West Hill schools and re-siting them at St Austell.	OC 12, no12, 49-52 & illus.
2005	St Austell	Information plaque designed and erected on the old West Bridge, St Austell to record the name 'River Vinnick'.	OC 13, no6, 62-63.
2006	St Austell	Assisted with the clearance and restoration of Roche Holy Well.	OC 13, no10, 2-5 & illus.
2018	St Austell	Improvements to the setting of the Mengu Stone in St Austell churchyard.	OC 15, no7, 11-12 & illus.

1970	St Columb	Clearance around the Cross Hands (Crossy Ann) cross on Tregonetha Downs.	OC 7, no7, 320.
1970	St Columb	Boundary stones found at St Columb Major, St Wenn and Roche boundaries.	OC 7, no7, 320.
1980	St Columb	Capstone of prehistoric Devil's Quoit preserved and information plaque set up at Quoit, St Columb Major.	Information from Mrs Bill Glanville of St Columb OCS.
1984	St Columb	Reconstruction of Ruthvoes Holy Well at Ruthvoes, St Columb.	OC 10, no6, 262-8 & illus.
2014-18	St Columb	Discovery of a late medieval cross-base at the northern entrance to the town and preservation in the town's cemetery.	OC 15, no7, 25-26.
1992	St Gerrans & Porthscatho	Replanted 80 sycamore trees to recreate Trewince Avenue, after Dutch elm disease.	Information from N Meek, Recorder St Gerrans & Porthscatho OCS.
2001	St Gerrans & Porthscatho	Re-siting of medieval stone coffin at St Anthony in Roseland.	Information from N Meek, Recorder St Gerrans & Porthscatho OCS.
?	St Gerrans & Porthscatho	Assisted in repairs and repainting of cast-iron fingerposts in the Roseland area, with the Area of Outstanding Natural Beauty team from Cornwall Council.	Information from N Meek, Recorder St Gerrans & Porthscatho OCS.
?	St Gerrans & Porthscatho	Clearing of the Cregoe table-top grave in Gerrans churchyard.	Information from N Meek, Recorder St Gerrans & Porthscatho OCS.
2020	St Gerrans & Porthscatho	Assisted with the clearance of Dingerein Castle, an Iron Age hillfort, with the Area of Outstanding Natural Beauty team from Cornwall Council.	Information from N Meek, Recorder St Gerrans & Porthscatho OCS.
1930	St Ives	Erected tablet to the memory of John Davey (Cornish language speaker) on Zennor church tower.	OC 1, no12, 34; OC 4, no7, 246; OC 11, no2, 61-65 & illus.
c1933-38	St Ives	Restoration and consolidation of the medieval culverhouse on Bussow Moor, Towednack.	FOCS Annual report, 1934-35, 16; OC 4, no7, 246; OC 7, no7, 321.
1938	St Ives	Financed the re-erection of a cross at Youlstone in Warbstow and plaque.	AG Langdon (1992) Stone crosses in North Cornwall, 65; AG Langdon (1997) Stone crosses in West Penwith, 7.
1940	St Ives	Rediscovery of the Trevethoe Cross.	AG Langdon (1997) Stone crosses in West Penwith, 7.
1951-58	St Ives	Re-erecting stone cross at Halsetown.	OC 5, no9, 391.
1955	St Ives	Successfully campaigning, over 20 years, for the removal of public toilets built over the site of St Ia's holy well at Porthmeor, and the restoration of the granite well structure.	St Ives Times October 14th 1955.
1957	St Ives	Re-erecting Polmanter Cross at Halsetown.	AG Langdon (1997) Stone crosses in West Penwith, 7.
1964	St Ives	Re-erecting of a Latin cross at Church Lane, Lelant.	OC 6, no8, 361 & illus.
?	St Ives	Erected plaques on unspecified buildings.	OC 7, no7, 321.
1972	St Ives	Repositioning and re-erecting the Polmanter Cross at Halsetown, following damage.	AG Langdon (1997) Stone crosses in West Penwith, 7.
1998	St Ives	Re-siting and restoration of Penbeagle Cross at St Ives.	OC 12, no4, 12-19 & illus.

2003	St Ives	Information plaque to the Hain (shipping) family erected at the Memorial Gardens, St Ives.	OC 13, no2, 56-58 & illus.
2010	St Ives	Re-set Lelant Lane Cross after it had slipped down in the hedge.	OC 14, no9, 20-21.
2016	St Ives	Clearance of vegetation from the roof and walls of the medieval culverhouse at Bussow, St Ives.	OC 15, no4, 55-59 & illus.
1968	St Just & Pendeen	Re-erecting the Nanquidno Cross at St Just in Penwith.	AG Langdon (1997) *Stone crosses in West Penwith*, 7.
1970	St Just & Pendeen	Helped to organise a search with Geevor miners for a chi-rho cross thrown down a well.	AG Langdon (1997) *Stone crosses in West Penwith*, 8.
1969-70	St Ladoca	Restoration of a memorial wheel-cross to Canon RF Wise at Ladock churchyard.	OC 7, no7, 323.
2011	St Ladoca	Restoration of Ladock Glebe Holy Well.	OC 14, no6, 23-26 & illus.
?	Saltash	Care (maintenance) of the 18th-century tombstone of Dr William Martyn at Botusfleming.	OC 7, no7, 317.
1996	Saltash	Joint project with Saltash Heritage to reposition a cross-shaft from near the old vicarage to the west entrance of the churchyard.	OC 12, no2, 30-31.
2005-07	Saltash	Restoration of Trematon Pound at St Stephen by Saltash in assocation with Saltash Heritage and Saltash Town Council.	OC 13, no5, 64; OC 13, no9, 65-66 & illus.
1970	Truro	Information tablet erected at The Green, Truro to mark the birthplace of explorer Richard Lander.	OC 7, no7, 324.
1988	Truro	Financed support for lengthening and re-siting the High Cross, Truro.	OC 10, no8, 406-9 & illus.
1964	Tywardreath	Memorial plaque and stone erected at Castle Dore hillfort, near Fowey.	OC 6, no8, 359-60 & illus.
1939	Wadebridge	Repair and re-erecting of Three Holes Cross at Egloshayle.	OC 3, no6, 221-3 & illus.; OC 3, no7, 304-5; OC 4, no7, 247.
1947	Wadebridge	Restoration of Trequite Cross on the green at Trequite, St Kew.	OC 7, no7, 325.
1952	Wadebridge	Restoration of Job's Cross in St Kew.	OC 7, no7, 325.
c1961-62	Wadebridge	Instigated moves to restore the Trevanion Culverhouse, including fundraising.	OC 6, no3, 134-5.
1965	Wadebridge	Excavation of a medieval midden at Burniere, Egloshayle.	OC 7, no7, 325.
1969	Wadebridge	Restoration and re-erecting the Penwine Cross at the crossroads at Longstone, St Mabyn.	OC 7, no7, 325.
1970	Wadebridge	Installation of a new fence around the Jesus Well at St Minver.	OC 7, no7, 325.
1975	Wadebridge	Re-erection of the prehistoric Long Stone at Longstone in St Mabyn.	Wadebridge OCS minute book 1969-1980 (October 8th 1975).
1981	Wadebridge	Clearance and maintenance of the Jesus Well, St Minver, including repointing the roof.	OC 9, no5, 210.

1984	Wadebridge	Supplying and funding the installation of a Holy Water stoup on the wall of the south aisle at Egloshayle Church.	Wadebridge OCS minute book.
1989	Wadebridge	Repositioning Trelights Cross-base at Trelights, St Endellion.	OC 10, no9, 429-30 & illus.
1994	Wadebridge	Financial support towards the restoration of the White Cross at St Breock.	AG Langdon, Cross records.
1995	Wadebridge	Financial support towards the restoration of the St Teath churchyard cross.	AG Langdon, Cross records.
1995	Wadebridge	Preservation of a granite mooring bollard and erection of a plaque at Bridgend, Wadebridge.	Wadebridge OCS Minute book 1992-2008 (September 20th 1995).
2016	Wadebridge	Restoration of a cast-iron fingerpost at Bridgend.	OC 15, no4, 53-54 & illus.
2017	Wadebridge	Repainting of the text on the Queen Victoria Jubilee Stone at Egloshayle.	Information and photographs from David Bartlett, Recorder Wadebridge OCS.
2018	Wadebridge	Regular repainting of the White Cross at St Breock.	Information from David Bartlett, Recorder Wadebridge OCS.

Endnotes

INTRODUCTION

1. *Royal Cornwall Gazette*, 6 October 1865, 24 January 1867 and 4 January 1878.

2. *The Cornishman*, 8 September 1904.

3. *Royal Cornwall Gazette*, 8 October 1880. *Cornishman*, 13 May 1880, 11 November 1880, 17 November 1881 and 13 October 1920.

4. Amy Hale, 'Genesis of the Celto-Cornish Revival? L.C. Duncombe-Jewell and the Cowethas Kelto-Kernuak' in Phillip Payton (ed.), *Cornish Studies: Five*, University of Exeter Press, 1997, pp. 100-111. Ron Perry, 'Celtic Revival and Economic Development in Edwardian Cornwall' in Phillip Payton (ed.), *Cornish Studies: Five*, University of Exeter Press, 1997, pp. 112-24. See also *Cornishman*, 30 June 1904, 29 September 1904 and 28 April 1938.

5. In contrast the Penzance Natural History and Antiquarian Society remained local while Cowethas Kelto-Kernuak operated at the Cornwall-wide level but without a communal basis. The Old Cornwall movement was able to forge a hybrid model that effectively brought the two approaches together.

6. *Cornishman*, 8 September 1932.

7. Garry Tregidga, 'The Politics of the Celto-Cornish Revival, 1886-1939' in Phillip Payton (ed.), *Cornish Studies: Five*, University of Exeter Press, 1997, pp. 137, 145 and 146.

8. *Cornishman*, 16 August 1945 and 11 October 1945. However, at times there were signs of tension between Young Cornwall and Old Cornwall as was demonstrated in the case of Helston (*Cornishman*, 6 May 1948).

9. Hale, 'Genesis of the Celto-Cornish Revival?', p. 100.

10. *Cornishman*, 10 January 1929.

11. David Stark, *The Banners of the Old Cornwall Societies*, Federation of Old Cornwall Societies, 2007.

12. *Cornishman*, 28 April 1920.

THE FIRST 100 YEARS OF 'OLD CORNWALL'

1. The Constitution has been amended on a number of occasions but its core principles have not changed.

2. A brief account of May (really Mary) James's life is found in (2010) *Cornish bards of the St Ives area / Berdh Kernow a ranndir Porthia*, [n.p.]: Gorsedh Kernow, pp. 19-20. With a few exceptions, biographical sources are not cited for the many individuals whose names occur in this book, though summaries of their lives can often be found in the above publication or in one of the others in the area-by-area series issued by Gorsedh Kernow. Obituaries and other tributes can also be found in the *Old Cornwall* journal, and articles on some of the more eminent people are included in the *Oxford Dictionary of National Biography*.

3. The fullest account of Nance's life is found in Peter W Thomas and Derek R Williams (eds) (2007) *Setting Cornwall on its feet: Robert Morton Nance, 1873-1959*, London: Francis Boutle. The chapter by Brian Coombes on Nance and the Federation of Old Cornwall Societies ('Keeping Cornwall Cornish', pp. 223-237) is of particular relevance here. Nance's letter to the *St Ives Times* is quoted (pp. 3-4) in Brian J Stevens (2006) '"Gather ye the fragments that are left, that nothing be lost": the

origin of the Old Cornwall Societies', *Old Cornwall*, vol. 13, no. 6, Spring 2006, pp. 2-11. Many other useful quotations, from the *St Ives Times* and elsewhere, can be found in this instructive article by the former Dialect Recorder of the Federation of Old Cornwall Societies. A personal account of the movement, written at an earlier stage, appeared in the 1990 'Special Edition' of *Old Cornwall* (pp. i-iii): 'Three score years and ten' by Stanley Cock, then President of St Ives OCS, who had lived in the same cottage as Nance in Nancledra.

4. *Old Cornwall*, vol. 2, no. 8, Winter 1934, p. 5.

5. R Morton Nance (1956) *The Cledry plays,* Marazion/Penzance: Federation of Old Cornwall Societies.

6. The most accessible and concise source of information on the Cornish Gorsedh (college of bards) is Rod Lyon (2008) *Gorseth Kernow / The Cornish Gorsedd: what it is and what it does,* [n.p.]: Gorseth Kernow. (The spelling 'Gorsedh' is now the 'official' one when referring to the Cornish body and is therefore the one used in this book. 'Gorsedd' is used for the Welsh body or in a general sense. In quotations or equivalent contexts, the spelling used at the time is of course retained.)

7. Quoted in *Old Cornwall*, vol. 7, no. 11, Autumn 1972, p. 480.

8. AK Hamilton Jenkin (1970) 'How it started' in *Old Cornwall*, vol. 7, no. 7, Autumn 1970, pp. 289-292.

9. The story of the St Ives Museum is told in Brian J Stevens (ed.) (2003) *St. Ives Museum*, St Ives: St Ives Museum; see also Cyril Noall (1977) 'The making of a museum' in *Old Cornwall*,

vol. 8, no. 9, Autumn 1977, pp. 450-456. Other Old Cornwall Societies have similarly fruitful relationships with their local museum (or equivalent), particularly in the essential business of Recording, while others again make equally suitable provision for their archives and associated material in different ways. The very active Liskeard OCS (founded 1928), for example, now has its headquarters within the town's Stuart House, where its minute books, photographs, maps and other research materials are kept (see *Old Cornwall*, vol. 12, no. 7, Autumn 2000, pp. 58-59).

10. The latest version of the booklet on this subject is Merv Davey (2019) *Tansys Golowan: the Cornish Midsummer Bonfire ceremonies*, St Agnes: Federation of Old Cornwall Societies. This was issued to mark the 90th anniversary of the revival of the custom by the Federation in 1929 and is based on research by Cyril Noall and Yvonne Gilbert for previous versions.

11. The fullest account of Jenner's life is found in Derek R Williams (ed.) (2004) *Henry and Katharine Jenner*, London: Francis Boutle. Again, the chapter by Brian Coombes ("Gathering the fragments…': Henry Jenner, the Old Cornwall Societies and Gorseth Kernow', pp. 161-181) is particularly relevant.

12. Williams, p. 161.

13. Minute book 1 of the St Ives Old Cornwall Society. This and subsequent minute books, as well as other valuable archival material, are kept at the St Ives Museum and have been used in the writing of this chapter. Some of these records incorporate press cuttings supplementing the written minutes.

14. Among reports of this notable event was at least one in Cornish: *An Gannas*, 519, Mis-Meurth 2020, p. 12.

15. See Brian Sullivan (1984) 'Hayle O.C.S. and Henry Jenner' in *Old Cornwall*, vol. 9, no. 11, Autumn 1984, pp. 522-525. This article follows 'The first Grand Bard of Cornwall' (p. 521), a description of two ceremonies commemorating the 50th anniversary of Jenner's death. See also CJ Appleby (1999) 'Hayle Old Cornwall Society at seventy five' in *Old Cornwall*, vol. 12, no. 4, Spring 1999, pp. 44-45. For the very successful Redruth OCS, see e.g. *West Briton* August 30th 2012, where the Old Cornwall Movement is likened, not for the first time, to 'a free university.'

16. Brian Coombes in Thomas & Williams, p. 227, including quotations from Jenner's presidential address to the Royal Cornwall Polytechnic Society 'The Renaissance of Merry England [sic]' as printed in the Society's *Annual Report 1921-22*, p. 60. Amy Hale, in her review of Williams, op. cit., feels that Jenner was perhaps more of a 'figurehead' than a 'strategist' in the emerging Cornish Revival, as implicitly acknowledged by Nance in the terms in which he invited Jenner to be President of the St Ives Old Cornwall Society (Amy Hale (2005) 'Rethinking Henry Jenner' in *Cornish Studies, Second series*, 13, pp. 307-312). In fact Jenner acknowledged as much himself (Williams, p. 168). He was after all 80 when he became Grand Bard so it is perhaps surprising that he played as active a role as he did in the fledgling Old Cornwall Movement and Gorsedh. This role, based on his iconic status, was by any measure enormously important in establishing the foundation on which their durability is based (Brian Coombes in Williams, pp. 175-177).

17. The Federation minute books to 1994 are held at Kresen Kernow, Redruth with other Old Cornwall research material, including the important record book covering 1924-30 kept by J Sims Carah as President of Camborne OCS. The minute books were used extensively in the writing of this chapter. (Until 2020 these records were held at the Courtney Library, Royal Institution of Cornwall, Truro, another important repository of Old Cornwall and Gorsedh material.) Unreferenced statements and quotations regarding the Federation in this chapter can be assumed to derive from these records, which include unsourced press cuttings supplementing the written minutes.

18. Both Federation and Society pilgrimages have remained a feature of Old Cornwall activity throughout the movement's history. Their purpose, as indicated by Nance, has often been submerged by a tendency to make them no more than companionable outings. A balance between the two was advocated by Terry Knight in *Old Cornwall*, vol. 12, no. 9, Autumn 2001, p. 1.

19. *Cornish Times*, December 14th 1928.

20. As reflected in the journal since the Spring 2012 issue, the organisation can now be referred to as the Federation of 'Old Cornwall' Societies, the addition of inverted commas making a subtle improvement to the potential impression given of the organisation's nature through its name.

21. Cuttings of both features comprise part of the contents of a book ('Henderson's Notes') among the St Ives Old Cornwall Society archives. Other contents include cuttings on Charles Henderson's university extension lectures in Penzance. A report on the first lecture begins: 'All who are interested in the Cornish people who lived on our hilltops in prehistoric times, should hasten to join the Old Cornwall Societies' (*Cornishman* November 19th 1924). Elsewhere in the book (p. 17) Jenner, Nance, Hamilton Jenkin and Henderson himself are shown to be supporters of the establishment of a university at Exeter as a development of the University College of the South West. For JH Rowe, see Hugh Miners & Treve Crago (2002) *Tolzethan: the life and times of Joseph Hambley Rowe*, [n.p.], Gorseth Kernow.

22. John ch. 6, v. 12b (English according to the King James Version). The spelling of this motto on the journal cover changed to that of Nance's Unified Cornish (UC) with vol. 5, no. 9, 1958. The original spelling is still sometimes used for the motto, as is UC spelling and that of the Standard Written Form of Cornish (SWF).

23. Francis Cargeeg, Deputy Grand Bard of Cornwall, in a paper read as a call to arms at the Closed Gorsedh in 1963. *New Cornwall* printed it as 'A Cornish approach to Cornish history' over three months that year. It is quoted in Derek R Williams (ed.) (2013) *Richard G. Jenkin: a great son of Cornwall*, London, Francis Boutle, p. 146.

24. Notwithstanding Nance's words it would be quite wrong to say that academic or 'learned' articles have had no place in *Old Cornwall*, though of course articles do not have to be academic to be well researched, interesting and useful. Jenner, Nance and Hamilton Jenkin were scholarly in their different ways, and other contributors have included GH Doble, Charles Henderson, Oliver Padel, Martin Picken, AL Rowse, Charles Thomas and James Whetter. Many members of Old Cornwall, speakers at OC meetings and other helpers continue to display a wide range of specialist knowledge, as such people have always done.

25. *Old Cornwall*, vol. 7, no. 7, Autumn 1970, p. 290.

26. *Old Cornwall*, vol. 14, no. 2, Spring 2010, pp. 2-7.

27. For the Federation's wish to establish a Gorsedh not merely for its own sake but as the core of a future Cornish Eisteddfod, see the *West Briton* January 10th 1927.

28. Philip Payton (1996) *Cornwall*, Fowey: Alexander Associates, p. 268 (Revised ed. (2017) *Cornwall: a history*, Exeter: University of Exeter Press, p. 286); original ed. quoted by Brian Coombes in Thomas & Williams, p. 230.

29. *Old Cornwall*, vol. 1, no. 2, October 1925, pp. 41-42.

30. Brian Coombes in Thomas & Williams, p. 229, referring to and quoting correspondence between Nance and D Rhys Phillips, then Secretary of the Celtic Congress, in 1925 (letters 3591 and 3592 in the Phillips 2 Collection, Llyfrgell Genedlaethol Cymru / National Library of Wales).

31. This 1927 pamphlet was updated and reissued, sometimes accompanied by a summarising flier, in 1977 and 1982. David Stark produced a revision of the pamphlet in 2003 and again, with further slight revisions, in 2004. A newly-written leaflet by Terry Knight, *Do you love Cornwall?*, was issued in 2009, revised slightly for a reprint in 2010 and redrafted by the author in 2011. This was again revised as *Old Cornwall*

Societies. What are they? What do they do? in 2018 and with minor updates again in 2019. A major purpose of such material is of course to attract new members to Old Cornwall.

32. Henry Jenner (1928) 'The Gorsedd of Boscawen-Un: a paper read at the meeting of the Federation of Old Cornwall Societies at Boscawen-Un, on June 25th, 1927' in *Old Cornwall*, vol. 1, no. 7, April 1928, pp. 1-6.

33. See WM Symons (1970) 'Camborne O.C.S. – an early project' in *Old Cornwall*, vol. 7, no. 7, Autumn 1970, pp. 299-300.

34. *Western Morning News* April 23rd 1928.

35. Henry Jenner (c. 1929) *Bards, druids and the Gorsedd*, manuscript in the RM Nance Collection at the Courtney Library, Royal Institution of Cornwall, part of which is reproduced in Williams (2004), pp. 190-196 (quotation from p. 190).

36. See David Stark (2007) *The banners of the Old Cornwall Societies*, [n.p.]: Federation of Old Cornwall Societies. The principal occasions on which the banners are displayed or paraded are of course Old Cornwall meetings and festivals.

37. Terry Knight, *West Briton* October 7th 2010.

38. Henry Jenner ([1928]) *Who are the Celts and what has Cornwall to do with them?*, St Ives: Federation of Old Cornwall Societies, p. 11. This was published in the same 'black on gold' livery as earlier issues of *Old Cornwall*.

39. See Thomas & Williams, p. 332; Karin Easton (2018) 'Dr Ralph Dunstan, 1857-1933' in *Old Cornwall*, vol. 15, no. 7, Autumn 2018, pp. 3-10, particularly pp. 8-9, including quotations from Merv Davey.

40. Ralph Dunstan (1929) 'The Cornish Song Book (Lyver Canow Kernewek)' in *Old Cornwall*, vol. 1, no. 9, April 1929, pp. 35-37.

41. The 'Ultimatum' was reprinted in *Old Cornwall*, vol. 14, no. 12, Spring 2015, pp. 2-3.

42. See Thomas & Williams, p. 189.

43. *West Briton* January 12th 1933.

44. The surviving letters from Sarre to Hooper are part of Gorsedh Kernow's Hooper archives, held at Kresen Kernow, Redruth. The letters were printed, with an introduction, in the *Journal of the St Agnes Museum Trust*; the one quoted here (February 3rd 1933) can be found in no. 17, 2010, pp. 42-44.

45. A version of the second lesson read at the 1933 service was printed in *Old Cornwall*, vol. 6, no. 12, Spring 1967, pp. 539-540.

46. This was not the only such troupe. 'Will Blewett's Old Cornwall Players' are mentioned in *Old Cornwall*, vol. 7, no. 5, p. 220.

47. *Old Cornwall*, vol. 2, no. 7, Summer 1934, p. 42; see also vol. 2, no. 8, Winter 1934, pp. 1-5.

48. See *Old Cornwall*, vol. 2, no. 9, Summer 1935, p. 40.

49. *West Briton* October 7th 1937, reporting on the Federation AGM of October 2nd.

50. Copies of the two reports are held at Kresen Kernow.

51. *West Briton* October 7th 1937.

52. *West Briton* (?) October 13th 1938 (cutting in Federation minute book 2).

53. *West Briton* March 2nd 1939.

54. *Old Cornwall*, vol. 2, no. 9, Summer 1935, p. 34.

55. See *West Briton* October 10th 1940.

56. See PAS Pool, revised and updated by Derek R Williams (2007) 'A bibliography of the writings of Robert Morton Nance' in Thomas & Williams, pp. 331-353.

57. Minute book 1 of the St Ives Old Cornwall Society, Annual Meeting October 6th 1942.

58. See *West Briton* October 7th 1943.

59. See *West Briton* October 10th 1946; separate cutting in Federation minute book 3.

60. See *West Briton* April 28th 1949.

61. The text referred to is JEB Gover (1948) *The place-names of Cornwall*, typescript, Courtney Library, Royal Institution of Cornwall. Ironically, although Gover's work remained unpublished, the English Place-Name Society was the publisher of a work which used it (with great caution) as one of its sources: OJ Padel (1985) *Cornish place-name elements*, Nottingham: English Place-Name Society. Though its English provenance may be frowned upon, this is an essential work for any in-depth study of Cornish place-names.

62. *West Briton* March 22nd 1951.

63. *West Briton* October 9th 1952.

64. *St Ives Times* September 11th 1953.

65. *Cornishman* March 7th 1957.

66. An obituary was of course published in *Old Cornwall*: JL Palmer (1960) 'Nyns-yu marow Mordon', vol. 5, no. 11, 1960, pp. 450-451. Despite its Cornish title the tribute is in English.

67. Amy Hale (1998) *Gathering the fragments: performing contemporary Celtic identities in Cornwall*, DPhil. dissertation, University of California Los Angeles, p. 77.

68. *Old Cornwall* vol. 6, no. 5, Autumn 1963, pp. 196-205.

69. 'The strength of the movement lies in the freedom of the individual societies to develop their individual interests. This has led to a healthy diversity while following the objectives of the founders' ('Federation and Society notes' in *Old Cornwall*, vol. 9, no. 4, Spring 1981, pp. 159-160 (p. 160).)

70. In one sense this motto can hardly be called new. A form of it was used by Henry Jenner and was adopted as the motto of Tyr ha Tavas in the early 1930s. See *Old Cornwall*, vol. 2, no. 5, Summer 1933, p. 29.

71. *Old Cornwall*, vol. 7, no. 7, Autumn 1970.

72. See *Old Cornwall*, vol. 9, no. 7, Autumn 1982, p. 364. The meeting was held at Redruth and had been suggested by Redruth OCS at the Federation Spring Meeting. Other Recorders whose work is described in the journal are Frank Carpenter, St Agnes (vol. 11, no. 1, Autumn 1991, pp. 25-27) and John Rapson, Liskeard (vol. 11, no. 9, Autumn 1995, pp. 434-436).

73. *Old Cornwall*, vol. 7, no. 7, Autumn 1970, p. 327. The gesture was reciprocated in *Old Cornwall* by the then President of the FOCS, Hugh Miners, for the 50th anniversary of the Gorsedh (vol. 8, no. 11, Autumn 1978, p. 519).

74. *Falmouth Packet* November 6th 1970.

75. Charles Thomas (1971) 'The next fifty years' in *Old Cornwall*, vol. 7, no. 8, Spring 1971, pp. 337-349.

76. The closest approach to a complete Cornish place-name survey is Padel (see note 61), a work totally

unconnected with Old Cornwall in which very local names, unrecorded in writing, are of course not covered. Dr Padel usefully summarises 'the rules of place-name study' in his *Old Cornwall* article 'Bolventor, Pennycomequick, Dunheved' (vol. 8, no. 10, Spring 1978, pp. 480-484). At the Federation Spring Meeting in 1971 it was urged that Societies should be pro-active in taking advantage of local authorities' willingness to use Cornish names for new building developments, by suggesting and thus perpetuating traditional names used by local people.

77. This is reflected in the Federation's securing various Holyer an Gof awards, which are presented for Cornish publishing. It has also acted as a sponsor of the awards. In 2013 the Federation won the Holyer an Gof trophy itself, for Andrew Langdon's *Wade-Bridge* (2012), which also won in its class. See *Old Cornwall*, vol. 14, no. 9, Autumn 2013, pp. 1-2; *Western Morning News* July 27th 2013; *West Briton* August 1st 2013.

78. The structure was further expanded later and has now changed altogether.

79. Charles Thomas (2012) *Gathering the fragments*, Sheffield: Cornovia Press.

80. *West Briton*, January 25th 1973.

81. *Old Cornwall*, vol. 9, no. 6, Spring 1982, p. 261.

82. See *Old Cornwall*, vol. 14, no. 1, Autumn 2009, p. 63.

83. See *Old Cornwall*, vol. 10, no. 4, Spring 1987, p. 157.

84. *Old Cornwall*, vol. 13, no. 10, Spring 2008, p. 41.

85. *Old Cornwall*, vol. 10, no. 10, Spring 1990, pp. 469-470.

86. During the hiatus following Joan Rendell's resignation as Secretary, Terry Knight, as Deputy President, took on many of her duties to help President Ron Opie. These included a concentrated attempt to amend the Federation Constitution, work which was completed by Ivor Corkell after he became Secretary in 2009. As Secretary he proved to be a real asset to the Federation, a clear thinker who was prepared to take on numerous tasks which led to marked enhancements of the organisation's efficiency. He and Terry Knight were prime movers in the important rethink which injected new life into the Old Cornwall Movement in the first decades of the 21st century.

87. *Old Cornwall*, vol. 14, no. 3, Autumn 2010, pp. 64-65.

88. Email message from Stephanie Thomas, President and Hon. Secretary of Bodmin OCS, to Terry Knight, February 10th 2020.

89. See note 17.

90. One of the new features under Alan Pearson's editorship was a Cornwall-centred crossword, which started in 1993. A puzzle of some kind has appeared in the journal regularly ever since that time.

91. See also his editorial in *Old Cornwall*, vol. 13, no. 8, Spring 2007, p. 1.

92. Hale, pp. 74, 78.

93. Bernard Deacon (2007) *A concise history of Cornwall*, Cardiff: University of Wales Press, p. 188.

94. Newspaper cutting October 8th 1953, in Federation minute book 4.

95. Thomas & Williams, p. 229.

96. Hale, p. 79.

97. *Old Cornwall*, vol. 13, no. 5, Autumn 2005, p. 1.

98. *Old Cornwall*, vol. 13, no.10, Spring 2008, p. 1.

99. *West Briton* March 6th 2008. For evidence of continued growth, with statistics, see *West Briton* March 12th 2009.

100. *Old Cornwall*, vol. 14, no. 1, Autumn 2009, p. 1.

101. See *Old Cornwall*, vol. 14, no. 9, Autumn 2013, pp. 2-3; *Western Morning News* July 9th 2013; *West Briton* July 11th 2013; *Cornishman* July 25th 2013.

102. Two examples of more advanced study in the 20th century are: Martyn F Wakelin (1975) *Language and history in Cornwall*, Leicester: Leicester University Press; David J North & Adam Sharpe (1980) *A word-geography of Cornwall*, Pool: Institute of Cornish Studies. The card database for the latter is held at Kresen Kernow, Redruth.

103. *Old Cornwall*, vol. 14, no. 4, Spring 2011, p. 4.

104. The aims of the movement were reiterated as a call to action ('Are you a do-er?') in *Old Cornwall*, vol. 15, no. 10, Spring 2020, p. 67.

105. *Old Cornwall*, vol. 14, no. 8, Spring 2013, p. 3; see also vol. 13, no. 3, Autumn 2004, p. 1.

106. See also *West Briton* December 5th 2013.

107. Terry Knight was the first holder of this position, which had been set up during his Presidency (2009-12) with the help of Secretary Ivor Corkell and at the instigation of Bill Glanville. With Barrie Bennetts concentrating on press publicity for successive issues of the journal, the Federation Publicity Officer sought coverage of Cornwall-wide OC events – a thankless task in view of the increasing parochialism of the traditional media.

108. Terry Knight, *Western Morning News* July 21st 2015.

109. See *Old Cornwall*, vol. 15, no. 8, Spring 2019, pp. 1-2.

110. See Terry Knight's editorial in *Old Cornwall*, vol. 12, no. 12, Spring 2003, p. 1.

111. Terry Knight (as Federation President), *Western Morning News* July 19th 2010.

112. Terry Knight, *West Briton* October 7th 2010.

113. Terry Knight's editorial in *Old Cornwall*, vol. 14, no. 7, Autumn 2012, p. 1.

Acknowledgements: My thanks are due to the other contributors to this book for all the help they have given me in compiling this chapter and editing other contributions. I am also grateful to Clive Benney; Ivor Corkell; Karin Easton; Dr Amy Hale; Ellie Jones; Tony Mansell; Len Sheppard; Jane Tutte; Derek Williams; Angela Broome at the Courtney Library, Royal Institution of Cornwall, Truro; Margaret and Brian Stevens at St Ives Museum; Brian Oldham of Liskeard Old Cornwall Society; and David Thomas at Kresen Kernow, Redruth. Without their willing assistance the task would have been much more difficult.

OLD CORNWALL AND THE CORNISH LANGUAGE

1. *Old Cornwall*, vol. 7, no. 7, Autumn 1970, p. 290.

2. 'Cornel', the Cornish word used here for 'corner' (in some systems spelt 'kornel'), is now listed in dictionaries as feminine in gender, so that the second word in this phrase would currently be spelt with an initial 'G' rather than 'K'.

3. See note 56 (previous chapter).

4. R Morton Nance ([1929]) *Cornish for all*, St Ives: Federation of Old Cornwall Societies.

5. WD Watson ([1931]) *First steps in Cornish*, St Ives: Federation of Old Cornwall Societies; ASD Smith (1931) *Lessons in spoken Cornish. Part I*, St Ives: Federation of Old Cornwall Societies.

6. Mordon [RM Nance] ([1932]) *An Balores*, St Ives: Federation of Old Cornwall Societies.

7. *Old Cornwall*, vol. 2, no. 6, Winter 1933, p. 43.

8. R Morton Nance & ASD Smith (1934) *An English-Cornish dictionary*, St Ives: Federation of Old Cornwall Societies.

9. Edwin Chirgwin (1937) *Say it in Cornish*, St Ives: Federation of Old Cornwall Societies.

10. Federation minute book 3; *Western Morning News* October 6th 1941. Later in life Rowse was very complimentary about the Old Cornwall Movement. See *Old Cornwall*, vol. 8, no. 5, Autumn 1975, p. 220.

11. *West Briton*, March 22nd 1951.

12. *Old Cornwall*, vol. 4, no. 11, Summer 1950, pp. 429-430 & 431-434.

13. R Morton Nance (1951) *A guide to Cornish place-names*, Marazion: Federation of Old Cornwall Societies.

14. Publications Fund flier; *Old Cornwall*, vol. 5, no. 1, Summer 1951, p. 12; *Cornishman* October 11th 1951.

15. *St Ives Times*, October 17th 1952.

16. See PAS Pool (1968) 'The Cornish Language Board' in *Old Cornwall*, vol. 7, no. 2, Spring 1968, pp. 97-99.

17. *Cornish Language* (IBC/LP/3624). See *Old Cornwall*, vol. 7, no. 5, Autumn 1969, p. 193.

18. The fullest account of Richard Jenkin's life is found in Williams (2013).

Jenkin, like Hooper, served the Federation in various capacities over many years, and his major role in the Old Cornwall Movement as a whole (with particular reference to Helston) is described in the chapter 'A voice heard all over the parish' by Ann Trevenen Jenkin (pp. 107-123), and his involvement with *New Cornwall* in the chapter 'Breathing the fire of Cornish patriotism' by Derek R Williams (pp. 125-164). The Helston Society's Trevenen Jenkin Lecture is an annual event.

19. *Old Cornwall*, vol. 10, no. 9, Autumn 1989, pp. 431-440.

20. *Old Cornwall*, vol. 10, no. 11, Autumn 1990, pp. 531-535.

21. *Old Cornwall*, vol. 6, no. 5, Autumn 1963, p. 198.

PRACTICAL WORK UNDERTAKEN BY OLD CORNWALL SOCIETIES

1. Henry Jenner (1925) 'The preservation of ancient monuments in Cornwall' in *Old Cornwall*, vol. 1, no. 1, April 1925, pp. 7-9.

2. John ch. 6, vv. 8-13.

3. 'Safeguarding of Cornwall's ancient monuments' in *Old Cornwall*, vol. 2, no. 8, Winter 1934, p. 29.

4. H O'Neill Hencken (1932) *The archaeology of Cornwall and Scilly*, London: Methuen, pp. 291-320.

5. Wadebridge OCS records.

6. Letter from Mrs Winifred Groser, Recorder of Wadebridge OCS, to Mr J Clemo at Bodmin OCS (Wadebridge OCS records).

7. Charles Thomas (1962), Editorial in *Cornish Archaeology*, 1, pp. 2-4.

8. Jacqueline A Nowakowski & Henrietta Quinnell (2011) T*revelgue Head, Cornwall*, Truro: Cornwall Archaeological Unit.

9. Societies subscribing to the Castle Dore excavations were St Austell, Bodmin, St Ives, Liskeard, Penryn & Falmouth, Penzance, Redruth, Truro and Wadebridge.

10. CA Ralegh Radford (1951) 'Report on the excavations at Castle Dore' in *Journal of the Royal Institution of Cornwall, New series*, vol. 1, Appendix.

11. Nowakowski & Quinnell, pp. 7, 8, 23.

12. Charles Woolf (1978) *Newquay Old Cornwall Society / Cowethas Kernow Goth Towan Blystry, 1928-1978: fifty years of events, personalities and records*, Newquay: Newquay Old Cornwall Society, p. 8.

13. A slate plaque next to the Longstone records the event.

14. William Borlase (1754) *Observations on the antiquities historical and monumental, of the county of Cornwall*, Oxford: W. Jackson, p. 364.

15. William J Stephens (1939) 'Inscribed stone at Indian Queens' in *Old Cornwall*, vol. 3, no. 6, Winter 1939, p. 247.

16. Charles Thomas (1994) *And shall these mute stones speak?*, Cardiff: University of Wales Press, pp. 282-283.

17. Thomas (1994), p. 328.

18. Elisabeth Okasha (1993) *Corpus of early Christian inscribed stones of South-West Britain*, London: Leicester University Press, p. 324.

19. John Watts Trevan (2010) *Summary memoirs of the parish of Endellion, prior to the year 1834*, Port Isaac: Port Isaac Local History Group.

20. https://www.atlasobscura.com/places/doyden-castle.

21. HJ Willmott (1933) 'Long Cross restored to Long Cross' in *Old Cornwall*, vol. 2, no. 6, Winter 1933, pp. 17-18.

22. Thomas (1994), p. 264.

23. Arthur G Langdon (1906) 'Early Christian monuments' in William Page (ed.) *The Victoria History of the County of Cornwall. Vol. 1*, London: Archibald Constable, p. 420.

24. JT Blight (1861) *A week at the Land's End*, London: Longman, p. 179.

25. Okasha, pp. 205-207.

26. Joseph Polsue (1868) *A complete parochial history of the County of Cornwall. Vol. 2*, Truro: William Lake, p. 293.

27. Arthur G Langdon (1896) *Old Cornish crosses*, Truro: Joseph Pollard, p. 271.

28. Helen Derrington (1970) 'St. Just and Pendeen O.C.S.' in *Old Cornwall*, vol. 7, no. 7, Autumn 1970, pp. 321-322 (p. 322).

29. Phyllis Head (1992) 'The restoration and rededication of a Celtic cross' in *Old Cornwall*, vol. 11, no. 2, Spring 1992, pp. 72-74.

30. 'Cornish cross removed from Lelant hedge', *St Ives Times* June 2nd 1964; Andrew G Langdon (1997) *Stone crosses in West Penwith*, [n.p.]: Federation of Old Cornwall Societies, p. 8.

31. Ashley Rowe (1936) 'Re-erection of Polmennor Cross' in *Old Cornwall*, vol. 3, no. 4, Winter 1938, p. 163.

32. Information from correspondence with George Ansell, January 5th 2004.

33. Andrew G Langdon (2005) *Stone crosses in East Cornwall*, 2nd ed., [n.p.]: Federation of Old Cornwall Societies, p. 48.

34. GE Ellis (1939) 'Middle Moor Cross' in *Old Cornwall*, vol. 3, no. 6, Winter 1939, pp. 237-239.

35. CKC Andrew (1939) 'Three Holes Cross, Egloshayle', ibid., pp. 221-223.

36. Arthur G Langdon (1896), p. 166.

37. *Cornish & Devon Post*, Launceston, June 10th 1950.

38. Arthur G Langdon (1896), pp. 213-214.

39. Photograph in the *Cornishman* February 28th 1957.

40. 'Cornish cross removed from Lelant hedge', *St Ives Times* June 2nd 1964.

41. Andrew G Langdon (2013) 'Cornish cross 2009-2011 update' in *Old Cornwall*, vol. 14, No. 9, Autumn 2013, pp. 13-22 (pp. 20-21).

42. Andrew G Langdon (1997), pp. 8, 60.

43. 'Pendrea Cross, St. Buryan' in *Old Cornwall*, vol. 5, no. 11, 1960, pp. 477-478; *Cornishman* May 14th 1959.

44. William J Stephens (1914) 'A hitherto undescribed cross at St. Colan' in *Journal of the Royal Institution of Cornwall*, vol. 19, pt 3, pp. 395-399.

45. Woolf, pp. 20-21; Charles Woolf (1972) 'Colan Cross' in *Old Cornwall*, vol. 7, no. 11, Autumn 1972, pp. 518-519.

46. Andrew G Langdon (2017) 'White crosses' in *Old Cornwall*, vol. 15, no. 4, Spring 2017, pp. 45-52 (p. 47).

47. 'Something done' in *Old Cornwall*, vol. 4, no. 7, Summer 1948, pp. 241-247 (p. 244).

48. Andrew G Langdon (2017), p. 46.

49. See survey of Purbeck marble coffin-shaped slabs in the Church Monuments Society newsletters.

50. Peter King (2013) 'Gathering up the crumbs' in *Old Cornwall*, vol. 14, no. 9, Autumn 2013, pp. 45-48.

51. 'Monk's granite coffin resited by Cornish history enthusiasts', *Western Morning News* November 29th 2001.

52. Charles Henderson (1925) *The Cornish church guide*, Truro: Oscar Blackford, p. 51.

53. Nicholas Orme (2010) *A history of the County of Cornwall [The Victoria History of the County of Cornwall]. Vol. 2: Religious History to 1560*, London: Institute of Historical Research, p. 75.

54. PO Leggat & DV Leggat (1993) *A tale of two mediaeval chapels in Lammana parish (Looe)*, West Looe: the authors, pp. 9-11.

55. 'Helston O.C.S.' in *Old Cornwall*, vol. 7, no. 7, Autumn 1970, pp. 302-304 (p. 304).

56. Ann Preston-Jones (2005) *Towan Holy Well, St Austell, Cornwall: recording and repointing*, Truro: Cornwall County Council, Historic Environment Service, p. 12; RE Evans & GW Prettyman (1994) *Pictorial Pentewan*, Pentewan: Pentewan Publications, p. 37.

57. MM Prettyman (1992) 'Towan Well gets a spring clean' in *Old Cornwall*, vol. 11, no. 3, Autumn 1992, pp. 126-127.

58. David Stark (2004) 'Society News: Pentewan' in *Old Cornwall*, vol. 13, no. 2, Spring 2004, pp. 58-59.

59. Ann Preston-Jones, op. cit.; David Stark (2005) 'Towan Holy Well' in *Old Cornwall*, vol. 13, no. 4, Spring 2005, pp. 63-64.

60. George J Lomer (1970) 'St. Austell O.C.S.' in *Old Cornwall*, vol. 7, no. 7, Autumn 1970, pp. 318-320 (p. 319); David Stark & Carole Stark (2005) *St Austell Old Cornwall Society: a celebration of its 80th anniversary, 1925-2005*, St Austell: St Austell Old Cornwall Society.

61. F Hoyle (1970) 'Looe O.C.S.' in *Old Cornwall*, vol. 7, no. 7, Autumn 1970, pp. 305-306 (p. 305).

62. Rachel E White (1970) 'Madron O.C.S.' in *Old Cornwall*, vol. 7, no. 7, Autumn 1970, pp. 307-308 (p. 307).

63. Conveyances and newspaper reports in Liskeard OCS Archives.

64. M Quiller-Couch & L Quiller-Couch (1894) *Ancient and holy wells of Cornwall*, London: Chas. J. Clark, p. 196.

65. Richard Cole (2007) *Roche Holy Well, Cornwall: consolidation work and archaeological recording*, Truro: Cornwall County Council, Historic Environment Service; see also David Stark (2008) 'The restoration of Roche Holy Well' in *Old Cornwall*, vol. 13, no. 10, Spring 2008, pp. 2-5.

66. MHN Cuthbert Atchley (1938) 'Report upon preservation works done by Old Cornwall Societies ... 1936-7' in *Old Cornwall*, vol. 3, no. 3, Summer 1938, pp. 128-129 (p. 128); quoted in Alfred Lane-Davies (1970) *Holy wells of Cornwall*, Penzance: Federation of Old Cornwall Societies, p. 82.

67. Woolf (1978), pp. 17, 19, 20; *Old Cornwall*, vol. 7, no. 7, Autumn 1970, p. 310.

68. Quiller-Couch & Quiller-Couch, p. 192.

69. 'Wadebridge O.C.S.' in *Old Cornwall*, vol. 7, no. 7, Autumn 1970, p. 325.

70. Quiller-Couch & Quiller-Couch, p. 90.

71. Michael Cole (2012) 'Ladock's holy well restored' in *Old Cornwall*, vol. 14, no. 6, Spring 2012, pp. 23-26.

72. Charles Henderson (1953-56) 'The ecclesiastical history of the 109 parishes of West Cornwall. 1' in *Journal of the Royal Institution of Cornwall, New series, vol. 2, Supplement 1*, pp. 86-87.

73. St Columb Old Cornwall Society (1988) 'Ruthvoes Holy Well project' in *Old Cornwall*, vol. 10, no. 6, Spring 1988, pp. 262-268.

74. Quiller-Couch & Quiller-Couch, pp. 211-213.

75. Beryl Tapp (1995) 'The restoration and re-dedication of Scarlett's Well', in *Old Cornwall*, vol. 11, no. 9, Autumn 1995, pp. 433-434.

76. Bill Burnett (2001) 'Ludgvan OCS & Tregellast Well' in *Old Cornwall*, vol. 12, no. 9, Autumn 2001, pp. 56-58.

77. MM Prettyman (1992) 'Gathering up the crumbs' in *Old Cornwall*, vol. 11, no. 2, Spring 1992, p. 74.

78. John McCann & Pamela McCann (2003) *The dovecotes of historical Somerset*, Martock: Somerset Vernacular Building Research Group, p. 27.

79. Rosemary Robertson & Geoffrey Gilbert (1979) *Some aspects of the domestic archaeology of Cornwall*, Pool: Institute of Cornish Studies / Cornwall Committee for Rescue Archaeology.

80. TW Cleave 'Trevanion "Culverhay"' in *Old Cornwall*, vol. 3, no. 1, Summer 1937, pp. 1-2; with 'Further note' by CKC Andrew, pp. 2-4.

81. WF Trestain (1962) 'Trevanion Culverhay' in *Old Cornwall*, vol. 6, no. 3, Autumn 1962, pp. 134-135.

82. Andrew G Langdon & Brian Stevens (2017) 'The culver-house at Lower Bussow, St Ives' in *Old Cornwall*, vol. 15, no. 4, Spring 2017, pp. 55-59; a photograph of the building appears on the front cover.

83. 'Helston O.C.S.' in *Old Cornwall*, vol. 7, no. 7, Autumn 1970, pp. 302-304 (p. 303).

84. N Perry (1999) 'Cross is link to the past', *West Briton* May 6th 1999.

85. Donald R Rawe & Jack Ingrey (1984) *Padstow and district*, Padstow: Lodenek Press, pp. 49-50.

86. Enys Tregarthen (1906) *North Cornwall fairies and legends*, London: Wells Gardner, Darton, pp. 141-148.

87. Daphne Hicks (2011) 'The Mounted Horsemen of Padstow' in *Old Cornwall*, vol. 14, no. 5, Autumn 2011, pp. 23-24.

88. 'Mullion O.C.S.' in *Old Cornwall*, vol. 7, no. 7, Autumn 1970, p. 309.

89. 'Redruth O.C.S.', ibid., pp. 314-316 (p. 315).

90. Terry Knight (2005) 'Society News: Saltash OCS' in *Old Cornwall*, vol. 13, no. 5, Autumn 2005, p. 64; Peter Gwynn (2007) 'Society News: Saltash' in *Old Cornwall*, vol. 13, no. 9, Autumn 2007, pp. 65-66.

91. Email correspondence from Linda King of Hayle OCS along with photographs of the project.

92. WL Bransgrove (2004) 'Society News: Newquay OCS' in *Old Cornwall*, vol. 13, no. 3, Autumn 2004, p. 61.

93. David Stark (2001) 'Society News: St. Austell' in *Old Cornwall*, vol. 12, no. 8, Spring 2001, pp. 58-59.

94. 'St. Agnes O.C.S. honours Passmore Edwards' in *Old Cornwall*, vol. 6, no. 12, Spring 1967, p. 571.

95. 'Old Cornwall in action' in *Old Cornwall*, vol. 1, no. 12, Winter 1930, pp. 34-35 (p. 34).

96. 'News from the Societies' in *Old Cornwall*, vol. 8, no. 10, Spring 1978, pp. 515-516.

97. 'Old Cornwall in action' in *Old Cornwall*, vol. 1, no. 12, Winter 1930, pp. 34-35 (p. 34); *Old Cornwall*, vol. 4, no. 7, p. 246; PAS Pool (1992) 'John Davey of Boswednack' in *Old Cornwall*, vol. 11, no. 2,

Spring 1992, pp. 61-65.

98. AJ Lyne (1970) 'Truro O.C.S.' in *Old Cornwall*, vol. 7, no. 7, Autumn 1970, pp. 323-324 (p. 324).

99. 'Homage to Nevil [sic] Northey Burnard' in *Old Cornwall*, vol. 7, no. 4, Spring 1969, p. 153.

100. Mary Martin (1978) *A wayward genius: Neville Northy [sic] Burnard*, Padstow: Lodenek Press, plate 70, opposite p. 49.

101. Hoyle, p. 305.

102. Peter King (2007) 'News from the Societies: Looe' in *Old Cornwall*, vol. 13, no. 8, Spring 2007, pp. 55-57; 'Looe OCS commemorates Joseph Thomas' in *Old Cornwall*, vol. 13, no. 9, Autumn 2007, pp. 62-65.

103. 'Penzance O.C.S.' in *Old Cornwall*, vol. 7, no. 7, Autumn 1970, pp. 312-313 (p. 313).

104. Barbara Seed (2010) 'Reuben Chappell plaque' in *Old Cornwall*, vol. 14, no. 3, Autumn 2010, pp. 30-31.

105. Federation of Old Cornwall Societies (1935) 'Penryn and Falmouth' in *Reports. 1934-1935*, St Ives: Federation of Old Cornwall Societies, pp. 13-14 (p. 14).

106. Lawrence Maker (1970) 'Callington O.C.S.' in *Old Cornwall*, vol. 7, no. 7, Autumn 1970, pp. 298-299.

107. David Stark (2018) 'Commemorative plaques on the route of the former St Austell & Pentewan Railway' in *Old Cornwall*, vol. 15, no. 7, Autumn 2018, pp. 27-29.

108. Personal comm., John Neale, Secretary of Launceston OCS.

109. Peter Beacham & Nikolaus Pevsner (2014) *The buildings of England: Cornwall*, New Haven: Yale University Press, p. 624; 'Unveiling of a memorial plaque, Stamford

Hill' in *Old Cornwall*, vol. 7, no. 10, Spring 1972, pp. 449-450.

110. 'Castle Dore' in *Old Cornwall*, vol. 6, no. 8, Spring 1965, pp. 359-360.

111. 'The Tristan Stone' in *Old Cornwall*, vol. 6, no. 1, Autumn 1961, pp. 35-38.

112. David H Thomas & Ivor Corkell (2016) 'The Trevithick – Teague – Budge memorial tablet at Camborne parish churchyard' in *Old Cornwall*, vol. 15, no. 3, Autumn 2016, pp. 55-60.

113. Roy Blewett (2014) 'Resolution for a bal maiden: Elizabeth Jane Hall 1857-1873' in *Old Cornwall*, vol. 14, no. 10, Spring 2014, pp. 71-73.

114. 'Par O.C.S.' in *Old Cornwall*, vol. 7, no. 7, Autumn 1970, pp. 310-311.

115. Wadebridge OCS, Committee minute book, 1934-50 (November 25th 1947).

116. Correspondence between CKC Andrew, Federation Archaeology Recorder, and Mrs Winifred Groser, Secretary of Wadebridge OCS (letter of May 2nd 1939).

117. Woolf (1978), pp. 18-19.

118. 'Old Cornwall in action' in *Old Cornwall*, vol. 1, no. 12, Winter 1930, pp. 34-35 (p. 35).

119. R Morton Nance (1935) 'The proposed Landewednack tablet' in *Old Cornwall*, vol. 2, no. 10, Winter 1935, p. 44.

120. Wadebridge OCS, Committee minute book, 1934-50 (1947).

121. 'St Keyne Well controversy – Old Cornwall Societies clash', *Western Morning News* January 18th 1936.

122. 'The Well of St Keyne', *Cornish Times* July 10th 1936.

123. Andrew G Langdon (2002) *Stone crosses in mid Cornwall*, 2nd ed.,

St Austell: Federation of Old Cornwall Societies, p. 50.

124. Andrew G Langdon (1995) 'Cornish crosses – 1994 update' in *Old Cornwall*, vol. 11, no. 8, Spring 1995, pp. 404-408 (pp. 405-406).

125. John Rowe (1996) 'Luxulyan O.C.S.' in *Old Cornwall*, vol. 11, no. 10, Spring 1996, pp. 490-491.

126. Andrew G Langdon (2011) 'Old Cornwall's post box survey 2009-2010' in *Old Cornwall*, vol. 14, no. 5, Autumn 2011, pp. 10-15.

127. Andrew G Langdon (2014) ''Old Cornwall' fingerpost survey 2011-2013' in *Old Cornwall*, vol. 14, no. 11, Autumn 2014, pp. 37-44.

128. David Bartlett (2017) 'Wadebridge: a sign at Bridge End' in *Old Cornwall*, vol. 15, no. 4, Spring 2017, pp. 53-54.

129. Locally, one can report to the Historic Environment Record at Cornwall Council on their enquiries email address her@cornwall.gov.uk.

Acknowledgements: To Ann Preston-Jones for reading through this work and offering amendments and corrections. Members who have supplied information include: Colin Roberts, Mullion OCS, Linda Beskeen, Redruth OCS, Neville Meek, St Gerrans & Porthscatho OCS, David & Margaret Bartlett, Wadebridge OCS, Brian Oldham & Jackie Jenkins, Liskeard OCS, David Stark, St Austell OCS, Daphne Hicks & John Buckingham, Padstow OCS, Audrey Aylmer & Alan McIntosh, Bude-Stratton & District OCS, Rob Evans, Pentewan OCS, Sue Theobald, Camelford OCS, Phil Davey, Carnon Downs OCS, Trevor Smitheram and Linda King, Hayle OCS, Steve Hebdige & Sheila Harper, Newquay OCS, Jean White, Derek Brooks & John Jackett, Goonhavern & District OCS, Peter Thomas & Clive Benney, St Agnes OCS, David Thomas,

Camborne OCS, Norma Dobinson, Looe OCS, Martin Matthews, Janet Spargo & Elaine Foreman, Helston OCS, Stephanie Thomas, Bodmin OCS, Diana Osborne, Par OCS, Margaret & Brian Stevens, St Ives OCS, Terry & Anne Knight, FOCS, Karin & Chris Easton, Perranzabuloe OCS, Gillian Hocking & Pamela Winterbourne, St Just & Pendeen OCS, Cedric Appleby, Penzance OCS, Leadville Parsons, Torpoint OCS.

FOLK TRADITION AND THE OLD CORNWALL SOCIETIES

1. For a detailed 21st-century perspective on Cornish folk tradition see Merv Davey (2011) *As is the manner and the custom*, Doctoral thesis, Institute of Cornish Studies, University of Exeter, http://hdl.handle.net/10036/3377.

2. R Morton Nance (1925) 'What we stand for' in *Old Cornwall*, vol. 1, no. 1, April 1925, pp. 3-6.

3. For example, his illustration for *Sweet Nightingale* in *Cornish Magazine*, vol. 2, 1899, p. 127.

4. Ronald M James (2018) *The folklore of Cornwall*, Exeter: University of Exeter Press, introduction.

5. William Bottrell (1873) *Traditions and hearthside stories of West Cornwall. Second series*, Penzance: the author, p. 1.

6. R Morton Nance (1956) *The Cledry plays: drolls of old Cornwall for village acting and home reading*, Marazion/Penzance: Federation of Old Cornwall Societies.

7. Philip Payton (2004) *Cornwall: a history*, Fowey: Cornwall Editions, p. 179.

8. Folk song and dance collectors such as Cecil Sharp and Peter Kennedy are often criticised for making the material they collected 'their own', sometimes to the point of its being subject to copyright.

9. Frederick James Thomas (1849-1934), obituary *Cornishman* March 1st 1934; Bessie Wallace (1883-1948), obituary *Cornishman* July 29th 1948; Tom Miners (1879-1940), obituary *Cornishman* November 7th 1940. William Daniel Watson (1887-1959) describes his involvement with the Celtic Revival in 'How Cornish came to me', *Old Cornwall*, vol. 5, no. 8, 1957, pp. 340-342. The author is grateful to Jason Semmens and Phil Ellery for pointing out these references (email correspondence 2013 & 2014).

10. William Bottrell wrote a regular newspaper column on Cornish folklore under the pen name 'Old Celt' in the mid-19th century, and these pieces were eventually published in two volumes: (1870-73) *Traditions and hearthside stories of West Cornwall*, Penzance: the author; see also note 5. A *Third series* was published in 1880 as *Stories and folk-lore of West Cornwall*.

11. 'The Cornish farmyard' (*Old Cornwall*, vol. 1, no. 1, April 1925, p. 21); 'Miner's song' (*Old Cornwall*, vol. 1, no. 4, October 1926, p. 18); 'Begone from the window' (*Old Cornwall*, vol. 1, no. 5, April 1927, p. 14). Jim Thomas is credited as Jas. Thomas in each case.

12. Ralph Dunstan (ed.) (1932) *Cornish dialect and folk songs*, Truro: Jordan's Bookshop.

13. See note 9.

14. 'Folk carols collected in the Camborne district', *Cornishman* November 16th 1915; 'Cornish carols', *Journal of the Folk-Song Society*, vol. 8, no. 33, December 1929, pp. 111-124.

15. For example: 'An old Cornish carol book' (vol. 1, no. 5, April 1927, pp. 22-25); 'Cornish "likes"' (vol. 1, no. 5, p. 39 & vol. 1, no. 6, October 1927, p. 36); 'Cornwall and the sea' (vol. 1, no. 6, pp. 26-27); 'Old Cornish Valentines' (vol. 1, no. 7, April 1928, pp. 18-22); 'Saturday night' (vol. 1, no. 7, p. 44); 'The Mummers' Play in West Cornwall' (vol. 1, no. 8, October 1928, pp. 4-16); 'Quaint marriage customs in old Cornwall' (vol. 1, no. 12, Winter 1930, pp. 22-24); 'Old May Day customs' (vol. 2, no. 8, Winter 1934, pp. 14-15).

16. Vanessa Beeman / Watson family correspondence with author, April 29th 2009.

17. For example: 'Nebes geriow moy adro dho Gernuak – A few words more about Cornish' (vol. 1, no. 3, April 1926, pp. 3-5); 'Lankyloo' (vol. 1, no. 4, October 1926, p. 29); 'The Black Bull of Mylor' (vol. 1, no. 7, April 1928, pp. 12-13); 'Covyon Keltek' (vol. 1, no. 11, Summer 1930, p. 15).

18. James Madison Carpenter Collection, Archive of Folk Culture, Library of Congress, Washington DC, AFC 1972/00William1.

19. James Madison Carpenter Collection, index 10565-10582: *Padstow Version of the St George or Mummers' Play*. Carpenter collected the play when he visited Cornwall in 1933/34 and notes correspondence with Robert Morton Nance, whose father could remember being scared by the dragon in the play as a child, circa 1845. Padstow Museum holds a copy of Carpenter's transcription of the Padstow Mummers' Play in its archive together with additional notes provided from local recollections dating back to the 1930s.

20. Fourteen stories by Bessie Wallace are printed in the *Old Cornwall* journal between 1937 and 1951.

21. *Mazed Tales*, 'Barbara Spooner 1893-1983': http://mazedtales.org/content/barbara-spooner-1893-1983, accessed 20-11-19.

22. Barbara C Spooner (1935) *John Tregagle of Trevorder: man and ghost*, Truro: A.W. Jordan (reprint: [n.p.]: Blackthorn Press, 1977; précised version: St Peter Port: Toucan Press, 1979); Barbara C Spooner (1950) *Queer tales of the Cheesewring; The Hurlers; The Other Half Stone*, [n.p.]: the author.

23. Barbara C Spooner (1961) 'Cloud ships over Cornwall' in *Folklore*, vol. 72, no. 1, March 1961, pp. 323-329.

24. Barbara C Spooner (1953) 'The stone circles of Cornwall' in *Folklore*, vol. 64, no. 4, December 1953, pp. 484-487.

25. Barbara C Spooner (1968) 'The haunted style' in *Folklore*, vol. 79, no. 2, Summer 1968, pp. 135-139.

26. The Great Western Railway in particular created an artificial image of Cornwall as a romantic fairyland holiday destination. See Philip Payton 'Paralysis and Revival: the reconstruction of Celtic-Catholic Cornwall 1890-1945' in Ella Westland (ed.) (1997) *Cornwall: the cultural construction of place*, Penzance: Patten Press, p. 34.

27. Jason Semmens (2005) '"Whyler Pystry": a breviate of the life and folklore-collecting practices of William Henry Paynter (1901-76) of Callington, Cornwall' in *Folklore*, vol. 116, no. 1, April 2005, pp. 75-94.

28. Introduction by Jason Semmens to William H Paynter (2016) *Cornish witchcraft*, Liskeard: privately printed, p. ix.

29. Jason Semmens (2008) *The Cornish Witch-finder*, St Agnes: Federation of Old Cornwall Societies.

30. Bodmin also retains the hurling tradition with a match being held every five years as part of the 'Beating the Bounds' ceremony.

31. *Cornishman* February 23rd 1921.

32. Mike O'Connor (2017) 'Crying the Neck: what we really know' in *Old Cornwall*, vol. 15, no. 5, Autumn 2017, pp. 55-57.

33. 'Crying the Neck', *Western Morning News* September 1st 1928.

34. Michael Tangye captures much of this in his article 'Customs remembered' in *Old Cornwall*, vol. 9, no. 6, Spring 1982, pp. 308-312.

35. In Cornwall, Midsummer is traditionally celebrated on or near June 23rd, which is the notional date for the end of the summer solstice. In 1929 this fell on a Sunday and it was decided to hold the ceremony on the evening of June 24th.

36. Merv Davey (2019) *Tansys Golowan: the Cornish Midsummer Bonfire ceremonies*, St Agnes: Federation of Old Cornwall Societies.

37. 'The Castle-An-Dinas Bonfire', *Cornishman* July 2nd 1931.

38. Richard Polwhele (1803-08) *The history of Cornwall*, London: Cadell and Davies, vol. 3, p. 58.

39. Fred WP Jago (1882) *The ancient language, and the dialect of Cornwall*, Truro: Netherton & Worth (entry under 'Guise-dance', p. 183).

40. See Peter Millington (2003) 'The Truro Cordwainers' Play: a 'new' eighteenth-century Christmas Play' in *Folklore*, vol. 114, no. 1, pp. 53-73. Cornwall has one of the earliest recorded versions of the combat play with characters including Father Christmas.

41. AK Hamilton Jenkin (1925) 'A Redruth Christmas Play' in *Old Cornwall*, vol. 1, no. 1, April 1925, pp. 29-31; FJ Roskruge (1925) 'A Guise-Dance Play, St. Keverne', ibid., pp. 31-32; Tom Miners (1928) 'The Mummers' Play in West Cornwall' in *Old Cornwall*, vol. 1, no. 8, October 1928, pp. 4-16.

42. S Winifred Paynter (1927) *Old St Ives: the reminiscences of William Paynter*, St Ives: privately published, p. 46.

43. Sampson Taylor Rowe 'Guise Dancing at St Ives', *St Ives Weekly Summary* January 6th 1900.

44. Report on Annual Licensing Session, *Cornishman* February 21st 1923.

45. 'Guise Dancing at St Ives', *Cornishman* January 17th 1929.

46. For example, the *Cornishman* of January 23rd 1936 carries a report from the Chamber of Commerce extolling the value of the Guise Dancers for St Ives.

47. William Barber, interview with author, October 30th 2009, St Ives, oral history research for PhD, Institute of Cornish Studies.

48. Dave Lobb, interview with author, July 26th 2006, Withiel, oral history research for PhD, Institute of Cornish Studies.

49. 'Old Cornwall Festival', *Cornishman* January 10th 1929.

50. Howard Curnow, interview with author, May 16th 2008, St Hilary. Howard played the part of Town Crier in the Hal An Tow and had also been involved with the play as a teacher at Helston School in the 1970s.

51. 'Madron Guise Dancers broadcast', *Cornishman* January 7th 1937.

52. 'Madron Guise Dancers: Cornish dialect the real thing: broadcast which made exiles think of home', *Cornishman* January 6th 1938.

53. See Richard McGrady (1993) *Traces of ancient mystery: the ballad carols of Davies Gilbert and William Sandys*, Redruth: Institute of Cornish Studies.

54. 'Old Cornwall – Gathering of the Clans', *Cornishman and Cornish Telegraph* January 13th 1926.

55. Alfred Perceval Graves (ed.) (1928) *The Celtic song book: being representative folk songs of the six Celtic nations*, London: Ernest Benn.

56. Ralph Dunstan (ed.) (1929) *The Cornish Song Book (Lyver Canow Kernewek)*, London: Reid Bros., introduction, p. 3.

57. Ralph Dunstan (ed.) (1932) *Cornish dialect and folk songs*, Truro: Jordan's Bookshop.

58. Scoot dancing is named after the metal plate used on the toe and heel of working shoes to prolong their life, called 'scoots' or 'scutes' in 19th-century Cornish dialect. See Jago, p. 260 (entry under 'Scute').

59. 'The Holidays', *Royal Cornwall Gazette* June 11th 1808.

60. 'Social at Boscastle', *Cornish & Devon Post* February 4th 1905; 'Boscastle', *Cornish & Devon Post* November 27th 1909.

61. Richard Dimbleby: BBC Sound Archive 6796 and 6918, recorded in October and December 1943; available on Topic Records 12T240.

62. Merv Davey, Alison Davey & Jowdy Davey (2009) *Scoot Dances, Troyls, Furrys and Tea Treats: the Cornish dance tradition*, London: Francis Boutle, p. 36.

63. Margaret A Courtney (1890) *Cornish Feasts and folk-lore*, Penzance: Beare and Son.

64. Charles Lee (ed. Ken C Phillipps) (1995) *The Cornish journal of Charles Lee, 1892-1908*, Padstow: Tabb House, p. 98; Charles Lee (1911) *Dorinda's birthday: a Cornish idyll*, London: J.M. Dent and Sons, pp. 238-247.

65. Merv Davey et al., p. 32.

66. Merv Davey & Alison Davey (2008) *Snail Creeps and Tea Treats: Clay Country customs*, St Austell: Rescorla Project.

67. R Morton Nance (1956), p. 84.

68. From research undertaken by Norma Dobinson of Looe Old Cornwall Society, shared with the author as part of a presentation to the Society on January 12th 2019.

69. Elizabeth Steed Shapcott (1930) 'Some Looe customs and incidents of last century' in *Old Cornwall*, vol. 1, no. 11, Summer 1930, pp. 19-26.

70. Davies Gilbert (1823) *Some ancient Christmas carols*, London: John Nichols and Son.

71. Mike O'Connor (2002) *No song, no supper: the music of John Old, Dancing Master of Par*, Wadebridge: Lyngham House Music.

72. Merv Davey et al. (2009), p. 116.

73. 'Gook' is a dialect expression derived from the Cornish word *kough* meaning bonnet, and *bal* is Cornish for a mine.

74. 'Cornish Gathering', *Cornishman* January 10th 1929.

75. Tartan Register: www.tartanregister.gov.uk.

76. Brian Wilton (2007) *Tartans*, London: Aurum.

77. The UK Government formally recognised the Cornish as a National Minority under the Council of Europe's Framework Convention for the Protection of National Minorities in 2014; press release April 4th 2014, Treasury Office, UK Government.

Index